Writing Visual Histories

Writing History

The *Writing History* series publishes accessible overviews of particular fields in history, focusing on the practical application of theory in historical writing. Books in the series succinctly explain central concepts to demonstrate the ways in which they have informed effective historical writing. They analyse key historical texts and their producers within their institutional arrangement, and as part of a wider social discourse. The series' holistic approach means students benefit from an enhanced understanding of how to negotiate the contours of successful historical writing.

Series editors:

Stefan Berger (Ruhr University Bochum, Germany), Heiko Feldner (Cardiff University, UK) and Kevin Passmore (Cardiff University, UK)

Published:

Writing History (second edition), edited by Stefan Berger, Heiko Feldner & Kevin Passmore
Writing Medieval History, edited by Nancy F. Partner
Writing Early Modern History, edited by Garthine Walker
Writing Contemporary History, edited by Robert Gildea & Anne Simonin
Writing Gender History (second edition), Laura Lee Downs
Writing Postcolonial History, Rochona Majumdar
Writing the Holocaust, edited by Jean-Marc Dreyfus & Daniel Langton
Writing the History of Memory, edited by Stefan Berger and Bill Niven
Writing Material Culture History, edited by Anne Gerritsen & Giorgio Riello
Writing History (third edition), edited by Stefan Berger, Heiko Feldner and Kevin Passmore

Forthcoming:

Writing Queer History, Matt Cook
Writing Transnational History, Fiona Paisley
Writing the History of Slavery, edited by David Doddington and Enrico Dal Lago
Writing Material Culture History, 2nd edition, edited by Giorgio Riello & Anne Gerritsen
Writing Gender History, Laura Lee Downs

Writing Visual Histories

Edited by
Florence Grant and Ludmilla Jordanova

BLOOMSBURY ACADEMIC
LONDON • NEW YORK • OXFORD • NEW DELHI • SYDNEY

BLOOMSBURY ACADEMIC
Bloomsbury Publishing Plc
50 Bedford Square, London, WC1B 3DP, UK
1385 Broadway, New York, NY 10018, USA

BLOOMSBURY, BLOOMSBURY ACADEMIC and the Diana logo are
trademarks of Bloomsbury Publishing Plc

First published in Great Britain 2020

Copyright © Florence Grant and Ludmilla Jordanova, 2020

Florence Grant and Ludmilla Jordanova have asserted their right under the Copyright, Designs and Patents Act, 1988, to be identified as Author of this work.

Cover images: Sarah Skinner Ward (needlework) and Samuel Folwell (design and painting), *Calliope and Clio*, 1810–3, silk needlework and tempera on linen,
62.87 × 46.67 cm (24¾ × 18⅜ in.). Winterthur Museum, Garden & Library, Winterthur, DE, 1991.0046 A
(artwork in the public domain; photograph ©
The Picture Art Collection/Alamy Stock Photo).

The East Portico of Sir Robert Smirke's building and the Queen Elizabeth II Great Court of the British Museum, London. The Portland stone of Smirke's classicizing design (completed 1852) meets the glass and steel roof of the Great Court (opened 2000) by Foster and Partners (photograph © Jon Bower- art and museums/Alamy Stock Photo).

All rights reserved. No part of this publication may be reproduced or transmitted in any form or by any means, electronic or mechanical, including photocopying, recording, or any information storage or retrieval system, without prior permission in writing from the publishers.

Bloomsbury Publishing Plc does not have any control over, or responsibility for, any third-party websites referred to or in this book. All internet addresses given in this book were correct at the time of going to press. The author and publisher regret any inconvenience caused if addresses have changed or sites have ceased to exist, but can accept no responsibility for any such changes.

Every effort has been made to trace copyright holders and to obtain their permissions for the use of copyright material. The publisher apologizes for any errors or omissions and would be grateful if notified of any corrections that should be incorporated in future reprints or editions of this book.

A catalogue record for this book is available from the British Library.

Library of Congress Cataloging-in-Publication Data

Names: Grant, Florence (Freelance writer), editor, author. | Jordanova, L. J., editor, author.
Title: Writing visual histories / edited by Florence Grant and Ludmilla Jordanova.
Description: London ; New York : Bloomsbury Academic, 2020. | Series: Writing history series | Includes bibliographical references and index.
Identifiers: LCCN 2020027587 (print) | LCCN 2020027588 (ebook) | ISBN 9781350023451 (paperback) | ISBN 9781350023482 (hardback) | ISBN 9781350023468 (ebook) | ISBN 9781350023475 (epub)
Subjects: LCSH: Historiography–Methodology. | History–Sources. | Material culture–Historiography. | Material culture–History.
Classification: LCC D16 .W955 2020 (print) | LCC D16 (ebook) | DDC 907.2–dc23
LC record available at https://lccn.loc.gov/2020027587
LC ebook record available at https://lccn.loc.gov/2020027588

ISBN: HB: 978-1-3500-2348-2
PB: 978-1-3500-2345-1
ePDF: 978-1-3500-2346-8
eBook: 978-1-3500-2347-5

Typeset by Deanta Global Publishing Services, Chennai, India
Printed and bound in India

To find out more about our authors and books visit www.bloomsbury.com
and sign up for our newsletters.

The editors would like to express their gratitude to close friends and family for their love and support and to dedicate this book, in Florence's case to her mother, Martha Hickman Hild, and in Ludmilla's to her daughter Zara Truscott.

Contents

List of illustrations ix
List of contributors xi
Acknowledgements xiii

Introduction 1

Essays 23

1 Heraldry topsy-turvy: Depictions and performances of dishonour and death *Marcus Meer* 25

2 Costume imagery and the visualization of humanity in early modern Europe *Katherine Bond* 45

3 Identity and continuity: The visual culture of an institution over 500 years *Ludmilla Jordanova* 68

4 Making an exhibition of himself: John Wilkes through visual sources *Jonathan Conlin* 88

5 Writing the history of the photographic book: Architecture in Weimar Germany *J. J. Long* 110

6 The picture magazine: *Life* and the limits of photography *Melissa Renn* 133

Concepts 147
    Agency 147
    Art 148
    Discourse 149
    Genre 149
    Iconography 150
    Medium 151
    Reception 151
    Reproduction 152
    Rhetoric 153
    Skill 154

Style	155
Visual culture	155

Practices
Description	157
Contextualization	158
Periodization	160

Practicalities
Using image databases	162
Organizing permissions	163
Writing captions	164
Publishing with pictures	164

Conclusions	166
Bibliography	169
Index	188

Illustrations

Figures

1 Master of the Housebook, *Coat of Arms with a Peasant Standing on His Head*, c. 1485–90   26
2 Letter of defamation against the City of Cologne, 1441   30
3 Public degradation ceremony including a reversed shield of arms, 1648   42
4 Mary Gertrude Stockbridge Allen, *Portrait of Narcissa Prentiss Whitman*, 1926   43
5 'That Farage Coat of Arms', magazine caricature, 2016   44
6 François Desprez, 'Woman of Roncevalles', 1562   49
7 Christoph Weiditz, 'This is an Indian ...', and 'Thus he again catches the wood on his feet ...', 1530–40   53
8 Johann Froschauer after Amerigo Vespucci, *Dise figur anzaigt uns das volck und insel die gefunden ist ...*, 1505   54
9 'Basque Woman from Cantabria', from Hans Weigel, *Habitus Praecipuorum Populorum*, 1577   61
10 Lucas de Heere, 'Naked Man with Fabric and Shears', 1570/80   64
11 Jost Amman, 'Frontispiece', from Hans Weigel, *Habitus Praecipuorum Populorum*, 1577   65
12 Screenshot from the Royal College of Physicians' website, showing the Dorchester Library with portrait of William Harvey   69
13 A view of the main staircase in Denys Lasdun's building for the college, opened in 1964   74
14 The Censors' Room   76
15 A procession, including the president in his robes of office, with the mace being carried in front of him   83
16 Cuttings in Frederick Farre's scrapbook   84
17 Badge in the form of number '45', c. 1763   95
18 James Watson after Robert Edge Pine, *John Wilkes Esqr*, 1764   99
19 William Hogarth, *John Wilkes Esqr*, 1763   100
20 William Sharp, trade card for Cotterell, tobacconist, c. 1764   103

21	'Dyeing plant of a hat factory ...', from *Bauten der Arbeit und des Verkehrs*, 1926	118
22	'Bahlsen Biscuit Factory Administration Block ...', from *Bauten der Arbeit und des Verkehrs*, 1926	119
23	Bathroom fittings in the experimental house designed by the Bauhaus, from Adolf Meyer (ed.), *Ein Versuchshaus des Bauhauses in Weimar*, 1925	124
24	Living room and study area in the experimental house designed by the Bauhaus, from Adolf Meyer (ed.), *Ein Versuchshaus des Bauhauses in Weimar*, 1925	128
25	Dining room in the experimental house designed by the Bauhaus, from Adolf Meyer (ed.), *Ein Versuchshaus des Bauhauses in Weimar*, 1925	129
26	Electrical installations in the experimental house designed by the Bauhaus, from Adolf Meyer (ed.), *Ein Versuchshaus des Bauhauses in Weimar*, 1925	130

Plates

(Between pages 87 and 88)

1. Letter of defamation against John III of Bavaria issued by John III of Nassau-Dillenburg, c. 1419–21
2. Letter of defamation against Louis of Hesse, 1438
3. Christoph Weiditz, 'This is also an Indian, a Nobleman ...', and 'This is also the Indian manner ...', from the 'Trachtenbuch', 1530–40
4. 'Indian Nobleman' and 'Indian Woman', from 'Kostüme der Männer und Frauen in Augsburg und Nürnberg, Deutschland, Europa, Orient und Afrika', fourth quarter of the sixteenth century
5. Johan Zoffany, *William Hunter at the Royal Academy*, 1770–2
6. Robert Hannah, *William Harvey Demonstrating to Charles I the Circulation of the Blood from the Heart of a Deer*, 1848
7. Robert Edge Pine, *John Wilkes*, 1768
8. Johan Zoffany, *Mary Wilkes; John Wilkes*, exhibited 1782
9. *Bauten der Arbeit und des Verkehrs*, 1926, front dust-jacket

Contributors

Katherine Bond is a postdoctoral researcher and Irish Research Council, Government of Ireland fellow based at the School of History, University College Cork. Following an MA in Art History from the University of Auckland, New Zealand, Katherine completed her PhD in early modern History at the University of Cambridge on the subject of sixteenth-century costume albums in the reign of Habsburg emperor Charles V. Between 2018 and 2019 she was a postdoctoral researcher on the Swiss National Foundation-funded project 'Materialized Identities: Objects, Affects and Effects in Early Modern Culture 1450–1750', investigating the materiality and cultural significance of veils in Renaissance Europe. Her research interests centre around the visual and material culture of the early modern world, with a particular focus on dress practices, ethnography and cross-cultural exchanges.

Jonathan Conlin is a senior lecturer at the University of Southampton and a historian of British cultural history from around 1750 to the present. His first book, a history of the National Gallery (London), led him to consider the development of other cultural institutions on the margins of history/art history: from eighteenth-century pleasure gardens to television documentary series such as *Civilisation* (1969). He is also interested in exploring how Victorians employed concepts of evolutionary 'development' in a range of 'non-scientific' contexts, including art history and architecture. His books include *Tales of Two Cities: Paris, London, and the Making of the Modern City* (2013) and *Evolution and the Victorians* (2014) as well biographies of Adam Smith and Calouste Gulbenkian.

Florence Grant is an independent writer and editor with a background in history of science, art history and studio practice. She completed her PhD at King's College London, where her research addressed the material culture of experimental philosophy in eighteenth-century Britain, through focused study of a collection of instruments made for George III in the 1760s. After a postdoctoral appointment at the Yale Center for British Art, she moved to the mountains of Western North Carolina. Her upcoming projects include hand-printed letterpress work exploring toponyms in the local Toe River watershed, conceived both in terms of social history and as a deep personal engagement with place.

Ludmilla Jordanova is Emeritus Professor of History and Visual Culture at Durham University, UK, where she directed the Centre for Visual Arts and Culture between 2015 and 2019. She writes about historical practice, the history of science and medicine, visual and material culture, and portraiture.

Her books include *History in Practice* (3rd edition, 2019), *Physicians and Their Images* (2018), *The Look of the Past: Visual and Material Evidence in Historical Practice* (2012) and *Defining Features: Scientific and Medical Portraits, 1660–2000* (2000). She is a trustee of the Science Museum Group (2011–21) and is currently working on a book about portraiture since 1600.

J. J. Long is Professor of German and Visual Culture at Durham University. He has published extensively on twentieth-century German literature and photography, including the monograph *W. G. Sebald: Image, Archive, Modernity* and articles on photography in the work of Franz Kafka, Bertolt Brecht, Thomas Bernhard and Monika Maron. He is a regular contributor to *Source: Thinking through Photography*. His current research focuses on the photographic book in the Weimar Republic.

Marcus Meer is a researcher at the German Historical Institute. He completed a BA in History and Linguistics at Bielefeld University and a MSt in Medieval History at Oxford University before obtaining his PhD as a Leverhulme Doctoral Scholar at Durham University's Centre for Visual Arts and Culture. He is particularly interested in a comparative perspective on the towns and cities of late medieval Europe, with a special focus on England and the German-speaking lands, analysing how townspeople used texts, images, objects, architecture and rituals to represent, construct and contest social groups, urban hierarchies and political structures.

Melissa Renn is Collections Manager, HBS Art and Artifacts Collection, Harvard Business School. She has published widely on *Life* magazine, including 'Time, *Life*, and the Flag Raisings on Iwo Jima', in Breanne Robertson (ed.), *Investigating Iwo: The Flag Raisings in Myth, Memory, and Esprit de Corps* (2019); '*Life*'s Pioneer Painters: Dorothy Seiberling and American Art in *Life* Magazine, 1949–1968', in Rachel Esner and Sandra Kisters (eds), *The Mediatization of the Artist* (2018); '*Life* in Color: *Life* Magazine and the Color Reproduction of Works of Art', in Regina Lee Blaszczyk and Uwe Spiekermann (eds), *Bright Modernity: Color, Commerce, and Consumer Culture* (2017); '"The Famous Iwo Flag-Raising": Iwo Jima Revisited', in *History of Photography* (2015); and 'Within Their Walls: *Life* Magazine's *Illuminations*', in the *Archives of American Art Journal* (2014). Renn is co-editor, with Monica E. Jovanovich, of *Corporate Patronage of Art & Architecture in the United States, from the Late 19th Century to the Present* (2019).

Acknowledgements

The editors are grateful to the contributors for their patience, good humour and hard work, the staff at Bloomsbury Academic for their assistance and support, the anonymous reviewers for their insightful comments, Finola Finn for compiling the Bibliography, those who provided images for giving us permission to use them here and each other for the enjoyable companionship that preparing this volume has provided. With the exception of Chapters 1 through 6, all the material in this book has been written jointly by the editors. J. J. Long assisted with the chapter on contextualization, for which we thank him.

Introduction

'The visual'

Visual agency and apprehension are central to human experience. Significant material resources, meanings and moral force are often invested in decisions about how things look. People form complex judgements about other people and the world around them by engaging visual skills and habits. Matters of vital interest to historians, including individual and collective identities, social processes, cultural change and political conflict, are shaped, not simply recorded or illustrated, in a visual register. All histories are potentially visual histories. In this book we are trying to be as explicit as possible about practices of history-writing that incorporate visual dimensions, and the kinds of histories that can result. By laying bare what we do in this way, including routine aspects that often go unremarked, it is possible to pay closer attention to and thereby refine historical practice. The things we take as self-evident are always worth noting, in order to facilitate critical reflection.

'The visual' is a vast and often unexamined category. Used in a loose way it can give a false sense of coherence to what is a wildly diverse field – methodologically, materially and culturally. We use the term here to refer to certain kinds of focused skill and attention, exercised both by historical actors and by historians. In doing so we are attempting to address historically specific modes of perception and understanding, including the techniques of trained observation exercised by artists, natural historians, anatomists, physicians, connoisseurs, designers and others whose occupations are highly invested in looking, as well as the skills, habits and codes deployed by a far wider range of people in their daily lives.

Accordingly, visual artefacts might be thought of as those objects in which visual interest has become remarkably concentrated. Such objects seem to embody heightened visual skills, attention and decision-making, and for that reason invite and repay close scrutiny. We are not suggesting a hierarchy of media or genres here; such materials might include prints and photographs, maps, paintings, magazines, sculpture, clothing, coats of arms, jewellery, political posters, tobacco labels, websites and so on. Rather, we are describing a kind of focused emphasis, that is, an approach that organizes understandings of disciplines, genres and media around questions of visual interest.

Texts, contexts, materiality

One of the assumptions that is often implied when historians use the phrase 'visual sources' is that this does not include texts. Historians, like readers of all kinds, spend many hours each day looking at text. Perhaps because the act of reading itself is so habitual, they rarely remark on letter shapes, page design or the visual qualities of paper, ink and bindings – as J. J. Long does here in his essay on photobooks – or on digital displays, unless these somehow hinder legibility. Nonetheless visual and textual sources are profoundly connected, and as Marcus Meer's discussion of inverted coats of arms demonstrates, we risk serious misunderstanding if we draw from one to the exclusion of the other. The writing of visual histories involves not only the recovery of such connections but also the use of practices such as description, through which historians link their own written arguments with images and objects from the past.

Visual things, as well as texts, are also material; the boundaries between 'visual' and 'material' histories are fluid. One potent intersection of the material and the visual can be seen in histories of intentional damage and destruction. Physical attacks on monuments, paintings and religious images, as well as the ritualized production and destruction of effigies, such as those still burned on Guy Fawkes Night in Britain, indicate these objects' complex status in relation to power, belief and action. Taking another approach, painted portraits might be addressed through material histories, giving attention to the substances used, such as pigments (lapis lazuli, ochres, soot), mixing mediums (linseed oil, whale oil), grounds (gesso) and supports (wooden panels, canvas, linen), as well as to frames and dimensions. These kinds of analysis underpin work in conservation and technical art history, and are becoming increasingly familiar in the broader art-historical literature.[1]

To focus in this way on painted portraits is to recognize that they are also made through the exercise of visual decision-making, in the expectation that they will receive certain modes of visual attention and within contexts that abound with visual conventions. Painters' and sitters' visual decisions and expected audiences' visual habits jointly shape the appearance of the picture.[2] The quality of concentrated visual interest can accrue in such artefacts as they are made, displayed, observed, commented upon and reproduced over time. For example, provenance sometimes links objects with well-known individuals whose past ownership adds a level of interest. Provenance studies and the history of collecting also enable the reconstruction of networks of objects that

---

[1] On visual and material culture, see Harvey, *History and Material Culture*; Rampley, *Exploring Visual Culture*. On iconoclasm, see Freedberg, *Power of Images*. On conservation, see Marstine, *New Museum Theory and Practice*, ch. 3. On materials, see Abrahams, *Beneath the Surface*, and Penny, *Materials of Sculpture*.

[2] Woodall, *Portraiture*, contains a range of approaches; the chapter by Angela Rosenthal explores negotiations between artists and sitters.

were collected and valued by a single individual, thus suggesting a kind of visual interrelatedness among potentially diverse items. A case in point is the wide-ranging collection of the eighteenth-century Scottish medical practitioner William Hunter, whose paintings, books and manuscripts, coins, and anatomical and natural-historical specimens were the subject of a recent exhibition at the University of Glasgow and the Yale Center for British Art.[3] Specimens in the natural sciences are selected, scrutinized, described, represented and displayed in ways that change over time, and are thus potential materials for visual histories. The category extends far beyond 'art'. Visual processes are embedded in social relationships; in order to uncover them, historians must engage visual skills of their own, and be attuned to those that were exercised in the past.[4] We advocate using historical contexts to understand visual materials, in order to integrate these materials more effectively into historical accounts, thereby informing new interpretations of their contexts, in an iterative and continuing process.

The ways in which appearances and meanings relate to each other are historically specific and change over time. For this reason, historians' interpretations of visual materials are best constructed through the careful building-up of analytical frameworks, step by step, outwards from the object into its immediate contexts and beyond. Such caution helps us to avoid making assumptions based on our own present-day visual habits and points of reference. Paying attention to genre, medium and context provides ways of building frameworks that usefully break up the 'visual' into smaller, more coherent pieces. Genres are cultural forms with recognizable conventions: the period drama, the portrait, the photobook, the novel, the sonata. Medium is not simply a matter of the materials that make up a particular artefact. Rather, media are recognized categories that entail conventions of representation or presentation, demand specific materials, technologies and skills, are often assigned value in relation to one another, have specific social characteristics and elicit particular expectations in audiences.[5]

A printed book and its digital counterpart pose very different design problems and possess distinct visual qualities, while patently conveying the same content. A portrait might be executed in oil on canvas and then reproduced in other formats: as a print on paper bound into a book, in a printed or online magazine, as a fridge magnet or within a museum's online catalogue. All are recognizable as nominally the 'same' image, even though they are physically distinct and arise from contexts of production that can be chronologically and geographically distant. Each iteration, potentially across a span of hundreds

---

[3] Campbell and Flis, *William Hunter*, contains examples of items Hunter purchased from Richard Mead, a famous medical collector, who died in 1754 (77–86).
[4] Baxandall, *Painting and Experience*, explores such visual habits; we return to this work later in the Introduction.
[5] Harris, *Art History*; West, *Guide to Art*.

of years, invites different audiences and types of interaction, operates within a distinct economic structure and construes a particular kind of relationship with the person portrayed. Comparable items in a given genre or medium form an important part of the context through which the significance of any single example becomes clear – other paintings, books, collections and websites, for example. Hence comparative analysis is essential in identifying what is particular, or not, about a given artefact.[6]

Institutions

Context can be thought of as the web of people, things, circumstances and associations that give an object meaning in a specific place and time. The locations where visual materials appeared and how they were encountered are crucial in this regard. Institutional settings are particularly rich, since they speak to collective identities, combine multiple media, genres and types of activities, tend to persist in time and are often well documented. Recent interest in salon criticism and lectures given in academies as well as projects such as the Paul Mellon Centre's RA 250, which documents every summer exhibition held at London's Royal Academy between 1769 and 2018, demonstrate the scope and depth that an institutional focus can bring to visual histories.[7] Similarly, visual culture can shape our understanding of how institutions develop and how they present themselves to both their members and broader publics.

Museums play a crucial role in the acquisition, preservation, display, documentation and interpretation of visual materials. At their inception and throughout their lives, these institutions have specific purposes that can change over time. Many explicitly aim for social and cultural change. For example, London's Victoria and Albert Museum was founded in 1852 to raise national standards in design and manufacturing, while the National Museum of African American History and Culture in Washington, DC, opened in 2003 with the goal of transforming public perceptions of US history, citizenship and national identity. The professional activities of museum directors, educators, curators, registrars, conservators, art handlers, designers and others take place within these purposeful frameworks. Some understanding of museums' internal organization and processes is essential for historians working with visual materials. These structures determine the conditions of access to artefacts themselves, as well as what is known about them through catalogues, websites and unpublished object files. They also respond to and shape the audiences that

---

[6] Jordanova, *Look of the Past*, ch. 5.
[7] See https://www.paul-mellon-centre.ac.uk/about/ra250, accessed 7 July 2019. This is information about the project rather than the site itself.

such institutions serve. Museum websites offer some of the most immediately accessible sources of images of and information about visual artefacts, often extending beyond so-called 'tombstone' details (maker, title, date, medium, dimensions and location) to sophisticated resources such as British Picture Framemakers, 1600–1950, which is an online database developed by the National Portrait Gallery, London. Such documentation tends to have high levels of accuracy and contains physical details about artefacts that are essential if they are to be cited in essays, dissertations and publications.[8]

As Ludmilla Jordanova's case study in this volume shows, the identities of institutions are articulated and shaped over time through visual means. Collections of portraits and other materials, as well as architecture and rituals, such as ceremonial meals, work together to express a collective sense of legacy and of the past. The point serves to remind us that the past is not solely the domain of historians; professionally written histories form just a small part of any culture's sense of the past and its significance for the present. Theatre, film and television, public monuments, museums, cemeteries, historic houses, and battle re-enactments, as well as family albums and other more private sites of commemoration, now play a part in many regions of the world, as do markets in antiques and fashions in vintage and retro clothing and design. Visual styling is central to many of these phenomena, and the look of a thing or an environment holds many cues that viewers use to situate it in time. The complex notion of style plays a fundamental role in these processes, indicated by the fact that terms such as 'baroque' are often used to designate both visual styles and historical periods.[9]

Evidence

The power of context and the sense of period style in shaping visual histories extend far beyond the academic community and reinforce the point that historians need to be thoughtful about periodization and contextualization when approaching visual materials – practices that are always fundamental to historical writing, whether or not they are discussed explicitly. Such self-awareness needs to include a critical understanding of the assumptions built into habitual forms of periodization and contextualization. Description is crucial to both; it provides the links between written texts and the images displayed alongside them, highlighting the salient features and translating them

---

[8] On museology, see Marstine, *New Museum Theory and Practice*; on the V & A, Baker and Richardson, *Grand Design*; for frame makers, see https://www.npg.org.uk/research/conservation/directory-of-british-framemakers.php, accessed 7 July 2019.

[9] Hills, *Rethinking the Baroque*; Panofsky, *Three Essays*; and Lang, *Concept of Style*.

into terms that enable further analysis. By means of these practices, all kinds of materials are activated, transformed into evidence through which questions may be examined and answered, and arguments supported.

Evidence is anything taken to be an outward sign or proof of something else. It is created or mobilized through the processes of research, from relevant sources. The letters, coats of arms, books, paintings, ephemera, photographs and magazine spreads discussed in the essays that follow have the status of 'evidence' because historians have paid attention to them, focused on them in relation to their concerns and arguments, scrutinized and interrogated them. As the essays by Katherine Bond and Melissa Renn make clear in discussions of early modern ethnographic knowledge and twentieth-century war reporting, respectively, no image can be treated as direct evidence of the thing it portrays. Rather, visual materials should be considered as evidence of past decisions and the social contexts in which they were embedded.

The activation of visual evidence involves complex and layered analyses that integrate visual materials with texts and other types of sources. Recovering the ways in which such materials embody social relationships is key to establishing connections between them and the phenomena that historians are interested in. Within the broad field of history, the history of science and the history of medicine have developed some of the most sophisticated approaches to visual evidence – perhaps because people writing on such topics are interested in the past construction and representation of evidence about nature and human bodies.[10] It is therefore helpful to read widely not only within the broad church that is history but also in other disciplines. Accordingly historians working with visual evidence may draw upon a range of fields, such as art history, visual culture studies, museology, history of photography, and word and image studies, that offer important conceptual and empirical resources.

Disciplinary landscapes

The phrase 'visual phenomena' covers many things – as evinced by the range of examples in Jonathan Conlin's essay on the eighteenth-century politician John Wilkes – from roughly chalked numbers to painted portraits. This inclusivity is helpful in so far as it directs our attention to rich potential materials for historians, who are still generally encouraged to understand their discipline as rooted in the study of documents and the meticulous analysis of language. However, in order to reveal the possibilities that visual culture can offer, a clear focus is required. Considering the disciplines that specialize in visual sources

---

[10] For example Daston, *Things That Talk*; Daston, *Histories of Scientific Observation*; Smith, *Body of the Artisan*; and Mitman and Wilder, *Documenting the World*.

is one way forward. Even here we note the number and range of fields that rarely occupy centre stage in university-level history courses, such as dress and costume history, print studies, numismatics and architecture. Each has its own history and traditions, modes of operation and institutional settings, with some, such as architecture, yoked to professional training and others, such as numismatics, largely the province of museum curators.

The fields that historians draw upon depend on their areas of specialism. Coins are routinely used by those working on ancient and medieval times. They tend to survive, are visually complex in their own right, and can yield valuable insights for scholars whose sources are necessarily more limited than those available to colleagues working on the more recent past. The scarcity of conventional sources, although in some sense restrictive, can also be a spur to methodological innovation: those working on earlier periods tend to practice more integrative forms of history.[11]

We have noted the distinctly blurred dividing lines between visual and material culture. Two disciplines have been particularly active in the development of material culture studies and hence of interest to those working on visual culture: archaeology and anthropology. Indeed there are subfields called 'visual anthropology' and the 'anthropology of art'. While there are clearly overlaps and affinities between these fields and others concerned with art and visual culture, there are also significant differences. Both archaeology and anthropology involve fieldwork, for example, and the distinctive skills required to carry it out form a central part of the training. Archaeology is rooted in an understanding of space, since the precise location of a find provides clues that are central to its interpretation and the distribution of finds across a whole site is equally revealing. In the case of anthropology, much attention is paid to the demeanour and ethical stances adopted when working with informants and to ways of recording and interpreting experiences.[12]

The prolonged, meticulous scrutiny of items already endowed with cultural, aesthetic and economic value that is characteristic of connoisseurship and of some art-historical approaches differs markedly from archaeological and anthropological practices, and has its origins in discussions of the visual arts during ancient times, Renaissance habits of debating, commissioning and collecting, and more generally in styles of thought characteristic of the humanities. Commitment to a canon – those works deemed most central to specific genres, art forms and cultures – is characteristic of European ways of responding to art, and was exported through processes of colonization and empire building. While there have been fierce debates about the matter, in practice the majority of

---

[11] For example Nelson, *Visuality*.
[12] For 'visual anthropology', see the journal with the same name, 1987 onwards. See also Pink, *Future of Visual Anthropology*. There is no comparable field in archaeology, presumably because visual phenomena have always been integral to the discipline.

scholars work on figures within some sort of canon, especially if they construe their objects of study in terms of 'art'. In other words, we tend to study only a small proportion of people who made items of visual interest in the past.[13]

'Visual culture' as a category of materials and as a field of academic study has gained currency in recent decades, in part as a reaction against the perceived exclusivity and elitism that 'art' implies. Those who see 'visual culture' as their principal guiding term can work with any medium, and do not need to concern themselves with judgements about quality. 'Art' and 'visual culture', then, are distinct notions, and indicate different intellectual priorities, although the same artefact can easily come under both categories. There are reasons for giving careful consideration to both terms.[14]

No matter how generous a definition of art is deployed, it is clear that some phenomena are excluded or peripheral. 'Art' implies some sort of gatekeeping, not least by institutions that are open to the public. 'Visual culture' is, by contrast, more generous and inclusive, as is 'material culture'. One way of conceptualizing this broad remit is in terms of horizontality. When studying any given period, invoking 'visual culture' gives us permission to consider diverse artefacts – dress, interior design, everyday commodities, maps, websites, currency, advertising and so on – together. Such an approach chimes with the long-standing interest in style, which allows scholars to find common visual threads between disparate forms: between, say, modernist art, literature, buildings, fabric patterns, books and magazines and household items such as tableware, furniture and appliances. The centenary of the Bauhaus – the German art school that was in operation between 1919 and 1933 – has spawned much commentary making precisely the point that their approach shaped the look and design ethos of a wide range of art and objects.[15] We can discern visual similarities right across a society's diverse products with the same style and that style is recognized by later generations, available to be used, adapted and celebrated by them.

Work in visual culture studies can eschew canonical makers and elite products in favour of popular genres not celebrated in cathedrals of art. National galleries of art can be contrasted in this respect with design museums, which may display coffee pots, chairs and furnishing fabrics with the same relish that other institutions reserve for works by old masters and contemporary artistic titans.[16] In this respect there is a kinship between visual culture studies, media studies and material culture studies, even if each of these fields has its own distinctive characteristics, by virtue of the traditions from which they

---

[13] Perry and Cunningham, *Academies, Museums and Canons*; Pollock, *Differencing the Canon*.
[14] On visual culture, see Rampley, *Visual Culture*, and for an approach more rooted in the social sciences, Rose, *Visual Methodologies*.
[15] Droste, *Bauhaus*.
[16] See, for example, the Cooper Hewitt, Smithsonian Design Museum, in New York; for a newly founded institution (2018), see the China Design Museum in Hangzhou.

draw inspiration and their institutional locations: material culture studies is frequently located in social science faculties, media studies is often paired with communications, visual culture studies with the humanities.

Inevitably there is a measure of ambiguity associated with the term 'art', since it can be applied to music and literature, exponents of which are commonly called 'artists'. The phrase 'art song' is sometimes used to distinguish *lieder* performed as part of the classical music repertoire from popular and folk song, which immediately indicates that nestled within the term 'art' are judgements suffused with assumptions about cultural hierarchies, class and value. Noting this point does not imply approval of such uses, it merely recognizes their existence and acknowledges that their histories and implications need to be taken into account. 'Art' is hardly value-neutral, and the term itself remains ambiguous and contested. Art history as it is practised incorporates an understanding of the complexities of 'art' as a term and of the history of a field that is still *relatively* young, and also vulnerable. Departments are fewer in number and smaller in size than those devoted to history for example. The historical study of art has flourished since the Second World War, although it existed in Germany since the nineteenth century (some would say earlier).[17] When and how disciplines form and take hold are important historical questions. Just as historians are helped by having a grasp of the past of their field, so those committed to studying 'the visual' can benefit from understanding the lineages of key concepts and intellectual approaches.

As an area of academic study, art history possesses some distinctive features. For example, it underpins judgements made by dealers, auctioneers, collectors and institutions, above all when they interact with international markets and develop acquisition policies. The potential relevance of art history to multinational companies, major museums and galleries and super rich collectors, is quite unlike the ways in which literary study or musicological analysis are normally deployed. 'Art' implies aesthetic judgement in a way that 'visual culture' does not. Indeed the origins of art history lie in scholarly work on highly valued artefacts, such as antique sculpture and old master painting. But what is valued, whether in monetary terms or aesthetically, changes over time, sometimes quite dramatically. Hence what counts as 'art' and for whom is itself a historical phenomenon, one in which art historians are deeply interested. The reputations of artists feted as self-evidently exceptional in our own times are sometimes far more recent and hard-won than we might imagine.[18] By the same token, art history is not a static discipline; rather its key features are shifting all the time in response to art and artists, to broad cultural, economic and political shifts, and to trends within academic institutions.

---

[17] Pointon, *History of Art*, and Hatt and Klonk, *Art History*, are useful introductions to the field.
[18] Scallen, *Rembrandt, Reputation*.

Partly because art history remains a far smaller field than history, it would be possible to claim that it is simply one subfield within the discipline of history. In practice, however, they differ in some important respects – attitudes to theory are one example – while art history and history departments tend to be separate entities within institutions of higher education. Aspects of art history, aesthetic theories and art criticism, for instance, have strong affinities with philosophy and with literary studies, and this may account for practitioners' openness to theoretical perspectives from these disciplines, about which many historians are sceptical. Art history inevitably has a narrower focus than history, since only certain categories of objects are deemed 'art', no matter how generous a definition one uses. It requires some specific skills, focused visual attention, for instance, that historians tend to lack. If it is argued, as we are doing here, that it is fruitful for historians to engage closely with visual and material evidence, then it follows that we should learn from scholars who are most skilled in using that evidence. Art history, for example, has been refining ways of seeing and interpreting the visual arts for around two centuries; hence it possesses forms of intellectual refinement and maturity that can help historians understand art and its significance; it illuminates changing ways of paying attention to visual phenomena. The study of contemporary art practice is an integral part of the discipline, connecting practitioners directly with artists and galleries. It enriches academic art history when there are conversations with those who make, sell, display and promote the visual arts, and by extension they can enrich the understanding of historians interested in visual culture.[19]

The place of photography

Since 'visual culture' can include so many genres and media, the areas it subsumes are likely to possess different characteristics in terms of modes of production, social status, market position and institutions. Photography is the pre-eminent example of an area that can be considered part of visual culture while possessing many distinctive features as a medium that has made a huge impact on every aspect of the world since its invention. Photography is the focus for so many scholars that photography studies might be considered a field in its own right.[20] Although its history and associated technologies are complex, it is helpful to see both as vital for writing visual histories. We are now deeply

---

[19] On contemporary art, see Hopkins, *After Modern Art*, and Stallabrass, *Contemporary Art*.
[20] For histories of the medium, see Jeffrey, *Photography*; Clarke, *The Photograph*; and Haworth-Booth, *Photography*. For attempts at its conceptualization, see Burgin, *Thinking Photography*; Wells, *Photography*; and Benjamin, *Illuminations*.

reliant on photography for research and publication, and the practice of digital photography has become so widespread that we simply take it for granted.

Photography does not have a straightforward or uncontested place in the history and contemporary practice of art history and visual culture studies. This situation reveals our inconsistent relationship with media, since art historians specializing in mainstream painting since, say, the sixteenth century would rarely describe themselves as someone working on 'oil painting', yet those who work on print and photography would more commonly see their focus on a medium as defining their intellectual identity. This may partly be explained by the shorter history of photography by comparison with that of paint, which goes back many thousands of years: in the form the medium has taken in Western art traditions, it has become so central that 'art' can easily be taken to mean 'painting'. Prints, such as engravings and etchings, are normally given lower status than oil painting in these traditions. They take so many forms and are so numerous that their study poses real challenges somewhat in the way photographs do. The custom of using photography as an organizing principle for research may also be connected with its initially ambiguous relationship with painting. In the medium's early years photographers aspired to make their prints look like paintings, that is, photography conducted itself as a dependent field. This gradually changed, and grasping the significance of waves of technological and social innovation for the resulting images is a major challenge for historians. Furthermore, it is worth emphasizing the sheer diversity and volume of photographs that existed by the end of the nineteenth century – features that have become ever more dramatic through to the present day with the near ubiquity of digital cameras. One result is the entangled integration of photographs into daily life, so that the history of family photography is now a recognized subfield, one taken up by historians who are committed to understanding the lives of the many rather than those of the elite few.[21] It is revealing that what is sometimes called 'art photography' has emerged as a major element within art galleries and art history, although its boundaries remain contested and photographers once seen as barely deserving of monographic exhibitions in major institutions – Cecil Beaton is a good example – are now held in high esteem, and the cost of their work, especially original prints, has soared accordingly.[22] A further feature of photographs needs to be noted here – their integration into publications.

Photographic books in all their diversity are a major historical phenomenon (and the subject of Chapter 5). Like the use of photographs in newspapers and magazines, discussed in Chapter 6, they prompt questions about print runs and audiences, the role of publishers, design and layout, and the relationships

---

[21] Rose, *Doing Family Photography*.
[22] On Beaton, see https://www.npg.org.uk/whatson/exhibitions/20041/cecil-beaton-portraits.php, accessed 7 July 2019.

between texts and images. One of the most famous examples was based on an exhibition at the Museum of Modern Art in New York, among the earliest photographic exhibitions the museum had mounted. The accompanying book has never been out of print since 1955, when *The Family of Man* opened, and there is an extensive literature on both the book and the exhibition, which explores their Cold War context, the ways in which they were assembled and displayed, and their ideological dimensions. One of the most striking features is the use of brief quotations from sources as diverse as Virgil and John Masefield, the Bible and the United Nations Charter.[23] The words set the tone for viewers as they turn the pages and absorb images from all over the world and the whole of photographic history. This example reveals how closely visual histories are bound up with texts, and hence that the kind of attention we can call 'literary' is indispensable, whether this is to interpret captions, life writings that engage with images, scholarly accounts of visual culture, fiction and poetry inspired by visual experiences, or texts expressly selected and designed to accompany pictures.

Illustration

It is no surprise that there is a field – word and image studies – that explores, among a range of topics, the ways in which writers and artists have collaborated, of which book illustration is a pre-eminent example.[24] Examples spring to mind where texts and their illustrations have become so totally entwined – John Tenniel's illustrations to Lewis Carroll's books about Alice, for instance – that they cannot easily be separated in the minds of readers. Gustave Doré's wood engravings have shaped the ways in which we envisage social conditions in the second half of the nineteenth century. He illustrated the works of writers such as Cervantes, Rabelais, Milton, Balzac and Poe, while also producing satires and comics. Such influential figures help historians to bring together genres that coexisted harmoniously in the past but all too often have subsequently been studied separately and accorded different types of cultural status.[25] Another field – history of the book – is relevant here, since its focus is books in their entirety, including bindings and paper.[26] But a cautionary note must be sounded. It is common to juxtapose word and image as if they occupy different categories, whereas in practice words form images, as we know from shape poems. The overall look of manuscripts and publications affects the reading

---

[23] *Family of Man*, 150, 171, 94–5, 33, 184.
[24] See the journal *Word and Image*.
[25] Dolphin, *Gustave Doré*.
[26] Raven, *What Is the History of the Book?*, and Gameson, *Early Medieval Bible*, are examples of book history.

experience, with the size and font of type as well as layout, paper and the use of colour all playing significant roles. These features may be approached from a visual culture perspective, which can and should be applied to the secondary sources scholars use as well as to the primary ones. The design of a book that engages deeply with visual evidence has a huge impact on its reception, while the volume itself will make visual as well as verbal arguments. These points also apply to the emerging genre of graphic history, that is, books where any meaningful distinction between 'text' and 'illustration' has vanished.[27] Such publications can reach wide audiences, as we know from the success of Art Spiegelman's *Maus*. A visual culture approach to graphic history enables us to think about the ways in which non-specialist audiences respond to new genres that provide innovative accounts of the past.

Historiographical perspectives

We have noted the many fields that bear on and can inform historical work that deploys visual materials, each with its own history, habits of mind and intellectual traditions. Reading widely, yet critically, is thus essential. In order to focus such reading and reflection, it helps to know why and how historians engage with historical writings, past and present, as well as with those from cognate fields. Every historian is also a historiographer, who probes the ways history is written. Then there are techniques for assessing publications that are worth making explicit. At the most basic level, it is obviously essential to know what has already been written on any given topic, and to critically evaluate it, and this involves putting the work in question in its own historical context. In this case, 'context' would include the technologies available to reproduce images and an understanding of the priorities of publishers, some of whom are still extremely cautious about giving historians generous numbers of illustrations. Art-historical publications are valuable for their combination of close readings with high-quality reproductions. They also tend to draw upon distinctive ways of conceptualizing visual phenomena from a number of fields, such as philosophy, especially aesthetics, literature, critical theory and post-colonial studies. In a similar manner, writings about digital media are able to take inspiration from communications theorists and about material culture from anthropological frameworks. In evaluating any given publication it is worth moving from its physical properties and subject matter through a critical assessment of its arguments and then on to its conceptual scaffolding and rhetorical features. The kinds of critical reading we are advocating are

---

[27] Jordanova, *History in Practice*, 257–61, discusses 'graphic histories'.

likely to include classic works in a relevant field, reference books, exhibition catalogues, textbooks as well as journal articles and monographs. As readers develop frameworks for historiographical evaluation, they acquire the tools to consider diverse genres and topics. The insights thereby gained are transferrable to other examples and areas. The works cited by the authors of the essays provide readers with a starting point for moving into literatures that engage closely and directly with visual materials, and with the conceptual issues that they raise. Peter Burke's *Eyewitnessing* has been pioneering in this respect. Here, we do not attempt to survey the literature on a field that is, as we have already suggested, too broad and varied to summarize in a meaningful way. Instead, we address four works that are significantly different in scope and approach, drawing out from each some historiographical points we wish to emphasize.

Readers respond to all aspects of a publication, including its size, layout and cover in the case of books, much as we do to any source. We may be struck, for example, by the small format, numbered sections within chapters and the limited number of colour plates in Michael Baxandall's hugely influential *Painting and Experience in Fifteenth-Century Italy*, first published in 1972. This small book grew out of lectures he gave to history students, which 'were meant to show how the *style* of pictures is the proper material of social history'.[28] Baxandall had initially studied English literature and worked in a museum, before he became one of the most significant art historians of his time. Among the most remarkable features of his body of work is the range of subjects, media, periods and places that he addressed, developing a precise and clearly articulated approach apt for each one. It is because *Painting and Experience* is measured and accessible that it has become so widely adopted in teaching. Evidence and the use to which any given piece of it can, and cannot, be put is a central concern. He lays out with exactitude the ways in which paintings at that time and place can be understood, not just by analysing them but by using documents, such as contracts between artists and patrons, to examine their genesis and to make inferences about prevalent ways of looking. The first sentence of the book – 'A fifteenth-century painting is the deposit of a social relationship' – indicates his interest in the historically specific practices surrounding the making and viewing of works of art.[29] In other words, he shows what a thoroughly *historical* approach looks like. Baxandall considers materials and money as well as the subject matter and style of paintings. This work ventures into a heavily occupied field, and it does so without the cumbersome apparatus of footnotes and bibliography, while still providing details of the main primary texts it deploys. Its force lies in the intellectual rigour of the arguments, each step manifestly following the preceding one, with

---

[28] Baxandall, *Painting and Experience*, 'Preface to the First Edition', n.p. Emphasis in original.
[29] Ibid., 1.

unfamiliar terms carefully explained. We might deem it a 'textbook' if it had to be assigned to a specific genre, although this term does not adequately express the vision that it articulates about the ways in which 'social history' and 'art' can illuminate each other. Baxandall's book demonstrates the value of being as explicit as possible about how an author is thinking and working. He is by no means unusual in doing so.

Art Spiegelman's acclaimed *Maus* is open about its maker's life, and the lives of his parents, while sharing with his readers some of the processes by which it was produced. This is a graphic history, that is, it works like a comic book, although the subject matter could not be more serious. It provides a historical narrative of the experience of Jews before, during and after the Holocaust, and recounts the terrible suffering of actual historical figures. This is hardly uncharted territory for historians, but Spiegelman delivers his account in highly unusual ways, using words and pictures in intimate union. He also eschews telling the story of his parents in chronological order; rather there are injections, doublings back and forth, and he is ever present, never a detached narrator. His principal source is his father and his memories, and he does not hesitate to show the complexities of their sometimes quite strained relationship. As the title suggests, mice are involved – he shows Jews as mice (wearing clothes), just as the Nazis are menacing cats, and other groups are represented by dogs and pigs. *Maus*, then, is an influential and acclaimed visual history that lays bare its sources and genesis. Its foundations, however, are personal and emotional. There is no detached, cool analysis here; rather the author uses his specifically visual skills to elicit powerful reactions in readers. Given its subject matter, *Maus* can be labelled 'political', and it would be easy to simply put it in the same categories as, for instance, cartoons in newspapers or persuasive posters, to which it bears a certain visual similarity. However there are many distinct ways in which visual histories, like the sources they use, deal with the nature of power and its myriad manifestations, which it is the job of scholars to draw out. In its own manner, *Painting and Experience* is a political book – it shows the ways money was used and patrons operated with respect to painters – and it demonstrates the potential of forms of art history that turn away from narrow iconographic analysis and embrace social history. The point applies to even the supposedly neutral genre of the exhibition catalogue, with which those writing visual histories need to engage, since these too touch on money and power, if often indirectly.

Catalogues of exhibitions and collections need to perform a number of seemingly mundane tasks. For example, they provide 'tombstone' details for works displayed, including provenance, if known. They certainly contain information about the owners, whether individual or institutional, who have lent treasured possessions for an exhibition quite possibly thousands of miles away. It is also necessary to acknowledge those who fund and insure the venture. In fact all of this is important and relevant, and even more so in a context where sponsorship in the visual arts is being hotly debated, where many items are bought for investment and may be unavailable for inclusion in a public show, and where some owners are reluctant to allow their possessions to travel, resulting in delicate negotiations between curators and administrators, on the one hand, and individuals, families and institutions, on the other. All this is 'political' in a number of senses, and these phenomena mean that catalogues are a veritable treasure trove for historians.

All those involved in exhibitions demand a high level of accuracy in the printed matter that they generate – labels, panels, leaflets and fliers as well as catalogues – which are, as a result, invaluable for scholars. While there are variations, such publications mostly include a foreword by the institutions involved, pitching the exhibition's virtues and giving thanks; descriptions of objects on display; a list of lenders; a bibliography; and shortish essays by experts in the field, including the lead curators. In a sense they become reference books, while presenting a clear thesis. Exhibitions that lack an easily graspable narrative of some kind tend to fail, and given the huge costs they typically involve, this is a risk few organizations can take. Such narratives are in any case essential for marketing purposes. Exhibitions about collecting practices offer particularly rich resources for historians.

Like a number of successful eighteenth-century medical men, William Hunter amassed a huge, valuable and diverse collection, which he left to the University of Glasgow.[30] Such bequests are hardly unproblematic, and make considerable demands on their recipients. A collection's history after the death of the owner reveals a great deal about how artefacts and naturalia are classified and displayed. Given that Hunter owned fine paintings as well as anatomical specimens, coins and medals as well as medieval manuscripts, it is immediately apparent that there are both practical and intellectual challenges in displaying the collection so as to indicate Hunter's vision, passion and project. *William Hunter and the Anatomy of the Modern Museum*, which opened in Glasgow during the tercentenary of the collector's birth in 2018, set out precisely to bring together items from his collection and tell a clear and coherent story about an individual and his possessions.[31]

The Hunterian Museum together with Yale University Press produced a magnificent volume to accompany the exhibition, in a large format with a generous amount of colour illustrations. Part I contains eight fully illustrated essays, while Part II consists of the catalogue of the exhibition, with eleven short essays between the entries on specific items. Since the work is 440 pages long, it represents a massive, profoundly collaborative undertaking, while necessarily containing a small selection from Hunter's vast collections. The high-quality

---

[30] Hans Sloane and Richard Mead are other examples; see Delbourgo, *Collecting the World*, and Hanson, *English Virtuoso*.
[31] Campbell and Flis, *William Hunter*.

design, for which this press is famous, makes a massive contribution to the reading experience, while details of the type face, the company that typeset the volume and the designer may be found on the very last page. This note also outlines the history of the font, and of a publishing company that used earlier versions of it, of which Hunter was a patron. Thus we learn a great deal about the design of books and the visual attention the makers expect of readers. Making these comments in no way lessens the value of analysing the content of publications; rather it draws attention to the ways in which we can extend our study so as to appreciate their visual properties, which play a central role in communicating arguments that are rooted in images, artefacts and specimens. A key notion here is 'attention', and the ways in which it can be mobilized in the service of writing – or even more broadly speaking, constructing – visual histories, in which words and pictures, ideas and arguments, reproductive technologies and the physical properties of displays and publications are considered together in an integrative manner.

This integrative approach is well demonstrated by Debora Silverman's book *Art Nouveau in Fin-de-Siècle France*, where she is explicit about the intellectual traditions upon which she draws and the choices she has made in framing the work. Silverman has the distinction of working historically and paying close attention to visual and material culture as well as to ideas, somewhat in the manner of Carl Schorske, with whom she undertook her doctoral research.[32] Her admirable conceptual precision allows readers to perceive her manner of working, and in this respect the book bears comparison with *Painting and Experience*. Yet it is clearly a monograph that grew out of her postgraduate research, with full scholarly apparatus and a highly specific focus – 'the institutional and intellectual origins of French art nouveau'.[33] The art nouveau in question is a historically specific style, examined in one country, with respect to interior design, and over a limited period of time, that is, the 1890s. Silverman's careful control of her subject matter and her willingness to explain her approach assist readers in grasping what this form of visual history actually consists of. For example, her focus on style requires her to undertake, in her phrase, 'formal analysis', while her historical project demands that she consider nineteenth-century writings about art and design, the political setting in which key developments in art nouveau occurred, the development of luxury crafts, ideas about the boundaries between public and private, and debates about modernity, which included medical psychology.[34] Thus she examines in a single volume themes that are present in many kinds of history-writing, including intellectual history, the history of science, technology and medicine, histories of art, design, nationalism and the fin-de-siècle phenomenon, for

---

[32] See Schorske, *Fin-de-Siècle Vienna*.
[33] Silverman, *Art Nouveau*, 10.
[34] Ibid., 1–13, 10.

instance. The body of the book contains black-and-white illustrations, with a colour insert of fifteen plates. The text is tightly argued, wide-ranging as well as finely descriptive, so that the rich context of the style is melded with close readings of its material manifestations.

Our argument here is that historiographical perspectives necessarily inform everything we do when writing visual histories and that these are gained by meticulous and wide reading of existing work, which is not only scholarly in its usual sense but includes graphic publications and all the materials generated by museums, galleries and institutions that display visual culture. It is in this spirit that readers are invited to engage with our book, its contents, its illustrations and above all with its ideas.

Writing visual histories

This book is intended to provide a number of ways of thinking about the writing of visual histories. Its structure, combining case studies with chapters on salient concepts, historians' all-too-often tacit practices, and practical matters concerned with publishing and research, invites a form of reading that is attentive not just to what is being said but to how questions are framed, evidence is constructed, and arguments are made and supported. We propose an integrative approach to all these matters while at the same time bringing each into focus for careful consideration. Each section (essays, concepts, practices and practicalities) is intended to carry equal weight, and we conceive of the book itself as an ensemble.

The six essays exemplify the approaches that we advocate. Their selection is limited by necessity, hence there are topics, genres, media, times and places that are not included; as a group they are intended to indicate the richness and potential range of visual materials and what historians can do with them. They cover a period between the fourteenth and the twentieth centuries, draw together accounts based in Britain, continental Europe, and the United States, and range in scale of analysis from depictions of a single individual to the role of printed representations in a global process of categorizing and describing peoples. Decisions about chronological and geographical scope have been made with the manageability and coherence of the volume in mind – certainly not to suggest that other periods or regions are of less interest or importance. Even a casual reader will notice that the essays focus on Western materials from the late medieval period to the twentieth century. In planning the volume, we as editors faced the fact that just as 'visual' has to be broken into pieces to be meaningfully discussed, so too does 'history'. Thus we chose to include material that we felt we could address in an informed and rigorous manner. The results reflect our disciplinary backgrounds, and the areas within which we are equipped to work responsibly on the topic of visual histories. These choices should not be taken as an assertion of the special value of the Western canon or Western ways of looking and thinking but rather as an acknowledgement of our own particular limits as historians.[35] Many medievalists and classicists working on Western materials have developed integrative forms of writing that tie comparatively scarce texts to material and visual evidence, and history to related disciplines such as archaeology. Historians working in non-Western fields adopt conceptual frameworks appropriate to their materials, reaching beyond the repertoire of ideas that has developed alongside European and US art worlds and arenas of visual culture.

The case studies are arranged in chronological order but need not be read in this way; we are not suggesting any predetermined route through the book. Instead, each section represents a different facet of the writing of visual histories. The essays make methodological points 'in action', while at the same time indicating broader literatures and fields of study. Marcus Meer considers the ways in which honour and dishonour were seen and shown through heraldry in late medieval Europe, focusing on the apparently simple action of turning coats of arms – and occasionally persons – upside down. This manipulation of symbols was powerful and widely understood but was also used in the context of funeral rituals, where it denoted honour in death, rather than shame in life. Thus the interpretation of a visual phenomenon with performative and material dimensions is profoundly dependent on context and on surviving textual evidence. Katherine Bond addresses the role of costume imagery in the development of ideas about human difference and national identities through the sixteenth century, charting the production, circulation and reception of travel sketches, costume books and ethnographic prints in a period of enhanced transnational exchange and cross-cultural encounter. Such imagery was crucial to the construction of popular ideas about 'other' cultures globally but presents particular challenges to historians, especially with regard to issues around observation, authenticity and the frequent reuse of derivative images. Within the costume book genre, certain motifs were repeatedly copied and adapted, eventually coming to stand in for cultural types and shaping social categories in turn. These images might be thought to represent more directly the practical and economic concerns of the printing trades than the customs of the peoples they nominally represented, demonstrating the need for cautious interpretation underpinned by comparative analysis.

---

[35] There is much important work on visual culture beyond Europe and North America; the recent contributions mentioned here provide useful and stimulating perspectives. Tang and Hori, for instance, include film in their interdisciplinary studies and insist on the complexities of visual culture in China and Japan respectively, in order to challenge a common assumption that existing models and approaches can be applied to all cultures; Ogbechie focuses on a collection of African art based in Lagos, Nigeria (https://femiakinsanyaartcollection.com, accessed 6 May 2020), precisely to show its diversity and richness. See Tang, *Visual Culture in Contemporary China*; Hori, *Promiscuous Media*; Ogbechie, *Making History*.

Ludmilla Jordanova's study of the Royal College of Physicians in London, from its founding in 1518 to the present day, shows how such institutions develop elaborate visual cultures that encompass buildings, portraits, books and manuscripts, silverware and other artefacts, including objects owned by renowned members that can approximate the status of relics. Such visual cultures are vital to the expression of professional identities and the sense of continuity that underpins them. Their diverse and layered nature makes them particularly ripe for the kind of integrative study we are advocating in this volume, as well as for reflection on the ways in which collective senses of the past are articulated in the present. Jonathan Conlin's study of John Wilkes surveys the visual symbols surrounding the controversial eighteenth-century British politician, including illuminated windows, the number '45' chalked on doorways, painted portraits, prints and tobacco labels. Tracing the development of such imagery across Wilkes's career, he argues that its political significance can only be established when the relationships between medium, genre and audience, as well as between originals and reproductions, are understood in detail. These factors, in turn, raise significant questions about trends in political participation in the eighteenth century.

In his essay on architectural photobooks in Germany's Weimar Republic, J. J. Long takes a detailed look at two very different examples of this genre. Developing an approach to these materials through the Foucauldian notion of discourse, Long highlights the visual conventions that guided the translation of three-dimensional buildings and models into two-dimensional images, as well as choices concerning materials, design and typography that framed the images' meanings within printed and bound books that were produced collectively by many individuals and for distinctive markets. Questions about German national identity were worked out in part through debates about architecture during this period, and the photographic representation of buildings took on an element of agency in this wider context. Melissa Renn's case study analyses the role of imagery in *Life* magazine (published weekly 1936–72) through the commissioning of paintings, drawings and three-dimensional models, all of which played a role alongside photography. Focusing on choices about particular artists and visual media in American coverage of the Second World War, she reveals the complex relationship between documentary photography, news reporting and the influential magazine's visual programme, conceived in the broadest terms. In doing so, she raises fundamental questions about the ways in which various visual media were thought to contribute to the 'truthfulness' of news reporting at a crucial historical moment for the genre.

The case studies are to be read as much for their historiographical moves as their historical arguments: other parts of this volume provide a toolkit for opening them up and seeing how visual histories work, as well as pointing towards broader issues and sources. These offer short, descriptive definitions of concepts central to writing with visual sources, along with reflections on the kinds of logical and rhetorical manoeuvres that historians make when they describe visual materials, place them in context and categorize them by period, and practical guidelines for using image databases, organizing permissions, writing captions and publishing with pictures. These can be read with reference to the case studies or independently, as occasion arises. We hope that readers will approach this book as a flexible resource: an invitation to reflect on fundamental questions concerning the role of visual experience in historical understanding and writing visual histories.

Essays

1

Heraldry topsy-turvy: Depictions and performances of dishonour and death

Marcus Meer

At first sight, this drypoint etching (Figure 1) by the fifteenth-century Master of the Housebook looks clearly heraldic: it features a shield (the escutcheon) on which is placed a helmet, in turn crowned by the elaborate and distinctive three-dimensional arrangement of the crest, all draped with the ornamental linen of the mantling.[1] On a second look, however, the image seems strangely out of order. Normally, the coat of arms placed on the shield consists of a unique combination of charges (for example beasts, flowers, weapons or architecture) and geometrical figures known as ordinaries (such as crosses and chevrons), often partitioned into more or less complex divisions (into halves, quarters and so on) of the field on the shield. While the absence of any distinctive colours (tinctures) is easily explained by the monochrome nature of the artwork, its other heraldic elements still seem to defy everyday expectations about 'proper' heraldry: the shield shows a figure in a headstand, while the crest consists of two equally curious figures, namely a woman sitting on the back of a man.

In the late medieval period, roughly spanning the later thirteenth to the early sixteenth century, nothing seemed to convey a humorous reversal of the natural order of things quite as much as the idea of a woman being on top and thus 'in charge' of a man.[2] The man's depiction with a distaff further underlined this sentiment, since this tool, typically associated with female work, had become a symbol attributed to emasculated, 'shameful' men.[3] After all, in the Middle Ages, shame was defined in opposition to the idea of (male) honour, which next to inherited status crucially relied on the strict adherence to social norms and values, from Christian piety to martial prowess and sexual dominance.[4] Little was therefore more shameful and dishonourable to medieval men than the kind of gender role reversal portrayed by the crest.

---

[1] Comprehensive overviews of heraldry as a medieval (and modern) sign system include Hablot, 'Heraldic Imagery', and Cheesman, 'Heraldry'. Among the many 'textbooks' on heraldry, see especially Woodcock and Robinson, *Guide*; Neubecker, *Heraldry*.
[2] Davis, 'Women on Top'; Moxey, *Peasants, Warriors, and Wives*, 101–26; Kunzle, 'Upside Down', 42–3.
[3] Biscoglio, 'Unspun Heroes'; Grössinger, *Picturing Women*, 115–21.
[4] Aurell, 'Honour'; James, 'Honour'. See also Stewart, 'Honor'.

Figure 1 Master of the Housebook, *Coat of Arms with a Peasant Standing on His Head*, c. 1485–90, drypoint etching printed on paper, 13.8 × 8.5 cm (5⅜ × 3⅜ in.). Rijksmuseum Amsterdam, RP-P-OB-947 (artwork in the public domain, photograph provided and released into the public domain by Rijksmuseum, Amsterdam).

The theme of reversal also dominates the shield. In the Middle Ages, a body turned upside down was an attack on the natural order of things par excellence, not least because society itself was often conceptualized as a body governed by the king as its head.[5] 'Unnatural' bodily reversal was a punishment reserved for criminals held to have stained their honour, which is why any honour-conscious person tried to avoid being hung upside down 'in the manner of a thief'.[6] The artist's decision to depict such motifs associated with shame and dishonour in a coat of arms further added to this overarching theme of reversal. In the Middle Ages, heraldry and honour went together, so that contemporaries saw and

---

[5] Lanfranchi and Rollinger, *Body of the King*; Najemy, 'Body Metaphors'; Hale, *Body Politic*.
[6] Merback, *Thief*, 174–89; Mills, *Animation*, 39–43.

presented coats of arms as outwardly visible expressions of this key quality, which defined a person's status and thus their identity within the hierarchical order of late medieval society.[7]

Curiously, just as the artist of the drypoint etching turned the purpose of a coat of arms on its head, late medieval contemporaries all across Europe repeatedly turned these signs of honour themselves upside down. The purposeful reversal of coats of arms – the *subversio armorum* – appears time and time again throughout the source material, both in the form of images and in the shape of tangible shields turned upside down.[8] But why were coats of arms turned upside down? What were the intentions of those who reversed arms, what were the interpretations of those who saw them, and what were the reactions of those whose arms had been reversed? Does this practice relate to negative connotations of bodily reversal and ideas of honour and identity so closely associated with heraldry, for instance? In short, how were coats of arms turned upside down *perceived* by late medieval contemporaries?

Among the first studies to embrace such questions concerning the visual culture of the late medieval period was Michael Baxandall's *Painting and Experience in Fifteenth-Century Italy*, discussed in the introduction to this book, and David Freedberg's *The Power of Images*, which was likewise dedicated to 'the extraordinarily abundant evidence for the ways in which people of all classes and cultures have responded to images'.[9] Today, to quote Kathryn Starkey, 'from the perspective of the medievalist, understanding visual communication and concepts of perception in the Middle Ages is crucial to understanding medieval culture'.[10] However, as part of this broader quest, a visual history of topsy-turvy heraldry in particular cannot solely rely on visual sources typical for the study of heraldry (seals, stone- and wood-carvings, stained glass windows, manuscript illuminations and so on). Instead, in order to understand this visual phenomenon and its contemporary perceptions, it is necessary to take a close look at textual sources, too, from literature and chronicles to administrative documents and court records. Texts preserve displays of the past for which no visual evidence has survived, either because they have been lost over the centuries or because they were never meant to be permanent. Perhaps more importantly, texts also allow for contemporary perceptions to be approximated as closely as retrospectively possible: often

---

[7] Rubin, 'Identities', 387; Keen, *Chivalry*, 9; Ailes, 'Markers of Identity'. See also the contributions in Sutter, *Identity*.
[8] The most comprehensive study of the *subversio armorum* is Hablot, 'Blason de la trahison'. See also Strickland, 'Disinvestiture', 294–7; Keen, *Chivalry*, 174–7.
[9] Baxandall, *Painting and Experience*, esp. 40; Freedberg, *Power of Images*, xix. For the impact of visual culture scholars on medieval history, see Jaritz, 'Images'. For a wide range of examples, see also the contributions in Blockmans and Janse, *Showing Status*; Boone et al., *L'image*; Van Leeuwen, *Symbolic Communication*.
[10] Starkey, 'Visual Culture', 2. For examples of studies on medieval visual communication and perception, see Groebner, *Defaced*; Richmond, 'Visual Culture'; Camille, 'Gaze'.

their authors will present their own interpretations, ponder the intentions of others, and describe individual and collective reactions to visual matters. Finally, it is helpful to pursue a geographically wide approach to avoid premature generalizations about the representativeness or uniqueness of a specific area and instead promote examination of differences and similarities of the same phenomenon across borders, not least because different places produced and bequeathed different kinds of sources.[11]

For the curious case of reversed coats of arms, this multi-medial and comparative approach allows this chapter to trace late medieval perceptions of the phenomenon throughout Europe and in four different contexts: as a visual feature of letters of defamation, as an element of ephemeral rituals of punishment, as a means of equally short-lived but highly emotional public provocation and protest, and as part of the performance of funeral ceremonies. Throughout this process, it will become clear that perceptions of 'the visual', although they might appear universal and constant at first, remained at all times highly ambiguous and fundamentally dependent on the context(s) of their display.

Letters of defamation

In fifteenth- and sixteenth-century Germany, letters of defamation were commissioned, copied and later printed in large quantities for display in public spaces such as the marketplaces of cities. Their texts scolded persons who had failed to meet important obligations such as the repayment of debts,[12] and in this effort the letters frequently also incorporated images which depicted visual representations of the accused in shameful ways. Next to figural depictions similar to the infamous *pittura infamante* found in Italy,[13] these representations were often heraldic in nature.

In fact, in an acknowledgement of indebtedness the German count John V of Nassau (1455–1516) in 1488 explicitly agreed that his creditors may 'display our likeness and arms as maliciously as they can possibly imagine' should he default.[14] What this defamatory creativity looked like can be seen in a considerable number of extant letters vilifying the arms of the letter's

---

[11] Wickham, 'Comparative History'; Berger, 'Comparative History'.
[12] Lentz, 'Defamatory Letters'; Lentz, *Konflikt, Ehre, Ordnung*; Hupp, *Scheltbriefe*.
[13] Milani, 'Defamatory Paintings'; Edgerton, *Pictures and Punishment*, chs 2 and 3; Ortalli, *Pittura infamante*.
[14] Arnoldi, *Miscellaneen*, 116: 'Ind wan wir ... in maissen vurgeschrieuen nyet enhilden; So hayn wir ... erkoiren ... dat asdan Diederich syne eruen off heldere vurgeschr. sullen ind mogen yre gadonge van ind oeuer vns schryven, vnse figuren ind wapen upslaen ind mailen, so erchlichen sy dat vysieren ind erdenken konnen.' Unless otherwise stated, all translations are my own.

target,[15] frequently in combination with his seal as another important medieval means of identification.[16] Thus, when Duke John III of Bavaria (1374–1425) had failed to repay a loan, a letter of defamation lamented the 'deceptiveness' and 'malice' of the duke, who 'for such a small sum of money turned his back on his great name'.[17] In retaliation, the creditor stressed, 'I had the villain painted here with his deceptive seal',[18] and indeed the letter contains a depiction of a man with a seal stamp, marked with the arms of Bavaria, next to a pig (Plate 1). An additional taunt left no doubt as to the message this scene was supposed to convey: 'I stand before this sow's backside / And impress my seal onto it / Since it is no more use for letters and charters / And neither is my oath and honour.'[19]

The motif of reversal was employed for the same purpose. A letter of defamation issued against Landgrave Louis of Hesse (1402–58) in 1438 thus exclaimed that 'one shall leave him hanging here with his arms shamefully painted'.[20] 'Shamefully', in this instance, was notably 'upside down'. Although conspicuously clothed in aristocratic dress, the landgrave was depicted as hanging from the gallows by a rope tied around his feet in the manner of a thief (Plate 2).[21] In addition to this figural representation, the disgraced landgrave was also identified by the coat of arms of Hesse, which was likewise turned upside down and suspended by a rope. In Regensburg, the Jewish merchants Saydro and Isaac Straubinger in 1490 chose to depict their peer Hans Judmann in the same manner, 'to warn princes, counts, barons, knights and commoners and all others, that they should beware of this man who is without honour and faith, and who breaks promises made under his seal'.[22] Again, the lack of honour proclaimed in the text was accompanied by the accused's figure and arms turned upside down.

The *subversio armorum* in letters of defamation was not limited to the coats of arms of individual noblemen or merchants; it also targeted corporate bodies such as cities and their municipal arms. Thus, when Count John II of Wied (r. 1415–54) accused the City of Cologne of deliberately delaying the trial of an acquaintance, who had been imprisoned there in 1441, he threatened to 'publicly

---

[15] For examples, see the appendix of Lentz, *Konflikt, Ehre, Ordnung*, nos 24, 34, 37, 38, 46, 51.
[16] On the significance of seals, see Bedos-Rezak, 'Medieval Identity', 1511; Bedos-Rezak, *Ego*.
[17] Götze, 'Scheltbrief', 71–2: 'Ind wan ich froichte, daz hey so voll inwendiger valscheit, misdait ind Boysheit sy, daz er sich aller ere ind guetz geruechtes ertroist habe, daz doch umb so wenich geltz willen syme groissen namen nicht en voigt, so hain ich desen selven boiswicht mit synen valschen siegel doin malen, as sine tuyscherygen ind valscheit zo gehoirt …'
[18] Ibid.
[19] Ibid.: '[Ich] Sta vor dem hinder diser su, / En druck alda myn sigel an … Tot brieven et nyet mer is danck / Mit eydesgelofft en myner ere …'
[20] Letter of defamation against Landgrave Louis of Hesse, 1438: 'Dar vmb sol man yn hie schentlich mit sinem wappen gemallet hangen lan als lang biß er mir karung gethan hat nach erkentnyß fromer lude …'
[21] For 'hanging upside down' as a punishment in the Middle Ages, see note 6, above.
[22] Translated in Stewart, 'Honor', 17.

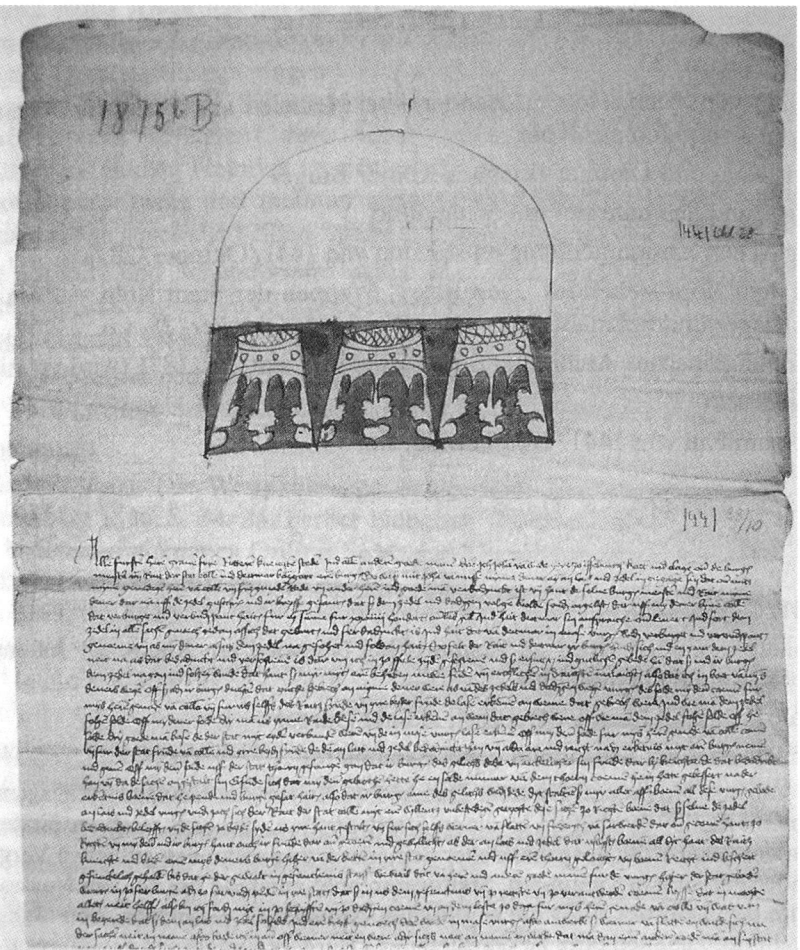

Figure 2 Letter of defamation against the City of Cologne, 1441, pen drawing on paper, 80 × 29.5 cm (30⅞ × 11⅜ in.). Historisches Archiv, Cologne, Briefeingang, 1875 b B (artwork in the public domain; photograph provided by Monasterium.net).

and continuously shame' the city if they did not expedite the procedure.[23] Since the townspeople did not comply with this 'request', the count issued letters with the municipal arms of Cologne turned upside down (Figure 2), much to the dismay of the townsmen, who felt that this display of their arms was not only an unjustified attack on their honour but also on the honour of God.[24] After all, they claimed, their arms depicted the crowns of the three Magi.[25]

---

[23] Kuske, *Quellen*, vol. 4, 81–3.
[24] Ibid., 87.
[25] The purported relics of the Three Kings were transferred to Cologne Cathedral in the twelfth century, later informing the city's visual culture. See Nagel, 'Ursula'.

In the context of letters of defamation attempting to shame and dishonour their recipient, then, the *subversio armorum* appears as part of an effort to publicize violations of the medieval code of honour. Coats of arms turned upside down – in the form of images depicted on paper or parchment documents – were meant to indicate their owners' shame and dishonour, warranted by a failure to comply with norms and values that required promises (and even more so oaths) to be faithfully delivered.

Shame and punishment

A much more performative part of late medieval life in which the *subversio armorum* appeared was the administration of official punishments for crimes against the code of honour. While such punishments were sometimes confined to a ritual removal of signs of honourable status, such as weapons and clothes, often they were but the portentous prelude to the destruction of the body's integrity through the gruesome climax of capital punishment.[26] In this context, too, honour was again linked to coats of arms, requiring the latter to be affected if the former was damaged or lost due to 'dishonourable' behaviour. Thus, when in 1515 the German nobleman Franz von Sickingen (1481–1523) was accused of having slandered Maximilian I (1459–1519), the emperor stripped the nobleman of 'all honour, nobility, lineage, dignity, pedigree, name, shield, helmet and badge'.[27] Deprived of these social qualities and their outward expressions, the decree continued, Franz von Sickingen was to be considered 'cast from the society and community of the nobility, and handed to the crowd of insensate beasts and dishonourable persons'. Similarly, in cases in which the accused was physically present, this removal of coats of arms and the honour they represented formed an important part of public performances of punishment rituals across late medieval Europe, as Matthew Strickland and Laurent Hablot show in their respective studies.[28]

Reversal, too, played its role in such performances meant to punish violations of the chivalric code of honour. A French treatise on public law, the *Songe du Vergier*, written between 1376 and 1378, warned everyone 'to not

---

[26] Cohen, 'Symbols of Culpability'; Royer, 'Body in Parts'.
[27] Senckenberg, *Selecta*, vol. 4, 544–50: 'Wir Maximilian ... von Römis. Keyserl. macht, volkomenheyt und rechtem wissen in krafft dieses brieffs ... ihne [Franz von Sickingen] und alle seine erben, und derselbig erbens erben, absteigender linien hinfür in ewige zeit aller vnd yeglicher ehren, adels, herkommens, wirdigkeyt, stammens, namens, schildt, helm, wapen, und kleynot darzu auch aller und yeder habe und güter ... zu unsern handen und gewalt anzunehmen, und einzuziehen bevolhen gentzlich und allerding priviret und entsetzt, sie des untüglich und unwirdig gemacht, auch aus der gesellschaft und gemeynschafft des adels gethan und geworffen und ... in die schar der unvernunfftigen thier vnd ehrlosen menschen ... zugeeygnet ...'
[28] Strickland, 'Disinvestiture'; Hablot, 'Emblèmes outragés'.

do anything resulting in the punishment of their arms being reversed ... for it brings shame to a noble lineage when their arms are turned upside down'.[29] Likewise, in about 1395, the English heraldic writer Johannes de Bado Aureo in his *Tractatus de Armis* held (and illustrated) that 'if an armiger is dishonoured due to treason, flight from battle or a broken oath, his arms are to be depicted upside down'.[30]

Ordinances of orders of chivalry and tournament societies, as associations of noblemen dedicated to ideals of chivalry and knightly honour, adopted the *subversio armorum* as a punishment for misconduct, too. In tournament ordinances issued by Philip VI of France (1293–1350), any contender exposed as an oath-breaker was to be 'shamefully excluded from the tournament' and 'to have his coat of arms reversed and trampled by the officers of arms [that is the heralds]'.[31] Shortly afterwards statutes of the chivalric Order of the Star, founded by John II of France (1319–64) in 1351, ordained along the same lines: 'If anyone dishonourably evades battle or a given task, he shall be suspended from the Order and not wear its habit, and his arms and his crest in the Noble Hall [of the Order] shall be turned upside down until he is reinstated by the Prince and his Council.'[32]

Individual knights fighting in the Hundred Years' War also repeatedly referred to the *subversio armorum* when emphasizing their sense of obligation by offering the integrity of their coat of arms as collateral. Thus, when Jean de Grailly (d. 1376) was captured by French soldiers in 1364, he referred to the shame his flight would bring in these terms: 'I want to be held for a false, evil-minded and disloyal knight, an oath-breaker and a liar, in signification of which my arms are to be reversed and shown turned upside down.'[33]

These were no idle threats or vague promises, as there are numerous instances in which such punishments were conducted. Members of the Order of the Golden Fleece deemed to have violated the code of chivalry got away relatively lightly. At the 1481 chapter meeting in the Church of St John in Brabantine 's-Hertogenbosch, for instance, Philippe de Crèvecoeur (d. 1494)

---

[29] Brunet, *Songe*, 183: 'Nul chevalier ou estrangier ne se peut obliger de faire aulcune chose sur peine que ses armes luy soyent renversées ... ; car c'est honte à toute une noble lignée quant les armes de leur hostel sont renversées.'
[30] Jones, *Heraldic Works*, 143: 'Item nota, quando portans arma debet dishonorari propter proditionem, fugam, vel fidem ruptam, tunc arma sunt pingenda per transversum.'
[31] Printed in Roy, *Chevalerie*, 127: 'Celui qui sera accusé et convaincu de foi mentie sera honteusement exclu du tournoi, et ses armes seront renversées et foulées aux pieds par les officiers d'armes.'
[32] Académie des inscriptions et belles-lettres, *Ordonnances*, vol. 2, 466: 'Et se il y a aucun qui honteusement ... se parte de bataille, ou de besoigne ordenée, il sera souspendus de la Compagnie, & ne pourra porter tel habit, & li tournera l'en en la Noble Maison ses armes & son timbre ce dessus dessous sans deffacier, jusques à tant que il fait restituez par le Prince & son Conseil ...'
[33] Secousse, *Mémoires*, 213: 'Je vueil et consens que je soie tenuz pour faux, mauvais & desloial chevalier, & pour parjure & foy mentie; & que en signe de ce, mes armes soient tournées & mises ce dessus-dessoubz ...'

was expelled from the order because he had defected to the French king. In public signification of his betrayal of the Burgundian crown, the disgraced lord's shield of arms, which had previously been displayed in the church alongside the shields of all other members of the order, was removed and placed outside, above the church's gate, for everyone to see and notably turned upside down.[34] Followers of anti-pope Benedict XIII, an Aragonese nobleman turned claimant to the throne of St Peter called Pedro de Luna (d. 1422/4), were subjected to a similar punishment by heraldic proxy. When he sent ambassadors to the French king in 1408, a chronicler recorded, they were apprehended, 'dressed in a tabard that bore depictions of the reversed coat of arms of Pope Luna, and shamefully and dishonourably put on a carriage', which was paraded through the cheering crowds of Paris.[35]

Others and their coats of arms met a more gruesome fate. When the former royal chamberlain Hugh le Despenser (b. c. 1286) was declared a traitor after the deposition of Edward II (1284–1327), his punishment, in the words of a fourteenth-century chronicler, was meant to 'extinguish all of his posterity, not just honour and rank, but the status he commands in the Kingdom of England forevermore'.[36] The punishment ritual, publicly staged at Hereford in 1326, saw Hugh le Despenser march through the city preceded by the king's marshal who carried the Despenser arms 'reversed upon a spear to show that they should be undone forevermore'.[37] Just as the Holy Roman Emperor had decreed in the case of Franz von Sickingen, the punishment extended not only to Hugh le Despenser but also to his 'posterity' – his successors who would otherwise have inherited his titles, arms and the honour they implied. The body of the shamed nobleman, too, was marked by means of topsy-turvy heraldry. Just like the followers of Pedro de Luna, he was 'dressed in a garment of his arms reversed',[38] and thus in the manner 'such as traitors and thieves were wont to wear', as the chronicler Jean Froissart (d. c. 1405) emphasized.[39] As Danielle Westerhof argues, Despenser, heraldically fashioned in this way, 'had to face the removal of his public identity and masculinity' in a shameful, excruciating and lengthy public execution that turned him into 'a symbol of his own corrupted nobility'.[40]

---

[34] Molinet, *Chroniques*, vol. 5, 291.
[35] Monstrelet, *Chronique*, vol. 1, 264–5: '[T]ous deux Arragonnois, mitrez et vestus de habillement où estoient figurées les armes de icellui Pierre de La Lune renversées, furent amenez moult honteusement et deshonnestement sur ung tumbereau, du Louvre en la court du palais.'
[36] Knighton, *Chronicon*, vol. 1, 436: 'Statimque tractatum est apud Herefordiam de morte Hugonis Spenser, et quomodo exstingui posset tota ejus posteritas, ne ad aliquem honorem, gradum, vel statum quis eorum deveniret in regno Angliae pro perpetuo.'
[37] Brie, *The Brut*, vol. 1, 240: 'Symunde of Redyng, bifore ham bar' her' armes oppon a spere reversede, in token þat þai shulde be vndone for evermore.
[38] Knighton, *Chronicon*, vol. 1, 436.
[39] Translated in Froissart, *Chronicles*, 11.
[40] Westerhof, 'Deconstructing Identities', 103, 105.

In the same way as letters of defamation, late medieval punishments and shame rituals thus related coats of arms to concepts of individual and collective honour. Next to the very tangible divestiture of material arms depicted on paper, shields or garments as a result of a loss of honour, in this context, too, the sight of arms turned upside down visualized violations of the medieval code of honour, especially with regard to values such as loyalty and fealty, which in some cases were so severe as to warrant the corporeal execution of their owner as well.

Provocation and protest

Just as late medieval penal contexts translated the loss of honour into damage or even loss of coats of arms, so did attacks on (and reversals of) heraldic signs as means of provocation, protest and vigilante justice. In the later Middle Ages, cities in particular provided a public sphere for the expression of disagreement and discontent by individuals and crowds alike, from spontaneous revolts against 'bad' government to the habitual rituals of *charivari*, which saw late medieval communities take to the streets (and to the visual) to partly mock, partly punish people deemed to have violated social norms, for example by burning their effigies or by forcing these 'dishonourable' persons – in the spirit of reversal – to 'ride backwards'.[41] But repeatedly such emotional outbursts also targeted coats of arms, often ending with their defacement or destruction.[42] On the occasion of the wedding of Richard II (1367–1400) and Anne of Bohemia (1366–94) in 1392, the destruction of heraldic decorations displayed 'in honour' of the couple caused 'great shame and scandal', as London court records noted.[43] Similarly, after the pretender Perkin Warbeck (d. 1499) had displayed the English royal arms outside a hostel in Antwerp to express his claim to the English throne, two Englishmen loyal to Henry VII (1457–1509), 'in order to defile, abolish, and defame the arms, the title, and the one who displayed them ... hurled dirt and other unspeakable things against them' in 1494.[44] The same motivations were at play when people in Cologne opposed

---

[41] On medieval forms of protest and provocation in general, see Dumolyn et al., *Voices*; Cohn, *Popular Protest*; Mullett, *Popular Culture*. On *charivari*, see Pettitt, 'Charivari'; Thompson, 'Rough Music'; Mellinkoff, 'Riding Backwards'.

[42] Hablot, 'L'iconoclasme héraldique'; Thiry, *Matter(s)*, ch. 5; Thiry, 'Heraldic Iconoclasm'.

[43] Plea and Memoranda Rolls, City of London, no. 26, 1381-3, membr. 2b: 'Inquisicio ... ad inquirendum quis vel que malefactores ... abradicarunt et deposuerunt ... circam mediam noctem tria scuta depicta tam cum armis dicti domini Regis quam imperatoris insimul ... et unum scutum depictum cum armis domini Regis ... in maximum dedecus obprobrium et scandalum tam ipsorum Regis et Regine ...'

[44] Molinet, *Chroniques*, vol. 5, 115–6; 'Donc pour dénigrer, abolir et diffamer tant les armes, le title, comme celuy lequel s'en paroit, deux compaignons englez, ... cuidans jecter contre lesdites armes ... terny de terre et autres immondices ...'

an attempt by Charles the Bold (1433–77), Duke of Burgundy, to claim the city by displaying the Burgundian coat of arms throughout the urban space in 1474. The proud townsmen 'threw faeces and other muck at the duke's letters and arms, ripped them off and dragged them through the dirt, thus shaming the proud prince ... in the worst way imaginable'.[45]

Again the *subversio armorum* was part of this repertoire of heraldic slander, and the emotional reactions of those affected demonstrate just how efficacious such visual manipulations of coats of arms were in the eyes of late medieval contemporaries. When the Breton knight Bertrand du Guesclin (d. 1380) was besieging a castle in Brittany in 1371, for example, he was insulted by the English captain of the fortress by means of topsy-turvy heraldry: 'Behold this misery,' lamented a late-fifteenth-century chronicle, 'the arms of Bertrand, although so great in courage, are shamefully hung as if he were a murderer, dragged to the middle of a crossroads, and reversed to show that Bertrand de Guesclin has the heart of a traitor!'[46] No doubt the Breton knight was outraged, too, for he ordered his men to seize the castle; they captured the English captain and hung him upside down instead.[47]

The arms of the Aragonese knight Bernat de Vilarig suffered a similar fate, although in this case the 'violation' of the chivalric code of honour was not quite as severe as alleged treason. In 1448, he had agreed to meet with the Castilian knight Gómez de Figueroa in Granada in order to settle a dispute by combat. However, while on his way to the city, Bernat was injured and brought back to Valencia – or so he claimed.[48] Certainly, his opponent believed the injury to be a pretence to avoid the confrontation. To signify this lack of courage, Gómez de Figueroa subsequently 'turned Bernat's arms upside down and so displayed them in public places'.[49] The same behaviour was echoed in chivalric literature such as the Catalan romance *Tirant lo Blanch* (1490), where the eponymous hero was challenged to battle: 'If you do not accept out of fear for me, rest assured, I will reverse your arms, and I will hang you like the traitor you are.'[50]

---

[45] Ehrenspiegel des Hauses Österreich, Augsburg, 1555/59, fol. 329r: 'Zudem lueff der gemain Man von allen orten do des Hertzoge brief, wappen vnnd Mandaten angeschlagen waren zu, warffen mit koth vnnd aller on sauberkait zu denselben, Rissen die herab, Drattens Inn das kot vnd schmäheten den stoltzen fuorsten vnnd Iren Bischoff auff das höhist ...'

[46] Cuvelier, *Chronique*, vol. 2, 217, n. 3: 'Oïl, dist l'escuier; regardez la doulour: / Les armes de Bertran, où tant a de vigour / Ont pendu laidement ainsi qu'un murdréour / et traïné ansois au lonc d'un carefour / Et les ont renversées en monstrant par fréour / Que Bertrand de Claquin a cuer de boiséeur.'

[47] Ibid.

[48] Salicrú i Lluch, *Documents*, 436.

[49] Ibid.: 'Lo dit mossèn Gómeç ... fer execució contra lo dit mossèn Bernat, revesant-li les armes e, axí revesades, posant-les o fent posar per lochs públichs ...'

[50] Martorell, *Tirant lo Blanch*, vol. 1, 227–8: 'E si per temor de mi acceptar no lo gosareu siau cert yo us reuersare les armes, e us penjare cap auall segons de trador se pertany, e per totes les corts dels grans feynors yo hire mostrant la gran tracio que feta haueu ...'

The infamous John of Gaunt (1340–99) was subjected to the same heraldic disgrace by the people of London in 1377. The latter had long been suspicious of the Duke of Lancaster, not least due to his role in the Bad Parliament, but when rumours spread claiming that the duke was about to restrict the city's liberties, the situation reached fever pitch: 'The commoners of London reversed the arms of the Duke of Lancaster, the base of the shield at the top and the chief at the bottom, placing one shield on the doors of St Paul's Cathedral, and another on the doors of Westminster Hall.'[51] That this was perceived to be a hostile and shameful act against the duke is underlined by the contemporary chroniclers' indicative choice of words: Thomas Walsingham (d. c. 1422) suggested that the shield upside down was to be understood 'in signification of treason',[52] while his colleague Jean Froissart held that it looked 'as though he was a traitor'.[53] Certainly, John of Gaunt was described to have reacted 'with great anger'.[54]

Just as Londoners furious about the Duke of Lancaster's policies targeted his heraldic signs, so the contempt for royal advisers and protégées fuelling a popular revolt in 1450 expressed itself in the form of attacks on coats of arms displayed in London. One of the victims was James Fiennes (c. 1395–1450), Lord of Saye and Sele, who had previously served on the King's Council and as Lord Treasurer. On account of these positions the rebels counted him among the 'enemies and traitors' believed to have used their access to the king's ear for their own gain, and held him responsible for the humiliating loss of England's territories in Normandy. Fiennes, too, was charged with treason, convicted, imprisoned, beheaded and his corpse dragged through the streets of London. Yet even in death the Lord of Saye and Sele – by proxy of his coat of arms – still prompted resentful reactions, as the chronicler Robert Bale (fl. 1461) recorded:

> On 21 July numerous soldiers that had been driven out of Normandy went to the Greyfriars' church in Newgate, where the said Lord Saye was worthily buried [in a tomb] with pillars decorated with his coat of arms, which the soldiers ripped off and turned upside down.[55]

---

[51] Galbraith, *Anonimalle Chronicle*, 104: 'Mesme celle temps au fyne du parlament, les comunes de Loundres reverserent les armes del duc de Loncastre, le poynt del escu amount et le test avale et mistrent une escu sour les huses del esglise cathedralle de seint Poule et une autre sur le huse de la sale de Wymoustre ...'

[52] Walsingham, *Chronicon Angliae*, 125: 'Tamen arma ducis, in signum proditionis, in pricipalissima strata urbis reversa suspendebantur, incertum a quibus vel quorum consilio hoc sit factum ...'

[53] Froissart, *Chroniques*, vol. 2, 165: 'Donc en aucun lieu en Angleterre on lui tourna ses armes ce dessus dessous, comme si il fût traître.'

[54] Walsingham, *Chronicon Angliae*, 125: '[Q]uod multum bilem ducis postea concitavit.'

[55] Bale, 'Chronicle', 134: 'Item the xxj day of July diverse and many of the Sowders that cam and wer dryven out of normandy toke upon them in þe chirch of the Greyfreres wtyn Newgate where as þe seid lord Say was worthely buried ... and his armes set on the pelours aboute drewe and pulled down the same armes and them reversed ...'

Here, reversal was combined with the iconoclastic *damnatio memoriae* of a disgraced military leader 'to make sure that what is dead has no chance of revival, whether in body or in spirit', as Freedberg writes with regard to the motives behind attacks on images.[56] In the case of James Fiennes, the target was not just his corporeal self but perhaps more importantly his honour as represented by his heraldic sign.

In the context of provocation and protest, too, the reversal of coats of arms thus conveyed failure to meet social expectations deemed to diminish or even obliterate the honour of the person in question. The words used by contemporary observers as well as the reactions of those affected by the *subversio armorum* recorded in the sources made it more than clear that it was this particular loss of honour, on grounds of violations of chivalric behaviour, such as treason or cowardice, that was meant to be rendered visible by means of topsy-turvy heraldry.

Death and (dis-)honour

At first sight, the perceptions of the *subversio armorum* encountered in the contexts of letters of defamation, rituals of punishment and expressions of provocation and protest seem to suggest that late medieval people always perceived reversed arms to represent an accusation of dishonour. However, a closer look at sources from an entirely different context, namely medieval funerals, paints a much more ambiguous picture. Funerals were, of course, a fundamentally 'honourable' occasion, meant to stage the honour of the deceased in all its visual and often heraldic splendour.[57] Yet coats of arms turned upside down were found in this context too, suggesting that the meaning of the *subversio armorum* was highly dependent on the specific context of its display.

In Germany, poet Peter von Suchenwirt's (c. 1320–95) account of the funeral ceremonies staged for Albrecht II (1298–1358), Duke of Austria, in 1358 is a case in point. Next to a sword borne point downwards, a sergeant-at-arms was equipped with a shield of the deceased duke's arms turned upside down and pinned to his chest.[58] Likewise, when counts Eberhard III and Ulrich V of Württemberg were buried in 1417 and 1480 respectively, again 'all coats of arms were reversed', just as 'all weapons pointed down'.[59] Affluent German

---

[56] Freedberg, 'Fear of Art', 71. See also Freedberg, *Iconoclasts*.
[57] For English examples of medieval and early modern funerals, see Woodward, *Theatre of Death*; Bassett, *Death in Towns*; Gittings, *Death*. On the 'heraldic funeral' which developed throughout the later Middle Ages, see also Kuin, 'Heraldic Funeral'; Litten, *English Way*, 173–94; Day, 'English Heraldic Funeral'.
[58] Suchenwirt, *Werke*, vv. 122–34.
[59] Boytsov, 'Funerals', 163.

burgesses staged the burials of their peers in a similar manner, as an account of urban funerals from fifteenth-century Frankfurt suggests:

> All bells in all churches and elsewhere are rung. A municipal messenger carries a candle [at the head of the procession], and after him follows the supreme judge with the shroud. Then follow the two oldest judges, one carrying the helmet, the other carrying the shield turned upside down.[60]

The reversal of coats of arms also occurred at funerals in France, and here sources underline that this practice was indeed perceived in a deeply symbolic way. When the aforementioned Bertrand du Guesclin was buried in the Cathedral of St Denis in 1389, a shield of his arms was displayed upside down 'in signification', as a chronicler emphasized, 'of the temporary loss of nobility'.[61] As in the case of arms reversed to punish and shame, the reversal of a shield of arms was perceived to signify a loss of honour. But in the case of funeral rituals, contrary to rituals of punishment, this loss was not final, as a description of Archambaud of Foix-Béarn's burial in 1414 suggests. Although this nobleman's shield was not turned upside down but instead turned only ninety degrees, this manipulation of the coat of arms' proper, that is upright, orientation was an important performative part of the ritual. The traversed shield was solemnly handed to the son and heir of Archambaud, who then restored it to its upright position.[62] The temporary loss of nobility implied by the reversing or traversing of the deceased's shield of arms was just that, a momentary interruption of the lineage, to paraphrase Pierre Tucoo-Chala.[63] After all, there was an heir who continued all of his ancestor's claims to status, from actual properties and legal titles to the intangible capital of honour they implied. Part of this inheritance was the coat of arms itself, which during such heraldic funerals was quite literally placed in the hands of the rightful heir. At the funeral of Richard Neville, Earl of Salisbury, and his son, Sir Thomas, in 1462/3, it was thus the Earl of Warwick, as the next in line, who received a shield of the Salisbury arms during the service, 'in token that it belonged to him as the heir'.[64]

Although in the latter case there is no mention of arms turned upside down, the association of reversed arms with death existed in late medieval England as well. In Matthew Paris's famous *Historia Anglorum* (1250–9), illuminations of reversed coats of arms marked passages that described the (honourable)

---

[60] Froning, *Frankfurter Aufzeichnungen*, 169: 'Item man ludet ime erlich in allen kirchen und zu allen andern glocken luudet man auch die storme. Item ein stedebote drug zuerst voran ein stantkirze. item darnach ein oberster richter uf beden armen das lichtuche. Item darnach zwene die eldesten richter einer den helme der ander den schilt, das underst ufgekart.'

[61] Pintoin, *Chronique*, vol. 1, 602: '[S]cuta cuspidem desuper habencia in signum temporalis nobilitatis amisse ...'

[62] Tucoo-Chala, 'Honneurs', 19.

[63] Ibid.

[64] Wagner, *Heralds of England*, 107.

death of an individual, for instance.⁶⁵ Again in stark contrast to the shameful connotations of reversed arms found in other contexts, here the *subversio armorum* merely indicated a temporary loss of honour and the momentary interruption of a line: on several occasions the description of the death of an English king is accompanied by the famous red shield charged with three golden lions, while shortly afterwards the same shield is displayed in an upright position when the text turns to the coronation of the new king who continued the line.

This does not mean that the association between reversal of arms and accusations of dishonour was necessarily unknown to Matthew Paris. When the case of William de Marisco is discussed, who was executed for piracy and treason in 1245, the Marisco arms are depicted upside down, too. However, in this instance the accusation of dishonour cannot have been implied by the reversed shield alone, as there are numerous reversed arms of 'honourable' deceased persons displayed throughout the same manuscript. In fact, next to William de Marisco's arms is painted the reversed shield of his father, Geoffrey, who had died ashamed of his son's fate but not himself stripped of all honour. The important qualitative difference between the two cases is communicated visually by the fact that Geoffrey de Marisco's arms were unscathed, whereas the arms of his son William were depicted split in half. Likewise, the shield is accompanied by a broken sword, a banner of the same heraldic design but fallen to the ground and a staff snapped in half – all important ensigns of knighthood that rituals of punishment so relentlessly targeted. The visual representation of their physical state was thus key: when a nobleman had died without the blemish of dishonour, his ensigns and arms might be displayed turned upside down but crucially they were depicted intact.

Finally, to complicate matters even further, contemporary perceptions of this display of 'damaged' heraldry were not fixed either. Indeed, in line with the emphasis on the existence of an heir as the recipient of the deceased's coat of arms, in Germany the destruction of shield, sword and staff of the last member of a lineage to die was sometimes part of funeral rituals, although again without any of the connotations of dishonour otherwise evoked by destructions and defacements. For example, in his *Mirror of Nobility* (1564), the theologian Cyriacus Spangenberg stated that 'in Germany it is customary that when the last nobleman of a line has died ... his coat of arms is painted on a wooden shield, which, just as his seal-ring, is broken and cast into the grave'.⁶⁶

---

⁶⁵ Cherry, 'Heraldry as Decoration', 132.
⁶⁶ Spangenberg, *Adelspiegel*, 287: 'Bey uns Deutschen ist der brauch / das wenn ein Edler der letzte des Geschlechts / oder der keine männliche Erben gelassen / gestorben / man hinder der Leyche seinen Leibhengst / mit schwartzem Tuch bekleidet / biß zum Grabe füret / vnd sein Wapen auff einen bretern Schild gemahlet / hinnach tregt / welcher / wie auch sein Pittschaft-Ring / bey dem Grabe zerschlagen / vnd ins Grab geworffen ...'

Late medieval visual culture thus allowed for considerable ambiguity and very different interpretations in different contexts. With regard to the *subversio armorum*, in the specific context of death, a reversed shield simply indicated the fact that its owner had passed away. Only if the bearer was still alive, it appears, were coats of arms turned upside down understood as accusations of dishonour.

Conclusions

Historians argue that late medieval contemporaries saw honour represented by heraldry, and the sources discussed in this chapter strongly suggest or even explicitly emphasize that this was the case throughout large parts of Europe, from Germany and Burgundy to England, France and the Iberian Peninsula. Everywhere the display of coats of arms was seen to render honour visible, just as their defacement or destruction was seen to express their owners' apparent or alleged lack of honour.

Between these two extremes, the *subversio armorum* – the practice of visually depicting or physically turning shields of arms upside down – occupied an ambivalent semantic position. In the contexts of letters of defamation, rituals of punishment, and public provocation and protest, coats of arms turned upside down were held to subvert the honour of their owners in a quite literal sense. After all, their treatment resembled the punishment of culprits whose bodies were reversed in order to show their shame. In a 'pre-portrait society' which viewed coats of arms as a 'second body', as Hans Belting argues,[67] the heraldic body was an obvious substitute in the absence of the physical body. However, in the context of funeral ceremonies as fundamentally 'honourable' performances, reversed arms were not at all perceived to communicate dishonour. Instead, they signified the death of their owner or, in a more abstract interpretation, the transitional state of their lineage's genealogical body.

In light of this contextual ambiguity it is thus too broad a claim that 'an inverted shield with the coat of arms was a universal symbol of death of its owner', as Mikhail Boytsov states.[68] Although Laurent Hablot similarly believes the *subversio armorum* to have been associated with death, his argument is more nuanced. He claims that it was this particular association which *also* allowed for reversed arms to communicate accusations of dishonour since dishonour was seen as a form of 'social death',[69] echoing Julio Caro Baroja's analysis of traditional European concepts of honour, where 'the loss of honour

---

[67] Belting, *Images*, 3.
[68] Boytsov, 'Funerals', 156.
[69] Hablot, 'Blason de la trahison', 348.

is equated with the loss of life'.[70] Still, it is impossible to define a clear-cut, chronological transition from a perception that saw reversed coats of arms to indicate corporeal death to one that understood them to indicate social death, as Hablot suggests elsewhere.[71] Both perceptions coexisted throughout the late medieval period, only determined by the specific contexts in which reversed arms appeared. The case of the *subversio armorum* is thus a reminder of Nicholas Mirzoeff's important caveat that any study of 'visual culture' ought to account for ambiguity and contextuality, as 'no one way of seeing is ever wholly accepted in a particular historical moment'.[72]

The same then applies to a visual history of heraldry, which is currently moving away from 'traditional' approaches to heraldry 'as a stable system of signification and even as a fixed system of meaning', as Fiona Robertson and Peter Lindfield suggest.[73] Instead, there is now a methodology more interested in contemporary perceptions that allowed for coats of arms to function 'as a communicative medium which is – necessarily – contingent, culturally and historically specific, and open to interpretation': 'In what ways and in which circumstances, historically and culturally, and under what assumed privileges and adopted constraints of knowledge, do heraldic signs "speak"? Who do they speak to, how, when, and why?'[74]

There is a performative and material dimension to visual culture, which often reveals itself only in written sources. As this chapter has shown, reversed arms were not just depicted in images but were part of performances that staged the reversal of shields as tangible artefacts whose perpendicular orientation added semantic dimensions beyond mere identification. Indeed, 'ensigns armorial had a specific materiality whose handling equally conferred meaning', as Steven Thiry shows with regard to 'heraldoclasms' more broadly in the early modern period, which still witnessed the *subversio armorum* (Figure 3).[75]

To some extent and in some contexts, similarly ambiguous depictions, performances and perceptions of coats of arms and reversal even survive into the present. As a residue of late medieval visual culture, they underline W. J. T. Mitchell's claim 'that the idea of the personhood of pictures is just as alive in the modern world as it was in traditional societies'.[76] Reversal as a signifier of death, for instance, featured in the state funerals of the US presidents John F. Kennedy (1917–63) and Ronald Reagan (1911–2004). 'In honour' of the

---

[70] Caro Baroja, 'Honour and Social Status', 85.
[71] Hablot, 'Ubi Armae', 48–9.
[72] Mirzoeff, *Visual Culure*, 44.
[73] Robertson and Lindfield, 'Speaking of Arms', 2. A 'tendency towards analysis of coats of arms using, for example, theories drawn from media studies, semiotics, sociology, and symbol theory' is also observed by Hartmann, 'Heraldry', 623.
[74] Robertson and Lindfield, 'Speaking of Arms', 2.
[75] Thiry, *Matter(s)*, 262.
[76] Mitchell, 'Pictures', 73.

Figure 3 Public degradation ceremony including a reversed shield of arms, 1648, copper engraving, from Vulson, *Théâtre d'honneur*, vol. 2, 558 (artwork in the public domain; photograph provided by Bibliothèque nationale de France).

deceased statesmen, the funeral processions featured displays of their riding boots turned upside down as a visual allusion to late medieval funerals, as Boytsov believes.[77] But negative connotations of reversal are alive still, too. On a more 'heraldic' level, a Nigerian newspaper noted that protesters in 2012 'carried the Nigerian Coat of Arms turned ... upside down to spite the government'.[78] The reversal of a national ensign also marks the epilogue of the film *BlacKkKlansman* (2018), which underlines the continuity of racist and antisemitic groups with real-life footage of a white supremacist terror attack in Charlottesville, Virginia, followed by a depiction of the US flag rendered in black and white and turned upside down.[79] Similarly, the upside-down motif recently responded to the defacement of likenesses of the founders of Whitman College, Washington.[80] In the wake of the attack, curators at the institution's museum created an exhibit showing a portrait of Narcissa Whitman (d. 1847)

---

[77] Boytsov, 'Funerals', 162. See also Santa Cruz, *Making JFK Matter*, 188; Raphael, *President Electric*, 197.
[78] Quoted in Onyekakeyah, *Crawling Giant*, 107.
[79] Lane, 'BlacKkKlansman'.
[80] Needham, 'Whitman Painting Defaced'.

Figure 4 Mary Gertrude Stockbridge Allen, *Portrait of Narcissa Prentiss Whitman*, 1926, oil on canvas, 91 × 169 cm (35⅞ × 66½ in.). Displayed in *A Proper Monument?*, Maxey Museum, Whitman College, 2018, curated by Libby Miller (image © Whitman College, photograph by Kynde Kiefel, provided by Libby Miller, reproduced with permission).

turned upside down, meant to serve as a symbol for acts of 'vandalism' directed against visual representations of people deemed questionable, despicable or 'dishonourable' in a more medieval sense (Figure 4).

In the same way, finally, the idea of turning the purpose of a coat of arms as a sign of honour on its head – as the late medieval Master of the Housebook had done – is also still very much alive.[81] The British satirical magazine *Private Eye*, for instance, regularly publishes hyperbolic heraldic caricatures mocking public figures. As an advocate of the United Kingdom's departure from the European Union following a referendum in 2016, the politican Nigel Farage was thus attributed with a shield – 'supported by swivel-eyed heraldic beasts' – comprising elements created in unflattering emulation of heraldic iconography and terminology (Figure 5). Just as the presence of the 'Pound Descendant' reminded viewers of the British currency's downturn in the wake of the referendum, the inclusion of 'Kippers Rampant' hinted at a pejorative term for members of the UK Independence Party then led by Farage, and perhaps also played on 'Brexit' supporters' fondness for

---

[81] See the contributions by Adrian Ailes and Kathryn Will in Robertson and Lindfield, *Display of Heraldry*, chs 5 and 6.

Figure 5 'That Farage Coat of Arms', magazine caricature, 2016. Published in *Private Eye*, 25 November 2016 (Reproduced by kind permission of PRIVATE EYE magazine).

fishing rights as a symbol of British sovereignty. Likewise, the depiction of cigarettes and beer in conjunction with the (badly) translated Latin motto 'One for the road, guv?' alluded to Farage's appearances in pubs as part of his attempts to appeal to 'ordinary' voters, while the crest, 'surmounted by the traditional gauntlets thrown down by Farageist champions before a fight in the EU carpark – executed in the distinctive heraldic colours of puce and bile', lampooned his scathing Eurosceptic performances as a member of the European Parliament. Such satirical depictions mocking and caricaturing a person's reputation by means of heraldry remain a curious aspect of contemporary visual culture, highly reminiscent of late medieval attitudes towards coats of arms, honour and shame.

2

Costume imagery and the visualization of humanity in early modern Europe

Katherine Bond

Addressed in a range of materials from travel sketches and ethnographic prints to lavishly illustrated costume books and albums, the subject of who wore what and where became an urgent priority in early modern Europe. The impulse to distinguish and classify populations by their dress launched a visual culture that sought to map human difference on a global scale. In an era of enhanced cross-cultural exchange and encounter, the typologies of dress formulated by costume imagery in the sixteenth century became a fundamental site for ethnographic enquiry and the evaluation of diverse populations, their qualities and clothing.

Visualizing the many faces of humanity was no simple feat. Populations at the outer reaches of Europeans' line of vision posed a particular challenge. The manner in which news of 'new' peoples was acquired, perceived and transmitted was mediated through contemporary visual strategies that need to be unpacked in order to chart developing ethnographic visions; practitioners sourced and shaped ethnographic information according to contemporary material constraints, working practices and audience expectations. The genesis and consequent recycling of a popular series of 'Indian' costume figures, originally composed by the southern German artist-traveller Christoph Weiditz (c. 1500–59), exemplify the tension that existed between perception and representation. The series commemorated a remarkable moment of cultural encounter between the artist and a visiting group of Nahua, people of the indigenous populations inhabiting pre-Columbian Mexico, that took place at the Spanish court of the Habsburg emperor Charles V (r. 1519–56) in 1529. Although the resulting images have been feted as highly naturalistic and objective, a critical reappraisal reveals that they offer a tailored view moderated by familiar motifs and accepted frameworks of knowledge that competed with eyewitness cognition. Recycled in later costume works, the 'Indian' costume figures made inroads into the period's visual culture, where their iconicity was augmented. Their transition illuminates the course by which costume icons entered into and shaped the ways of seeing shared by authors and audiences for envisioning, visualizing and comprehending human difference.

The dispersal of knowledge about global dress customs through visual icons fed into, and energized, ideas about dress, appearance, cultural difference and national identity. The popularity of costume books, indicated by the production of at least twelve printed publications in Western Europe between 1550 and 1600, exemplifies the period's confidence in dress as a signal of kinship and identity.[1] Publishers in Paris, Venice, Nuremberg and Antwerp embraced costume icons and motifs, filtering information about foreign clothing into typologies of national character.[2] Basque figures drawn from the costume books of Parisian François Desprez (1562) and Nuremberger Hans Weigel (1577), for example, demonstrate costume motifs' rhetorical capacity to augment ideas about foreign populations. Maintaining patriotic directives, these books added fuel to the contemporary notion that different peoples ought to conserve their own styles of dress. In this context, the motif of the naked man became a popular expression for the perilous condition of lacking a defined, national habit, and provided a symbolic counterpart to clothed costume figures.

This visual history charts the processes by which costume imagery established a framework for conceptualizing humanity in sixteenth-century Europe. By analysing the strategies of those producing and collecting costume imagery, and the means by which icons and images evolved through transmission, this paper dissects the role of visual media and pictorial practices in the fashioning of global identity. Visually dynamic, the iconographies of dress that emerged moulded and defined ethnographic visions and formulated social meanings about clothing, culture and nationhood. In this capacity the visual was active in shaping, and not merely documenting, social values, collective identities and popular discourses.

The versatile costume figure

The sixteenth century witnessed a shift in visual conventions regarding the approach to human difference. Ethnography departed the scholar's study to incorporate the acquired knowledge of travellers and artists. The pictorial arts became an opportune medium for investigating reality 'in an age when news of the newfound world was arriving thick and fast' and when consequently first-person observation and eyewitness testimony were emphasized.[3] Visual culture

---

[1] For a comprehensive list see Olian, 'Sixteenth-Century Costume Books', 20–1.
[2] An already sizeable body of scholarship about such works exists: Defert, 'Genre ethnographique'; Wilson, *The World in Venice*; Jones, 'Habits, Holdings, Heterologies'; Vecellio, *Clothing of the Renaissance World*; Jones, 'Impossible Present'; Paulicelli, 'Mapping the World'; Rublack, *Dressing Up*; Bridgeman, 'Origins of Dress History'; and Calvi, 'Cultures of Space'.
[3] On the development of observational practices in the visual arts, refer to Smith, 'Art, Science, and Visual Culture', 89.

found a new and important role documenting, cataloguing and classifying aspects of the world that were newly under scrutiny, whether the curious or commonplace, the familiar or the unfamiliar.

Among the singular methods that emerged in the sixteenth century to organize visual cognition of human difference was the representative costume figure.[4] Bronwen Wilson has interrogated the possible reasons for this, isolating the semiotic capacity of clothing, which met the demands of a growing European fascination with geographic classification. As Wilson explains, it was a period in which 'it was less the body than what was worn over the skin that was the focus of alterity', especially since 'physiognomy, as a signifier of race in its modern sense – as a sign of ethnic distinctiveness – was a concept not yet clearly articulated'.[5] Accordingly, dress habits, alongside social mores, religious customs and language, among other things, provided useful markers of ethnic identity and could be studied as part of 'the interpretive skills deployed to comprehend foreigners'.[6]

Emblems for sociocultural types such as a 'Venetian nobleman' or a 'French widow', the costume figures that populated the margins of maps and lined the pages of costume books, travel accounts and friendship albums (*alba amicorum*) were distinct from those in later centuries' fashion plates insofar as they did not promote seasonal fashions but were instructive about characteristic, customary apparel. 'Costume' is used to describe this understanding of dress because, linguistically related to 'custom', the term implies clothing which is habitual and traditional.[7] In the preface to Jean-Jacques Boissard's costume book *Habitus Variarum Orbis Gentium* (1581), the Mechelen-based publisher Caspar Rutz disclosed his view that picturing (the diversity of) mankind in 'his own costume and habit' was a useful method for showing how regions and their inhabitants differed from one another, precisely because 'through clothing, mental dispositions and local customs can be represented and easily recognized'.[8] Costume *was* custom, in this line of thought, externalizing a culture's internal character and qualities.

This principle guided ethnographic pursuits. A 'new spatial orientation towards bodies' incorporated costume figures into cartographic projects and travelogues as though these bodies might themselves be chartable terrain.[9] In her monograph examining Renaissance ethnography, Surekha Davies has underscored that early modern European readers took for granted that 'human variety was a function of place, a tenet that took on a visually persuasive form

---

[4] Observed by Leitch, *Mapping Ethnography*, 2.
[5] Wilson, *The World in Venice*, 80.
[6] Ibid., 70, 80.
[7] As was brought to attention by Defert, 'Genre ethnographique'.
[8] Caspar Rutz in Boissard, *Habitus Variarum*, 2r: '... mit seiner selbst Kleidung / vnnd dracht fürbilden ... vnnd durch die Kleidung die gemütter / vnnd sitten / gemeinlich abgenommen warden / vnnd leichtlich zuerkennen ist.' Translated in Klein, 'Mapping of Africa', 37.
[9] Traub, 'Mapping the Global Body', 46.

on illustrated maps'.[10] Georg Braun and Franz Hogenberg's atlas series *Civitates Orbis Terrarum* (Towns of the World), first published in 1572, populated its topographical cityscapes and maps with costume figures, while the maps of the cartographers John Speed and Pieter van den Keere regularly positioned costume figures within bordering frames or cartouches.

The idiosyncrasies of local clothing customs had long intrigued travellers. The vivid commentary of Burgundian chronicler Laurent Vital for example, in his account of the voyages of Charles V and Ferdinand I in the years 1517–8, vocalized his astonishment at the 'strange ... quite pagan' headdresses of women in Asturias, Spain, and the dress and (un)dress of female villagers in Kinsale, Cork.[11] The first costume series in book form, François Desprez's *Recueil de la diversité des habits* (A Collection of the Various Styles of Dress), published in Paris in 1562, claimed to have relied on the 'designs' of Jean-François de La Rocque (sieur de Roberval, c. 1500–60), a French corsair and colonizer of French Canada in the early 1540s, and those of an unnamed Portuguese traveller who had frequented 'several and diverse countries'.[12] As costume books increased in popularity, they were even envisioned as a tool to assist travellers, colonizers and traders with cross-cultural diplomacy. In 1580, the promoter of English colonization Richard Hakluyt (1553–1616) proposed that, along with maps, the explorers Arthur Pet and Charles Jackman ought to present a 'booke of the attire of all nations' when visiting the Chinese court of 'Cambalu'.[13] 'Bestowed in gift', he suggested, the book surely 'would be much esteemed'.[14]

It was, in fact, the costume drawings of a travelling artist that sparked the trend for such books in the first place. For Christoph Weiditz, a portrait medal-maker from southern Germany, the discernment and comparison of clothing customs proved a useful interpretive method when he embarked on a trip to Iberia. Travelling to and from the Spanish and Netherlandish courts of Charles V between 1529 and 1532, Weiditz illustrated the dress of locals he observed on the road, at sea, in the countryside and in urban settings. With descriptive labels announcing how these people 'thus' went about, the illustrated album known as his 'Trachtenbuch' (costume book) captured clothing's ability to visualize differences between places and cultures.

This notion reached its apogee with the emergence of printed and painted costume series in the second half of the sixteenth century, works designed to edify and entertain a public readership about the curious forms, remarkable

---

[10] Davies, *Renaissance Ethnography*, 5.
[11] Vital, 'Relation du premier voyage', 95: '... et leur achem et accoustrement de test sont estranges ... assez à la mode payenne'. Unless otherwise stated, all translations are my own.
[12] Desprez, *Recueil*, fols a2v–a3r: '... ayant suiuy quelque dessein ... d'vn certain Portugais ayant frequenté plusiers & diuers pays'.
[13] Hakluyt, *Original Writings*, 155; Mancall, *Hakluyt's Promise*, 83–4. Mancall hypothesizes that the costume book in question might have been Hans Weigel's *Habitus*.
[14] Hakluyt, *Original Writings*, 155.

variety and moral pitfalls of foreign fashions. Printed costume books like Cesare Vecellio's well-known *Degli habiti antichi et moderni* (On Clothing, Ancient and Modern) were the result of sustained collecting of imagery, oftentimes copied from pre-existing sources. Costume books' drive to catalogue humanity can be compared to the period persuasion to assemble, categorize, classify and order that contemporary scholarship on early modern collecting and natural history has exposed.[15] Pairing images with text descriptions or verse, costume books followed a representational method applied in many instructional works of the era (Figure 6). The costume book was at once a literary and a visual genre for which text and pictures together formulated images, created associations and upheld ideas. The pairing of word and image created a mutually reinforcing

Figure 6 François Desprez, 'Woman of Roncevalles', from *Recueil de la diversité des habits qui sont de présent en usage tant ès pays d'Europe*, 1562, woodcut on paper, 14.6 × 8.5 cm (5¾ × 3⅜ in.). Rijksmuseum, Amsterdam, RP-P-OB-33.878A (artwork in the public domain; photograph courtesy of Rijksmuseum, Amsterdam).

---

[15] See, for instance, Daston and Park, *Wonders and the Order of Nature*; Findlen, *Possessing Nature*; and Ogilvie, *Science of Describing*.

scheme that is a common feature of visual culture, deployed in this case to form a didactic system. An important strategy for knowledge-making, it enabled costume figures, arranged into comparative series, to outline and instruct upon clothing customs that were familiar or strange, local or foreign, virtuous or sumptuous.

Imaging the Nahua

Whether used for an ethnographic manual, a travelogue or a guide for moral dressing, costume imagery was mitigated by the material and intellectual constraints of gathering and reproducing knowledge about global wardrobes. The following two sections centre upon these issues by way of the important series of 'Indian' costume figures originating in Christoph Weiditz's 'Trachtenbuch'. From their inception through to their transmission in later works, these figures exemplify the tension between observation and representation, and authenticity and authorship that manifested itself in the visual landscape of sixteenth-century Europe.

The group is identified with a caption above one of the figures announcing, 'These are Indian people whom Ferdinand Cortez brought to his Imperial Majesty from India and they have played before his Imperial Majesty with wood and ball'.[16] In 1528 a delegation of Nahua travellers accompanied Hernán Cortés (1485–1547) to Spain. They were still at the Spanish court when Christoph Weiditz arrived the following year, seeking the emperor's support after a dispute with the Augsburg goldsmiths' guild. A trained wood-sculptor, his use of precious metals when he segued into making portrait medals had caused contention with the city's goldsmiths, who believed the right over such materials was exclusively theirs.[17] Pursuing imperial protection, Weiditz travelled to Toledo with the armourer Kolman Helmschmid in the early winter of 1529, sailing first to Portugal from the Netherlands and then journeying overland to join the imperial entourage in Castile.[18] Passing through the landscape, Weiditz sketched regional dress habits as well as customary activities from which illuminations were later produced, today preserved in the album known as his 'Trachtenbuch'. Its gouache, gold- and silver-gilt illustrations mostly cover subjects situated in Iberia but include others from

---

[16] Weiditz, 'Trachtenbuch', fol. 12: 'Das send die Indiannisch leit der verdinant Cordesyus K tt aus India heraus bracht hatt, vnnd haben also vor K gespilt mit dem holtz vnnd Ball'. Translated in Weiditz, *Authentic Everyday Dress*, 27.

[17] Habich, 'Christoph Weiditz', 26–7.

[18] This route is confirmed in a missing folio depicting Helmschmid that has been preserved in Hans Römer's copy after the 'Trachtenbuch'. See 'Kostümbuch – Kopie nach dem Trachtenbuch', fol. 74v: 'über mör gfaren in Portugal vnd darnach in hispania' / 'travelled across the sea to Portugal and afterward to Spain to his Imperial Majesty'.

Italy, France, the Low Countries, Germany, England and Ireland. The folios were potentially worked up to a decade after Weiditz's return to Augsburg in 1532, so their mediation by time and the influence of other visual examples warrants consideration.

Unlike contemporaries, whose travelogues concentrated on royal personalities, holy sites, local architecture and notable landmarks, Weiditz concentrated on people. His eye was drawn to the daily life of people from all social stations that he observed on the roads, in the cities and out in the countryside. It was not just the appearance of various folk that stood out but also the tools, animals and methods employed for everyday tasks. He depicted how corn was threshed in Castile and how bread was kneaded in Zeeland. He captured interesting characters such as penitent self-flagellants and men who collected donations to pay the ransom of prisoners captured by Ottoman pirates. Discussing Weiditz's approach, Ulinka Rublack has argued that it was the manner in which people wore their clothes and comported themselves while performing social tasks and identities that above all interested the artist.[19] By isolating these costume figures against bare backdrops that heavily reduced architectural and landscape features, emphasis was squarely placed upon the dress and bearing of different members of society.

Historians have tended to assume that the Indian figures constitute convincing examples of first-hand observation. Since Weiditz's trip to the Spanish imperial court coincided with the Nahua group's well-documented visit, the artist's opportunity for closely observed figural study is often accepted as self-evident. The series consists of six static costume figures wearing feather mantles (*tilmatli*) and breechcloths (*maxtlatl*) (Plate 3). A further seven engage in acts of entertainment: one pair play the Aztec ball-game *tlachtli*, another demonstrates the board game *patolli* and a final three figures juggle a large wooden log with their feet. These details have led scholars to enthuse about Weiditz's careful ethnographic rendering.[20] Gabrielle Mentges sees their 'complex and varied' portrayal as evidence of Weiditz's 'tactile gaze', which distinguished, rather than homogenized, different members' facial features.[21]

Although directly linking observation, naturalism and ethnography is tempting, there is also much that is contrived about Weiditz's figures. The group's various accoutrements are painted with a uniform palette of blue, green and crimson, meriting a rethink of the images' supposed naturalism. The artist's willingness to copy or adapt existing imagery is also apparent, since a number of the costume figures in the 'Trachtenbuch' are subjects of lands Weiditz is not believed to have travelled to.[22] The artist conflated New World cultural

---

[19] Rublack, *Dressing Up*, 188.
[20] Massing, 'Early European Images', 517.
[21] Mentges, 'Cartographie vestimentaire', 11–3.
[22] It is doubtful Weiditz journeyed to England, Ireland, Venice or Genoa, for example, destinations which are represented by only a handful of examples each. Although clear visual models for

markers too – something which has recently been highlighted by Elizabeth Hill Boone.[23] Finally, the manner in which the Nahua were presented in Spain was manipulated by courtly manoeuvres whereby members may have worn apparel that did not concord with their ethnic or social identity. By peeling back these layers of context, practice and authorial decision-making, this case study looks beyond the immediacy of the images' subject matter to review how and why Weiditz came to synthesize a range of ethnographic knowledge on the pages of his 'Trachtenbuch'.

The Nahua group reached Spain in May 1528.[24] They included seven nobles, twenty-nine lesser but named elite and an unspecified number of indigenous performers, assembling approximately seventy people in total.[25] The elite individuals, who had been baptized and taken Christian first names, travelled to demonstrate their vassalage to the Spanish crown.[26] These representatives of diverse ethnic groups and realms, including Mexico-Tenochtitlan, Tlaxcala, Cempoala, Texcoco, Tacuba and Culhuacan, jockeyed to safeguard the emperor's favour in the wake of their new political reality.[27] Charles V decreed that Seville's House of Trade would furnish the cost of clothing their guests.[28] The seven most notable among them, three of whom were sons of Moctezuma, were granted the title 'Don'. They were to be set apart through sumptuous yellow damask doublets, breeches of fine scarlet with a matching cape and blue velvet caps.[29] Those of lower rank were likewise to be gifted Spanish-style garments, but seven months after the wardrobe provisions were ordered, and after the emperor had ordered the group to await passage home, they still lacked their promised clothes.[30] Whether the Nahua ever received their outfits is uncertain, but it can be assumed that in the interim they were supplied with Spanish garments of varying description for use in and around court. Weiditz did not depict such provisions; nevertheless, the contrived nature of the clothing and accessories they are portrayed wearing works against an assumption that this dress was ethnographically accurate.

Direct observation nevertheless took place. Weiditz must have witnessed the log-juggling and the games *tlachtli* and *patolli* at the Spanish court, since his

---

these figures have not yet been identified, their inclusion suggests Weiditz encountered other pictorial sources and desired to have a larger set of national clothing examples for comparative purposes.

[23] Hill Boone, 'Seeking Indianness'.
[24] Cline, 'Aztec Indians', 71.
[25] Ibid., 70–1, 84.
[26] Hill Boone, 'Seeking Indianness', 47.
[27] See Jovita Baber, 'Empire, Indians'.
[28] Cline, 'Aztec Indians', 82. Decree dated 2 October 1528, Madrid.
[29] Ibid., 82–4.
[30] Ibid. Documents from Seville's House of Trade record that by April blue velvet had been purchased but that the outfits' construction was only just being organized. Three members had been missed off the initial order, moreover, and a related notice issued in May regretted that these three were going about 'naked'.

portrayal of these actions concord with written testimony about the diversions formerly practised in the Aztec Empire, described by European arbiters.[31] Before reaching court in Toledo, Cortés had showed off the 'dexterous' jugglers in Guadalupe. They were described by Cortés's biographer Bernal Díaz del Castillo to have 'passed the stick from one foot to the other'.[32] Weiditz's lively record demonstrates the precise movements in which the log was handled and tossed into the air with a sequence of three figures who throw and catch the log, 'as long as a man and as heavy', while lying on a leather mat (Figure 7).[33]

The figures have nonetheless been mediated by the influence of pre-existing visual models. When Christoph Weiditz encountered the subjects from New Spain he may already have had a preconceived notion about how these supposed Indians ought to appear, based on material items and pictorial information circulating through artistic, intellectual and commercial channels. Among such

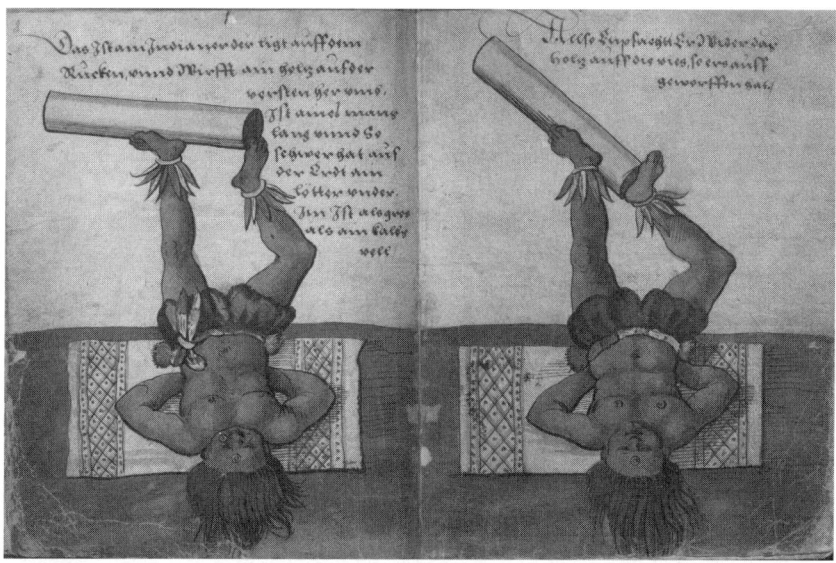

Figure 7 Christoph Weiditz, 'This is an Indian, he lies on his back and throws a block of wood around his heels, it is as long as a man and as heavy, he has on the earth a leather under him, it is as big as a calf skin', and 'Thus he again catches the wood on his feet as he has thrown it up', from the 'Trachtenbuch', 1530–40, pen and gouache, gold and silver leaf, 15 × 20 cm (6 × 7⅞ in.). Germanisches Nationalmuseum, Nuremberg (artwork in the public domain; photograph provided by Historic Images/Alamy Stock Photo).

---

[31] For example the testimony of Francisco López de Gómara in his *Historia general de las Indias* (1552).
[32] Díaz del Castillo, *True History*, 144.
[33] Weiditz, 'Trachtenbuch', fols 6, 8, 9: 'vnnd Wirfft ain holtz aus der versten heraus, Ist aines mans lang vnnd so schwer'. Translated in Weiditz, *Authentic Everyday Dress*, 28.

influences was the persuasive broadsheet published in Augsburg by Johann Froschauer in 1505, which purported to show inhabitants from coastal Brazil according to Amerigo Vespucci's descriptions. The broadsheet reported that 'the people are thus naked, handsome, brown; their heads, necks, arms, private parts [and the] feet of men and women are lightly covered with feathers. The men also have many precious stones in their faces and chests'.[34] The accompanying woodcut portrays Brazilian Tupinambá wearing various feathered garments including headdresses, collars, skirts, bustles and leg-bands, and following Vespucci's prompts, practising cannibalism (Figure 8). Weiditz's log-jugglers also wear feather anklets – a garment missing from Mesoamerican codices. Although they might have represented part of the jugglers' costume, to draw attention to the feet, it is noteworthy that the feather anklets of the woodcut, as well as the colourful stones or jewels inserted into figures' cheeks, chins, foreheads and noses, reappear in Weiditz's corpus. Although Aztec men wore

Figure 8 Johann Froschauer, *Dise figur anzaigt uns das volck und insel die gefunden ist ...*, after Amerigo Vespucci, 1505, woodcut broadsheet, 25.5 × 35 cm (10⅛ × 13¾ in.). Bayerische Staatsbibliothek, Munich, Einbl. V,2 (artwork in the public domain; photograph © Bayerische Staatsbibliothek).

---

[34] 'Die leüt sind also nackent hübsch. braun wolgestalt von leib. ir heübter halß. arm. scham. fuß. frawen vnd mann ain wenig mit federn bedeckt. Auch haben die mann in iren angesichten vnd brust vil edel gestain'. Translated in Davies, *Renaissance Ethnography*, 79–80.

nose-rods and lip- and ear-plugs, these were unlike the small, stud-like stones Weiditz depicts and were not placed into the cheek or forehead. These features, Hill Boone has argued, became motifs purposefully marshalled by Weiditz to 'satisfy expectations of how Amerindians should look'.[35]

The Nahua's fluffy, thick mantles are depicted with wavy, feathery surfaces in alternating rows of colour (see Plate 3). *Tilmatli* mantles in indigenous codices, however, are invariably portrayed with a smooth, flat texture. In the pre-Hispanic Valley of Mexico, luxury *tilmatli* – spun from cotton, and interwoven with feathers and rabbit fur – were part of a vibrant gift culture and diplomatic trade.[36] The Spanish had been gifted mantles in the cities of Cotaxtla and Cempoala as they edged towards Tenochtitlan and thus splendid mantles afterwards made their way to Spain, including mantles worked with feathers listed in Cortés's 1522 shipments of goods.[37] The Spanish jurist Alonso de Zuazo reported his compatriots' winnings as they ventured into the Yucatán peninsula: 'I saw many doubled-faced mantles, made with turkey feathers so smooth that in drawing the hand across the grain, they seemed nothing but a well-tanned sable marten skin.'[38] The smooth materiality of feather-garments sent to the emperor also struck Peter Martyr d'Anghiera, a court humanist and official of the Spanish Council of the Indies. Recalling the garments, he wrote,

> The people of that country only use three materials for their clothing; that is to say, cotton, birds' feathers, and rabbits' hair. They make the feathers and the hair into a pattern upon a foundation of cotton, working them with such ingenuity that we are unable to comprehend their methods of fabrication.[39]

D'Anghiera elsewhere observed that a feather-shield 'had coloured feathers resembling our raw silk'.[40] As these comparisons to sleek textiles affirm, Nahua feather-workers produced finely woven, smooth-surfaced fabrics that disguised individual feathers, confronting and contradicting the depiction in the 'Trachtenbuch' of bushy plumage fixed at its shaft and otherwise left loose and curling.[41] A more naturalistic portrayal of feather-work may have been surrendered in order to emphasize the mantles' principal material, the feather, by now a canonical marker of the New World. Moreover, the mantles' texture bears a strong resemblance to extant Brazilian Tupi cloaks and thus appear as amalgamations combining Tupi feather-work with the rectangular shape, shin

---

[35] Hill Boone, 'Seeking Indianness', 55.
[36] Umberger, 'Art and Imperial Strategy', 102–3.
[37] López de Gómara, *Cortés*, 59, 72; Russo, 'Cortés's Objects', 241.
[38] Alonso de Zuazo, translated in Rieff Anawalt, *Indian Clothing*, 30.
[39] Martyr d'Anghiera, *De Orbe Novo*, 197–8.
[40] Ibid., 198.
[41] A good example of this is the extant Aztec shield of c. 1500 housed in the Weltmuseum, Vienna, inv. no. 43380.

length and shoulder knot of Mexican *tilmatli*.[42] Thus they constitute artistic creations inspired by entangled visual and material stimuli. The synthesis of this ethnographic information may have been a purposeful, reinforcing tactic. Surekha Davies has noted that contemporary European mapmakers 'synthesized, transformed, and re-circulated' acquired information to construct 'socially acceptable' knowledge.[43] By combining existing visual tropes with first-hand observation, Weiditz, too, skilfully synthesized ethnographic knowledge, delivering cultural images acceptable to discerning peers familiar with the idea of the supposedly be-feathered and be-jewelled New World Indian.

From the time of the first Portuguese landing in Brazil in 1500, Tupi items were collected and shipped to Europe.[44] Cortés sent several shipments of Mexican goods back to Spain before his return that caused wonder among European spectators. Alessandra Russo has illuminated his influence over the material goods reaching Spain in the 1520s.[45] In a letter of 1520, Charles V is told that Moctezuma 'had made in gold' various things Cortés had designed, including 'images, crucifixes, medals, jewels [and] collars'.[46] Cataloguing his two shipments of 1524, Cortés again refers to his commission of certain pieces.[47] Items including the 'feather and hair mantles, fans [and] shields' brought to Spain in 1528 may thus have comprised custom-designed, matching pieces. Hybrid objects thus entered the Spanish court, where they were likely incorporated into ceremonial demonstrations and could have been modelled by the visiting Nahua.

The circumstances under which the Nahua wore indigenous apparel instead of Spanish courtly garb also require consideration. Peter Martyr reports an intriguing case of a Nahua slave who arrived at the Spanish court in 1522 with a shipment of gifts. Introduced by Cortés's secretary Juan de Ribera, the man was summoned for a demonstration. 'He had dressed himself in my room', Martyr retells, and wore a 'robe of woven feathers' and cotton trousers.[48] After a blood-curdling display of feigned human sacrifice, he changed into his 'gala costume' ahead of a musical performance.[49] The Nahua man was directed to dress up in indigenous garments for cultural demonstrations, indicating that courtly audiences anticipated the connection between native customs and costume. The manufactured nature of such court displays means that the dress put aside for demonstrations could have been worn by models who had little personal connection to the items. Feather-work costumes, arms and armour, headdresses

---

[42] As is argued by Hill Boone, 'Seeking Indianness', 54. Exemplified by a pre-Columbian example housed by the Musées royaux d'Art et d'Histoire, Brussels, inv. no. AAM 05783.
[43] Davies, *Renaissance Ethnography*, 13.
[44] Massing, 'Early European Images', 515.
[45] Russo, 'Cortés's Objects', 239.
[46] Cortés, *Letters*, 100–1.
[47] Russo, 'Cortés's Objects', 243.
[48] Martyr d'Anghiera, *De Orbe Novo*, 202.
[49] Ibid., 203.

and gold, turquoise and jade jewellery were among the mix of plundered, gifted and collected artefacts circulating at the Spanish court deriving from diverse ethnic groups across Mexico, Brazil and the Caribbean.

Weiditz's animated portrayal of Aztec entertainment suggests his observation of court performances. These were not neutral displays, however, and were concocted by and for European courtiers. The gouache illuminations in the 'Trachtenbuch' were probably produced several years after Weiditz's encounter. In the meantime, popular visual tropes of the New World 'Indian' may have skewed his memory or been purposefully employed to bolster the trustworthiness of his pictures. Despite their anomalies, his images speak of the way cultural knowledge was acquired and re-contextualized into a European sphere of ethnographic understanding supported by visual cues and descriptive terms.

The Nahua series' transcendency

Christoph Weiditz's Nahua series maintained its appeal and was copied, modified and dispersed through later printed and painted costume series. While Weiditz's originals have received a lot of scholarly attention, occupying a central position in the canon of European Renaissance ethnographic images, recycled copies after the Nahua series have been overlooked. These reinterpretations, decontextualized from the initial 1529 encounter, show the results of authorial agency and the transmission of knowledge over time. Reviewing such supposedly peripheral works makes it possible to grasp the threads connecting a visual style or movement and assess its broader social and cultural ethos. Not only that, it can show processes in the circulation of icons and ideas which, in the case of costume imagery, highlight how the pictorial study of dress settled into its position as a pre-eminent method for contemplating the diverse nature of humankind.

In two southern German costume albums from the second half of the sixteenth century, figures originating from Weiditz's Nahua series are presented as 'Moors'. One album identifies the *tilmatli*-wearing characters as 'Moors in Africa', while the other labels a log-juggler an 'Arabian Moor'.[50] Blurring distinctions between ethnic groups played into the formation of exotic stereotypes, whether intentional or not. In this case, the artist may have consulted an intermediary copy that had neglected to transfer textual descriptions about the figures' ethnic identity. But labels were also subject to many costume book producers' ambition to present extensive global collections, thus identifications were purposefully altered to encompass more populations.

---

[50] 'Kostüme und Sittenbilder', fols 30r–31v; 'Trachtenbuech', ills 30–1.

Stylistic choices also substantiated change. In an etched series of costume figures anonymously printed in Augsburg in the late sixteenth century, several of Weiditz's Nahua reappear with the long hair, beards and moustaches fashionable in contemporary Europe (Plate 4).[51] Two of the group are even painted with the pink skin of white men. A colourist painted the *tilmatli* with rows of narrow, dagger-like feathers, highlighting each individual plume and underscoring the material of the garment even more dramatically than Weiditz. Artistic alteration even occurred directly upon the original 'Trachtenbuch' when a new hand added long feathers – visible in a faded wash – to the waistbands of the Nahua group's breechcloths (see Plate 3). This transformed them into feather-skirts, the garment par excellence for epitomizing an 'Indian' identity, however erroneously applied. Although these changes further skewed the ethnographic knowledge contained, the results were part of the solidification of ethnic icons that occurred over the century. Sartorial cues for cultural identities were only magnified as imagery became embellished. As it migrated, it constructed a broader visual culture propagating popular stereotypes. Feather mantles and facial jewels became unambiguously associated with an 'Indian' identity, more so than brown skin or nudity, reinforcing paradigms that blurred real cultural and ethnic differences existing in the Americas.

Around the turn of the seventeenth century, the maturing Hans Römer of Munich stumbled upon the 'Trachtenbuch' and commissioned a complete copy.[52] A Bavarian native, Römer must have observed Weiditz's work in Augsburg or its surrounds. His motivations for the commission emerge in a couple of folios, positioned at the start of the album, in which the unfolding itinerary is reframed as the travels of his father, a Habsburg servant in the employ of Henry III of Nassau-Dillenburg, one of Charles V's closest advisers. On a title page presenting the Römer coat of arms, text upon curling ribbons announces that in 1523 Hans Römer (the elder) of Erfurt journeyed with his master to Charles V's court and went 'over the sea to India'.[53] Because the work purports to be the father's original creation, the text claims to show 'what I saw'.[54] Overleaf, a handwritten provenance notice claims that Hans Römer the younger was bequeathed his father's book.[55]

Stylistic differences on the part of Römer's unidentified artist account for reductions of detail. The ball-game and board-game playing Nahua are again portrayed with white skin but maintain the canonical face jewels. Although Weiditz's visual material had been extensively copied and recycled, Römer's copy was unprecedented because it dared to present itself as the visual

---

[51] 'Kostüme der Männer', fols 182v–185r.
[52] 'Kostümbuch – Kopie nach dem Trachtenbuch'.
[53] Ibid., fol. 1v: 'mit Karl. dem. v. Iber mör n India'. My grateful thanks to Stefan Hanß for his help transcribing Römer's annotations.
[54] Ibid.: 'vnd was Jch gesehen'.
[55] Ibid., fol. 2r.

recollections of Römer's father, hijacking Weiditz's personal travel experiences. It elaborated this travel, however, by insisting his father journeyed 'over the sea to India'. The Nahua were thus transported from a Spanish courtly environment into an overseas world, now evidencing the supposed travel to and first-hand knowledge of a faraway continent. Costume imagery, positioned in a personal, hand-illustrated album, maintained a cachet that, around seventy years on, still signalled worldliness and the prestige of travel and cultural knowledge.

Iconographies of national dress

The comprehensive geographic scope that costume books aimed for demanded the resourceful reuse of pictorial information. Certain iconic characters circulated for decades, transmitted between different works and media. As motifs increased in iconic potency through repetition, their authenticity was paradoxically augmented despite the effect this had on ethnographic precision. Discussing the translation of eighteenth-century fashion caricatures across national borders, Patrick Steorn has remarked that the adaptation of imagery was a 'knowing and discriminate act on the part of artists, collectors, and other audiences who assimilate various kinds of art and images into the local visual culture'.[56] As motifs were reinterpreted, new meanings were created and older meanings reaffirmed, positioning national and cultural identities within a growing iconography of global tastes and habits. Transmittable, recyclable costume imagery, in other words, underlay the growth and success of this visual culture and buoyed the costume book genre.

The costume books that developed in the second half of the sixteenth century used the iconic nature of costume for rhetorical ends. These printed volumes were more systematic, taxonomic and often outwardly instructive than earlier, intimate works like Weiditz's, promoting the notion that diverse clothing styles could be compared and studied as a means to ruminate on the many faces of humanity, society and culture. Many books swapped basic descriptive captions for poetic verse that alerted readers to the praiseworthy or lamentable appearance of the costume figures introduced. François Desprez's 1562 publication *Recueil de la diversité des habits* used costume imagery to critique the hierarchical ills and moral failings of the author's native French society during a period of intensifying religious and class conflict. By contrast, the 1577 costume book *Habitus Praecipuorum Populorum* (The Principal Habits of People), printed in Nuremberg by Hans Weigel and illustrated by Jost Amman, was more inclined to praise the upstanding, humble dress habits of the German nation, offering an alternative to the alluring dress of foreigners.

[56] Steorn, 'Caricature and Fashion Critique', 255–6.

Discourses about what constituted honourable, shameful or strange clothing were augmented by circulating visual tropes. A series of widely recycled figures illustrating Basque costume, initially popularized in Weiditz's 'Trachtenbuch', came to reinforce stereotypes about the region and Spain more broadly. The conspicuous height, volume and elaborate compositions of female headdresses (*tocados*) from these parts had long captured the imagination of foreign observers. The fashion for conical, sometimes twisted, horn-shaped headdresses was particularly commented on, regularly inviting phallic references from incredulous travellers. When Burgundian chronicler Laurent Vital observed local women in the province of Asturias, he remarked that 'it seemed as if they had planted on their heads ... those things with which men make children'.[57] Andrew Boorde, a Welsh pilgrim to St James's shrine in 1532, similarly noted that women along the route wore headdresses that reminded him of codpieces.[58] This interpretation was even echoed by close neighbours. Philosopher Michel de Montaigne, who hailed from a town bordering the Basque province of Gascony, commented that 'the married women near my place twist their headscarves into the shape of the male sexual organ to revel in the enjoyment they derive from it'.[59] The mockery this style endured from outside its own community is palpable; according to Vital, when he asked Charles V's and his Flemish lords' opinion of these headdresses they 'burst out laughing, saying that the ornaments were cheerful and of great novelty'.[60] Incorporated into Desprez's *Recueil*, this idea was manifested in the dress of a woman of Roncevalles, which is a Basque town at the foot of the Pyrenees (see Figure 6). Readers are directed to the woman's headdress as the verse asks whether 'this *coiffure* seems dirty to you'?[61] Arranged into a phallic protuberance, the headdress becomes the source of a joke made at the expense of Basque culture, designed, in part, to boost the Parisian author's readers' sense of their cultural and sartorial sophistication.

As costume series circulated the appearance of these idiosyncratic headdresses to a wider audience, the baggage of these views seeped into critical dialogues evaluating Spanish culture more broadly. In Weigel's *Habitus*, a female figure derived from Weiditz's woman of the mountains 'in the kingdom of Pamplona at the Basque frontier' has been reidentified as a generic Spanish 'peasant's wife'. Accompanying verse narrates her appearance 'when she comes in from the countryside / and thinks she's well adorned'.[62]

---

[57] Vital, 'Relation du premier voyage', 97: 'car il sembloit qu'elles eussent sur leurs testes ... de ces choses de quoy ces hommes font des enfans'.
[58] Boorde, *Fyrst Boke*, 1999.
[59] Montaigne, *Essays*, 969.
[60] Vital, 'Relation du premier voyage', 98: 'En parlant de ceste matière, le Roy et la seigneurie se prindrent à rire, disant que les atours estoient des joyeuses et nouvelles fassons'.
[61] Desprez, *Recueil*: 'La fême de rõceualle': 'si la coiffure vous semble sale'.
[62] Weigel, *Habitus*, plate CLVII, 'Ein hispanische Bäwrin': 'Wann sie kompt von dem Land herein / Und dunckt sich wol gezieret seyn'.

Now portrayed as an older woman, the figure's reinterpretation broadcasts the idea that this style of loose, now outdated, clothing and pointed cloth headdress represents backward peasant-wear worthy of ridicule. Overleaf, another Basque woman is dressed in festival-day apparel (Figure 9). The verse teases, 'and it is for them a beautiful costume / for us it would be thought

Figure 9 'Basque Woman from Cantabria', from Hans Weigel, *Habitus Praecipuorum Populorum*, 1577, woodcut on paper, 30 × 19 cm (11⅞ × 7½ in.). Bibliothèque nationale du France, Paris, ARS EST-1277 (artwork in the public domain; photograph © Bibliothèque nationale du France).

odd'.⁶³ Here the figure's transition from a young woman to an elderly crone is even more exaggerated. Her emphatically twisted, conical headdress, curling over her coarse features, is dramatized by the self-referential pointing gesture the woman makes – her proud insistence that her dress is beautiful. The mocking tone accompanying these two figures not merely schooled readers that the Basque region embodied the vulgar and uncultivated dress and people associated with rural Spain. The verses also addressed Weigel's imagined German audience, who could reaffirm their own value systems around what constituted normal, morally upright and attractive dress. Acknowledging that foreign populations maintained different aesthetic standards upheld another critical idea strengthened through recycled costume motifs: that people of different nations ought to preserve their own national costumes and, as such, be readily identifiable.

Naked men and national habits

Cultural identity was understood to be quite literally worn on one's sleeve. Its opposite – cultural nakedness – was expressed in a popular period anecdote whereby a painter, having illustrated the costume of various different nations, came to the depiction of his own only to be confronted with a dilemma: how could he render his kinsmen's costume when their inconstant dress habits and love of foreign dress permitted no single design? The artist-biographer Karel van Mander (1548–1606) offers an interesting account of his former teacher, the Dutch painter Lucas de Heere (1534–84) who, during a period in England between 1567 and 1577, was commissioned to paint 'all the costumes or clothing of the nations' in a gallery for the high admiral of England, Edward Clinton, Earl of Lincoln:

> When all but the Englishman were done, he painted him naked and set beside him all manner of cloth and silk materials, and next to them tailor's scissors and chalk. When the Admiral saw this figure he asked Lucas what he meant by it. He answered that he had done that with the Englishman because he did not know what appearance or kind of clothing he should give him because they varied so much from day to day; for if he had done it one way today the next day it would have to be another – be it French or Italian, Spanish or Dutch – and I have therefore painted the material and tools to hand so that one can always make of it what one wishes.⁶⁴

On his way to the tailor, the naked Englishman was depicted ready to have the latest fashions cut according to his whim.

---

⁶³ Ibid., plate CLVIII, 'Ein Weib in Pischeaien': 'Und ist bey im ein schöner Tracht / Bey uns würdens für seltsam geacht'.
⁶⁴ Van Mander, *Lives*, 281.

The now-lost gallery was likely a casualty of the 1666 Great Fire of London.⁶⁵ But while Van Mander's testimony is the only known record of its existence, a related manuscript collection of costume illustrations produced by De Heere during his English stay preserves the gallery's ambition to chart different countries' habits.⁶⁶ The surviving album contains 195 watercolour costume figures, both historical and contemporary, covering European territories in Italy, Spain, Germany, France, England and Ireland, as well as the Ottoman Empire and the New World (in the form of a fur-parka-wearing Inuit).⁶⁷ It ends with the naked Englishman carrying a length of fabric on his arm, wielding a pair of shears (Figure 10).

As Van Mander's description of the naked Englishman reveals, foreign fashions and inconstant behaviour were charged with disrupting clear national habits. The motif was not new to De Heere; it had earlier appeared in Andrew Boorde's *First Book of the Introduction of Knowledge*, composed in 1542 and published in 1547, in an illustrated poem describing 'the natural disposition of an English man', which correspondingly narrated the Englishman's predilection for new fashions. This inconstancy was not only an English trait, noted Van Mander, who accused his Flemish kinsmen of imitating the clothes of their neighbours.⁶⁸ This rebuke was soon parroted across Europe, as the motif was transferred to new settings. The naked man materialized in a 1571 embroidered chimney-hanging in the Leipzig town hall.⁶⁹ Lining up nine costume figures, including a Frenchman and an Italian, in their national habits, it predictably concludes with a naked German carrying cloth. He also reappeared anecdotally in the 1590 costume book of Cesare Vecellio. In Venice-based Vecellio's account, it is an Italian painter who was compelled to depict his kinsman naked, since he was 'so changeable, mutable and capricious in his dress'.⁷⁰

A broader version of this theme was the subject of the engraved frontispiece of Weigel's *Habitus* (Figure 11). Laying out the costume book's global scope, the continents Asia, America and Africa are imagined as men adorned in the clothes and accessories commensurate with their place of origin. Europe, by contrast, is stark naked, lacking any recognizable garb. Wielding a bolt of fabric and shears, he holds the necessary equipment to have made up any clothing styles he fancies. Afflicted with this identity crisis, his vulnerability to foreign influence is plain. At the top of the frontispiece, a scene depicting humanity's

---

⁶⁵ Hypothesized by Conrads, 'Het Theatre', 10. In his description of London, Thomas Pennant, the eighteenth-century Welsh traveller, remarks that in 1553 Edward Clinton obtained the large stone and timber residence on Old Fish Street Hill that once belonged to the Mounthauntes of Norfolk. The adjoining chapel, which became the Church of St Mary Magdalen, is recorded as having burned down in the Great Fire, leaving little doubt as to the fate of the house. Penannt, *Mr. Pennant's Account of London*, 34; Stow, *Survey of London*, 133.
⁶⁶ De Heere, 'Théâtre de tous les peuples'.
⁶⁷ De Heere sourced his information about Inuit from the abducted Greenlanders English privateer Martin Frobisher brought to Bristol in 1576. See Sturtevant and Beers Quinn, 'This New Prey'.
⁶⁸ See Yates, *Valois Tapestries*, 17.
⁶⁹ See Rublack, *Dressing Up*, 144–5, 149.
⁷⁰ See Vecellio, *Clothing of the Renaissance World*, 59.

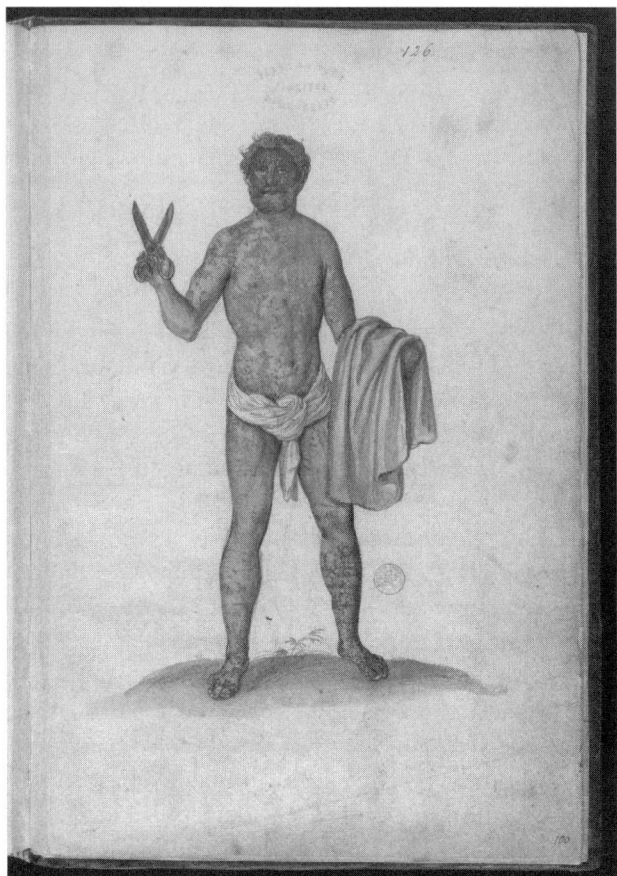

Figure 10 Lucas de Heere, 'Naked Man with Fabric and Shears', from 'Théâtre de tous les peuples', 1570/80, watercolour on vellum, 32.5 × 21.5 cm (12⅞ × 8½ in.). Ghent University Library, BHSL.HS.2466 (artwork in the public domain; photograph courtesy of Ghent University Library).

fall from paradise adds another layer of meaning to the naked European beneath. Banished from the Garden of Eden, a naked Adam and Eve attempt to cover themselves having lost innocence and learned shame. Now on Earth, they wrap themselves in animal skins, establishing clothing as a consequence of original sin. The European's nakedness – due to his inability to resist new and foreign fashions – brings shame upon his continent. And yet the motif is not only a critique about the danger of lacking a stable costume. The naked European strides forth with purpose in the direction of the other continents.[71] Advancing in this manner and taking the best of what other continents have

---

[71] Rublack, *Dressing Up*, 149.

Figure 11 Jost Amman, 'Frontispiece', from Hans Weigel, *Habitus Praecipuorum Populorum*, 1577, woodcut on paper, 30 × 19 cm (11⅞ × 7½ in.). Bibliothèque nationale du France, Paris, ARS EST-1277 (artwork in the public domain; photograph © Bibliothèque nationale du France).

to offer, he embodies the ingenuity and resourcefulness that Weigel's readers were encouraged to associate with Europe and its position on the world stage.

Weigel was nevertheless quick to critique the negative influence of foreign fashions, particularly their adverse effect upon the dress habits of his German kinsmen. His readership, Rublack has added, was cautioned to preserve the virtuous and unassuming clothing of 'our common fatherland', offering through visual example a patriotic code of dressing based on a modest application of plain but honourable textiles contrasted with the more ostentatious finery of other nations, above all Italy.[72] Where Italian women are typically portrayed sporting low décolletage and voluminous skirts flowing in ornate textiles, and carrying luxury accessories such as ostrich-feather fans and perfumed gloves, their German counterparts adopt high necklines, narrow skirts of plain fabrics and utilitarian accessories such as purses containing scissors.

Cesare Vecellio also warned against the influence of foreign fashion. Most worryingly for contemporaries, Vecellio regarded inconstancy in dress a consequence of political domination. Explaining that the Italian peninsula was subject to vacillating habits because of foreign invasions, he lamented,

> [H]ow often this beautiful country of Italy has been subject to ruin and how many diverse inhabitants and foreign invaders and barbarians have trod underfoot and plundered this most fertile region. ... Italy derived no benefit from them except its wide and changing array of languages, clothing and customs.[73]

Leafing through his costume book then, patriotic citizens across Italy and, indeed, wider Europe, could sort through and mull over its anthology of world dress, familiarizing themselves with the 'looks' of their countrymen, neighbours and faraway populations, aligning their own habits accordingly.

Dressing as an act of allegiance was reinforced by this visual culture. Costume imagery crafted by printers, artists, woodblock cutters and poets surpassed its immediate requirement to amuse armchair travellers in an era discovering the capital of global cultural knowledge. Many costume books open with hyperbolic introductory tracts and histories of dress that referenced the classical age, emphasizing to a wide readership the learnedness of the books' producers and their lofty, moralizing aims. Following the proto-nationalist rhetoric exhibited by Weigel's *Habitus*, for example, even the body politic's wardrobe was at stake. Following the transition of costume imagery from commemorative travel albums to later printed costume books, it is observable that the adaptable costume figure donned different guises and re-envisioned human society according to the demands and subjectivities of diverse authors, artists and audiences.

Conclusion

Circulating costume imagery, reinforced through repetition, contributed to the period's visions of what constituted human variety. Illustrators, engravers and printers had a stake in expanding global cultural knowledge, popularizing ethnography through the subject of dress. The transmission of costume imagery

---

[72] Translated ibid., 150–8.
[73] Vecellio, *Clothing of the Renaissance World*, 58.

through different forms permitted information about people, clothing and culture to migrate, gain currency and increase in conceptual weight, formulating iconographies and hierarchies of sartorial character. An important historical source, Christoph Weiditz's series of 'Indian' figures elucidates practices and processes of dealing with new cultural knowledge in this crucial period of global encounter, showing that constructing credible pictorial representations of the latest ethnographic information called not merely for close observation but also for engagement with familiar, accepted knowledge and popular visual and material icons. Artful synthesis provided Weiditz with a method for uniting all available knowledge, reinforcing rather than undermining the resulting costume figures. Reinterpreted through later works and patterns of circulation, the characters became formidable exotic types.

Costume images on the move popularized concepts about cultures and populations. Structured by the period's printed costume books, they partook in critical dialogue about compatriots and foreign populations alike, promoting evaluation of national traits, qualities and dress styles. The striking compositions of women's headdresses from the Basque region captivated foreign observers. The trope of the conical headdresses' supposedly phallic shape – an oft-repeated quip – was intensified through the consolidation of costume motifs and verse in the costume books of Parisian author François Desprez and Nuremberger Hans Weigel. Entering into the visual landscape of migrating costume imagery, these figures achieved pictorial currency as designs onto which assumptions and critiques about Spanish rural society could be projected.

Visualizing humanity with the costume figure raised the status of dress to something of political consequence and moral gravity. Costume books addressed (and fuelled) contemporary anxieties about the corrupting influence of foreign fashions and inconstant dress habits, reinforcing the concept that diverse populations ought to retain and be recognized by their own dress styles. Without a clear, traditional outfit, the motif of the naked man embodied this concern and circulated between media and across borders. Costume imagery was a visual culture that assisted early modern contemporaries in defining and redefining the boundaries of identity. What was local, what was foreign, what was virtuous and what was indecent could all be addressed by taking note of the costume figure.

3

Identity and continuity: The visual culture of an institution over 500 years

Ludmilla Jordanova

Portraits and icons

The very act of making a portrait has significance. It suggests that the sitter and her or his appearance are worth recording, and that others will want to look at them. Preserving, displaying, copying and discussing a portrait further assert the value of the person in question.[1] No painting demonstrates the point more vividly than a work by an unknown hand and probably from the 1650s. It shows a seated, balding man holding a hat, and behind him the billowing clouds, massive column and draped curtain suggest a person of some importance. This canvas is infinitely precious to the institution that owns it, those associated with it and people all over the world, since it depicts someone of exceptional distinction. Furthermore it was saved from the Great Fire of London in 1666, when other valued works were lost. This iconic survivor is hung in a place of honour as an institutional treasure (Figure 12). It is thus a symbol both of a long-lived organization, around which identities are formed, and of the intellectual achievement of an individual that has received worldwide recognition. A single item of visual culture can spawn many derivatives, such as prints, mugs and fridge magnets. Hence one work, an oil painting on canvas measuring 133.9 by 108.5 centimetres, is supercharged with significance, remaining capable of acting as a powerful centrepiece for an institution and as a focus for reverence.[2]

William Harvey (1578–1657), famous for discovering the circulation of the blood and sitter in only a small number of demonstrably authentic portraits,

---

My warmest thanks to Julie Beckwith, Simon Bowman, Lowri Jones and Felix Lancashire at the Royal College of Physicians for their generous help and support, especially with the images. Illustrations in this chapter are courtesy of the college.

[1] Works that cover portraiture as a genre include Woodall, *Portraiture*, and West, *Portraiture*. See also Pointon, *Hanging the Head*.
[2] Accession no. X183. Collecting portraits is characteristic of most institutions and especially of those associated with education, learning and specialized occupations. All the paintings in the Royal College of Physicians, London are on the Art UK website, which covers all public collections: https://artuk.org, accessed 22 June 2019. Earlier published volumes on the portrait collection remain useful: Wolstenholme, *Royal College*; Wolstenholme and Kerslake, *Royal College*; and Driver, *Catalogue*.

Figure 12 Page from the Royal College of Physicians' website, showing the Dorchester Library with the college's seventeenth-century portrait of William Harvey in situ. This screenshot shows how the college's history is promoted when selling the site as a venue for events. The portrait of Harvey is on the upper right.

remains of immense importance for the Royal College of Physicians in London.[3] Founded in 1518, its long history can be used to reveal the ways in which forms of visual culture are woven into collective life, remaining available for a remarkable range of uses over hundreds of years. While organizational continuity may help people to forge their professional identities, there are also major changes to be noted, of which the succession of buildings the College has inhabited is one of the most obvious. Its current home is a highly praised modernist structure, which shows off its collections, and especially its portraits, to excellent effect.[4]

---

[3] On Harvey, see Keynes, *Life*; Keynes, *Portraiture*; Bylebyl, *William Harvey*. Most of the people mentioned in this chapter have entries in the *Oxford Dictionary of National Biography*, which list portraits of the person in question. All fellows are included in Munk's Roll, which is freely available online: https://history.rcplondon.ac.uk/inspiring-physicians, accessed 16 June 2019. See also Briggs, *History*, ch. 9. Harvey used experimental methods, and hence was seen as a pioneer of ways of producing sound knowledge that were highly prized from the seventeenth century onwards. He was also renowned for his learning – a broader claim to distinction.

[4] On the history of the college there are the 'official' volumes, Clark, *History* (2 vols); Cooke, *History*; and Briggs, *History*. See also Pelling and White, *Medical Conflicts*; Cook, *Decline of*

By their very nature, institutions have their own visual culture, even if it is simply a website without place or possessions. In this chapter I explore one that has a notably elaborate life in structures, artefacts and images in order to show how the many facets of its existence repay visual attention. The argument suggests the value for historians of what I call an integrative approach. By considering a range of media and genres and of items made in diverse periods, and by engaging with their textual hinterlands, it is possible to reach a fuller, more satisfying sense of the past, one that chimes with the commitments of historical actors for whom relics, portraits, coats of arms, books, buildings and so on were profoundly significant.[5]

Commemoration

An economical way of sketching in my approach is through a description of the series of ten books issued to celebrate the college's 500th anniversary in 2018. The uniform format – all the volumes are fifteen centimetres wide and twenty-one high, with a little over 100 pages – affirms the significance of the anniversary. Each text is relatively short at around 20,000 words, accompanied by numerous illustrations, and draws attention to fifty items of significance in the college. The front cover bears a simplified coat of arms, which includes a disembodied hand with fingers taking the pulse of an equally disembodied arm, next to 'Royal College of Physicians'. These volumes also sport an anniversary logo in the top right-hand corner – '500 Reflections on the RCP 1518–2018'. Such features are all recognized devices for imposing uniformity on publications and generating a visual brand – standardized design features inside each book reinforce the point.[6]

The content of these volumes is also revealing, covering as they do the college's buildings, garden, collections – books, manuscripts, silver, furniture, portraits and so on – and history, as well as thematic treatments of war, quacks and the RCP's global impact. Taken together, and given the heavy emphasis on artefacts and illustrations, this series reveals how those active in the college now think about its visual culture. The slim volumes represent, embody and epitomize that culture. Authors are hardly conjuring up this visual identity afresh but drawing upon five centuries of collecting, displaying and

---

the Old; Davenport et al., *Royal College*. On the building, see Moore, *Anatomy of a Building*; Cherry and Pevsner, *London*, 620–2, plate 111; Calder, *Denys Lasdun's Royal College*.

[5] This approach is set out in Jordanova, *Look of the Past*, and Jordanova, 'Science, Memory and Relics'.

[6] Chinthapalli, *Physicians*; Compston, *Simples and Rareties*; Jordanova, *Physicians*; Moore, *Anatomy of a Building*; Oakeley et al., *Garden*; Thompson, *Curiosities*; Vaughan, *Grave and Learned*; Vaughan and Thompson, *Ever Persons*; Shorvon and Hodgson, *Physicians and War*; Strathern, *Quacks, Rogues*.

writing, even if that project effectively had to start anew after the Great Fire. Meetings, whether routine or ceremonial, at which valued artefacts are used and architectural settings inhabited, reinforce collective memories and sustain visual and material identities.

Aspects of the college's visual culture have been transmitted through many generations. When new items are added to the collections, those who make and commission them necessarily have that history in mind. They engage with texts as well as artefacts when developing a sense of the past. Paintings and prints, for instance, are better understood when texts and other associated artefacts are considered alongside them. Artefacts, books and manuscripts are equally forms of visual culture. An elaborately bound copy of Harvey's complete works, published in Latin by the college in 1766 and bound around 1786, is a good example, where the deep red leather, gold decoration on the front and back covers and spine, as well as painted paper edges provide considerable visual complexity.[7] Thus the boundaries around what we call 'visual culture' are inherently fluid.

William Harvey

To illustrate the point, we can return to William Harvey. Although he had been lecturing on his discovery for some time before publishing it, the slim volume in which he announced the circulation of the blood in 1628 is highly valued.[8] Harvey published other works, and in the eighteenth century the college produced an edition in Latin of his writings, one copy of which I have just described, containing a fine frontispiece based on the painting of him in old age in its collection. We can analyse this volume, its design, binding and frontispiece, in terms of their visual properties. It is possible to gauge just how special this volume was from the fact that a bound copy was placed in Harvey's coffin when he was reburied in 1883.[9] By the time his *Opera Omnia* appeared and Harvey had been dead for just over a century, he already had a huge international reputation, which depended on people reading his work, admiring his discovery, debating his ideas and valuing his likeness, as Richard Mead (1673–1754) had done in 1739 when he donated a bust of Harvey to the college. Integral to Harvey's renown was the claim that he had made a unique contribution to natural knowledge. The bust, now in the college's foyer, was based on a painted portrait in Mead's own collection and made by Peter

---

[7] I am describing a copy in the National Library of Scotland, H.25.c.7. According to the catalogue the red Morocco binding is by James Scott of Edinburgh. He was active in the eighteenth century.
[8] Harvey, *Exercitatio Anatomica*. See also Harvey, *Circulation*, in which p. 22 is an illustration.
[9] Munk, *Brief Account*.

Scheemakers, a sculptor with whom he worked on other commissions.[10] The bust, like the frontispiece, was a visual manifestation of a larger, heterogeneous phenomenon. Harvey's reputation, sustained by memories, conversation and artefacts including relics, images and publications, created an aura – an environment within which any given piece of visual culture could be endowed with meaning. Invoking the notion of 'visual culture' in this context serves to focus our attention on prints, portraits and busts among other categories of objects but should not isolate them from their hinterland, which is textual, certainly, and also social, in that it is composed of friendships, networks and institutions. Specific social relationships, which assume a variety of forms, underpin all visual and material culture.[11]

The portraits the college owns are in a never-ending conversation with accounts of the lives of those they depict. Such accounts could take the form of a biography, as in the case of Harvey's *Opera Omnia*, where the poet and physician Mark Akenside (1721–70) set out his life.[12] By the mid-eighteenth century, it was well established that biography and portraiture were closely connected, even codependent genres. Links between lives and likenesses were also made through sociable interaction, such as the sharing of anecdotes, and by friendship networks that included artists, writers and medical practitioners. Stories about well-known practitioners found their way into print. Portraits in printed form might be attached, or circulated as independent images, thereby demonstrating the constant traffic between media that is of great historical interest. We need to see visual culture, then, as a phenomenon that was integral to, never apart from, social, cultural and material forms.

Physicians, their careers and institutions exemplify the point. Some were well-known public figures, especially when they were also writers or had famous patients. Medicine itself was and is an area of wide interest touching the life of every human being. The college, with its regulatory function, royal connections and elite membership, has found itself constantly in the public eye, while its most senior fellows not only lead the profession but make statements on matters of general concern.[13] Furthermore, the college is also a business,

---

[10] Jordanova, *Physicians*, 33, 38–9; Jordanova, 'Portraits, People and Things'; Hanson, *English Virtuoso*, ch. 5 (on Mead). The college also owns a conversation piece showing Peter Scheemakers in his studio around 1739, holding a print depicting William Harvey while the bust sits near him on a plinth (accession no. 2008.6). See Jordanova, *Physicians*, 40. On the conversation piece as a genre, see Retford, *Conversation Piece*.

[11] The point about relationships is put forcefully by Baxandall, *Painting and Experience*; in the case of the college such relationships include family ones.

[12] Harvey, *Opera*, i–xxxviii. There is no indication of who the author was in the volume itself, but the college's library catalogue attributes it to Mark Akenside. There are many versions of *Opera Omnia* in its collection. On biography, see Shortland and Yeo, *Telling Lives*; Wendorf, *Elements of Life*.

[13] We can appreciate the ways in which fellows were public figures through their roles as royal physicians, as many prominent figures in the college have been; in debates about public health, of which smoking is a good example (Briggs, *History*, ch. 4); and the high profile of some presidents, such as Lord Moran. On Moran, see Lovell, *Churchill's Doctor*. On the college's initial regulatory functions, see Clark, *History*, vols 1 and 2.

hiring out its building for events and conferences, as the website reveals. There the historic resonances of the college and its visual identity are exploited to sustain commercial activity. We can claim that it has become a brand. All these phenomena have visual components, from items for sale in the foyer to the abundance of portraits in the building and from publications to coasters bearing the coat of arms.

So far I have made a number of historical and historiographical points. In the former category sits information about a specific work-related institution, the centrality of William Harvey as an influential figure and source of prestige, the celebrations associated with its 500 years of history, a gift to the college and remarks about its public profile. These pertain to one case, which is taken to exemplify a wider historiographical point: items of visual and material culture shed light on the history of institutions, professional associations and social relationships precisely because they are integral to historical phenomena. They express, represent and shape the lives of both individuals and groups. By paying attention to their visual characteristics and life histories, it is possible to grasp more fully the nature of the past and its legacy in the present. But visual and material culture never exist in isolation, and it is vital to interpret a portrait, say, in the light of texts associated with it, as well as other likenesses and related artefacts. Many forms of visual culture exist, and some are more supercharged with significance and various kinds of value than others. In the case I am examining here, architecture is a good example.

Modern architecture

In the south-east corner of London's Regent's Park sits a remarkable building designed by Denys Lasdun (1914–2001), who also worked on the capital's South Bank Centre and the University of East Anglia's well-known ziggurats. Recognized as one of Lasdun's masterpieces, it was opened in 1964 and is a Grade 1 listed building.[14] There has been considerable architectural interest in this structure, which provides a sense of immediate connection with the garden and nearby buildings of a much earlier period by virtue of the huge windows on one side. Its centrepiece is the triple-height marble hall with a large staircase around which there are walkways acting as corridors between rooms, offering plenty of space for portraits to be hung (Figure 13). Every person entering the

---

[14] See https://historicengland.org.uk/listing/what-is-designation/listed-buildings/ for an explanation of the system in the United Kingdom designed to protect and classify buildings: 'listing marks and celebrates a building's special architectural and historic interest'.

Figure 13 A view of the main staircase in Denys Lasdun's building for the college, opened in 1964, with portraits on the walls. The interior, including the carpet, is as Lasdun designed it, although the building has been modified and extended since its opening.

college becomes aware of its distinctive design and of its collections, especially the portraits.[15]

In the foyer the eighteenth-century bust of Harvey is set into a wall. It was not taken directly from life but was, as we noted, fashioned by a prominent sculptor, using as a template the portrait in the possession of a notably generous fellow. As Harvey is by far the most famous physician associated with the college, this bust creates a palpable link between his lifetime and those who step into the building now. Thus historical continuities are visually asserted, as they are by the portraits hung on all the floors and in most of the rooms of a building that, in terms of design and materials, is resolutely modern. Rooms

---

[15] On the building, see Moore, *Anatomy of a Building*; on Lasdun, see Calder, *Denys Landun's Royal College*. The building has been modified since its original design, and the hang of the paintings is changed from time to time, although the portrait of Harvey is generally in the Dorchester Library.

are named after illustrious fellows, which reinforces the sense of the past in the present.

On the lower ground floor is an enclosed display space in which treasures owned by the college can be seen. One of these, the Gold-Headed Cane, exemplifies the attention to the past that is a notable characteristic of this organization. It has been claimed that the cane belonged in succession to five physicians, all of whom played a part in the college, and whose coats of arms are engraved on the head.[16] The widow of the last owner, Matthew Baillie (1761–1823), presented the cane to the college; Sophia Baillie (1771–1845) also donated paintings, and later a portrait of her came into its possession. In 1827 a book appeared, written as if by the cane itself, detailing its life, experiences and observations. Although the volume was published anonymously in the first instance, the author was William Macmichael (1783–1839), writer, physician and fellow of the college. Several editions are available, many are illustrated, and in some the contours of the cane's head are embossed on the front cover. Around one object, then, there is a history that began in the seventeenth century, when its first alleged owner, John Radcliffe (baptized 1650–1714), was active, and continues to the present day, when the book is still read and the object itself admired.

One room within the new building, the Censors' Room, contains wood panelling from the college's earlier homes (Figure 14). It too is hung with portraits and adorned with portrait busts. Similarly, the main meeting room, lined with books, is named the Dorchester Library after Henry Pierrepont, Marquis of Dorchester, whose family donated some 2,700 books to the college in 1680; it is here that the canvas of Harvey is generally hung and further portrait busts displayed (see Figure 12). A modernist building and historical furnishings and contents sit happily together.[17]

This can only be a partial account, albeit one that, starting with the college's contemporary location, shows how its history is made visible at every turn. It has, in other words, an elaborate visual identity that has been created, sustained and remade over the centuries. In order to grasp more fully the specificities of this visual identity, we would need to consider the nature of occupations, specifically of learned professions, and the key players with whom they worked.[18] In this case, patients, royal patrons, other medical professions and

---

[16] Macmichael, *Gold-Headed Cane*. Several editions exist, for example, the one by Munk.
[17] On the coexistence of modern and historical that is also evident in the Censors' Room, which contains panelling from earlier buildings as well as portraits and busts, see Jordanova, *Physicians*, 10, 83, and https://www.rcplondon.ac.uk/news/censors-room-symbolic-gateway-ancient-institution.
[18] Collyer, *Palgrave Handbook*, esp. chs 19, 33, 39, and Cockerham, *Medical Sociology*, chs 11 and 12, approach the medical profession from a social scientific viewpoint. Corfield, *Power and the Professions*; Peterson, *Medical Profession*; and Digby, *Making a Medical Living*, take a historical perspective. So far there is little on the visual culture of professions in the manner I am hinting at here.

Figure 14 The Censors' Room with its historic panelling in the heart of the college, set up for a meeting.

institutions, including hospitals and medical schools, are major players. So is the state, which, especially since the formation of the National Health Service in 1948, interacts with the college on a regular basis, even if the latter is, in terms of governance, autonomous. The history of the college has been told in terms of its impact on medicine and on London life.[19] The ways in which visual culture is central to its history have not been so extensively explored.

Integrative visual histories

I have indicated that visual culture is integral to all institutions, so the claim that this holds for London's Royal College of Physicians is hardly surprising. The historian's job is to show how this works for a particular case, and also to demonstrate what the historiographical value of such a demonstration is. In order to do so it is helpful to set physic in its contexts. Physicians, who were university-educated in periods when other kinds of medical practitioners rarely were, had a strong sense of the medical past, nurtured until the nineteenth century by reading classical writers such as Hippocrates, Galen and Celsus, as

---

[19] For example Cook, *Decline of the Old*, and Pelling with White, *Medical Conflicts*. On the NHS, see Webster, *National Health Service*.

well as by works on medical history.[20] Many physicians have exhibited deep interest in the visual arts and literature. Practices of collecting and display sustained their visual experiences. Portraits exemplify the point, given the diverse media in which they exist and surrounded as they are by complementary artefacts. Given the growing ubiquity of print culture from the fifteenth century onwards, portraits could also be widely circulated.[21] The preoccupation of elite learned physicians with ancient authorities, their general interest in the past of their field and their propensity to amass collections thus resulted in a rich visual culture from which the college benefitted by virtue of gifts and legacies. What this obscures, perhaps more or less deliberately, is the conflicts around medical practice and ideas, since the college's origins lay in attempts to control who practised medicine in the London area. Over many centuries this proved both controversial and exceptionally difficult to police. The college was well known and physicians could be represented as figures of fun, hence the visual culture of the college also involves satirical prints.[22] In this context royal patronage enabled the college to associate itself with powerful elites, to affirm its status, and this impulse is evident in the portraits of monarchs in its collections.[23] Historical insights are all the more persuasive if they have taken seriously visual phenomena that were cherished by people in the past.

The possibilities for an integrative visual history are emerging. Starting with an organization, we can trace its existence through a cultural array that includes books, manuscripts, portraits in a number of media, collectables such as the cane, satirical prints, gifts of silver, buildings, interior design and so on. When contextualized and interpreted, such sources provide a vivid sense of institutional life – of who was celebrated; how and why; and, where evidence permits, of the economic value assigned to items of visual culture. At the same time this case study reveals networks of association between individuals and families, patrons and clients, and institutions. These could be at once intimately personal and professional as they were when sons followed in their fathers' footsteps and medical families intermarried. Sophia Baillie, for example, came from a medical family, and both she and her sister married medical practitioners. Her husband's uncles, William and John Hunter, were well-known medical men.[24] Many prominent fellows enjoyed the patronage

[20] The first history of physic to be published in England was by John Freind (1675–1728), a fellow of the college: Freind, *History of Physic*.
[21] The college owns an extensive collection of prints, which are also present in frontispieces; see Driver, *Catalogue*. On prints in general, see Griffiths, *Prints*, and Grifiths, *Print before Photography*.
[22] On satirical prints, see Donald, *Age of Caricature*; on medical prints there is Haslam, *From Hogarth to Rowlandson*. The print collections in the Wellcome Library and the British Museum are notably rich and both are searchable online.
[23] There are portraits of Henry VIII, George III and Edward VII in the collection.
[24] Sophia's father was Thomas Denman (1733–1815), a licentiate of the college and a physician-accoucheur. Her sister, Margaret, married Richard Croft (1762–1818), who had been a pupil of John Hunter and attended Princess Charlotte during her pregnancy in 1817. After Charlotte's

of the royal family, including William Harvey, John Radcliffe, Richard Mead, Matthew Baillie and Henry Halford.[25] Such connections brought physicians to public attention, which was inevitably a mixed blessing when things went wrong but also in itself a generator of status as is evident in the grandeur of some of their portraits.

The elegant depiction of Sir Henry Halford (1766–1844) from around 1825 by the prominent artist Sir Thomas Lawrence (1769–1830), portrait painter to British elites, is a case in point.[26] That Lawrence was president of the Royal Academy and interested in anatomy and medicine, while Halford moved in aristocratic circles and was president of his college for more than two decades, serves to illustrate their networks of association. For a significant part of its history there was considerable overlap between the college and the Royal Society, founded in 1660 under the patronage of Charles II.[27] An excellent example is Sir Hans Sloane (1660–1753) who was president of both bodies simultaneously and whose collections formed the basis of the British Museum.[28] Such affinities become visible not just through images and objects themselves but through gifts, provenance, commissions and bequests. We should note, however, that although the visual culture of the college arises from a specific profession, the actual work of physicians is rarely depicted.

Work and performance

The visual representation of work is a complex matter and has been historically diverse.[29] There are numerous examples in print culture of allusions to the ways in which people make a living, for example, in street scenes and landscapes, which include forms of labour that were visible in urban and rural locations.

---

son was stillborn and her death, he committed suicide. The significance of Matthew Baillie's connection with the Hunters is clear in Baillie, *Works*.

[25] On court physicians, see Nutton, *Medicine at the Courts*. Radcliffe's, Mead's and Baillie's royal associations are brought out in Macmichael, *Gold-Headed Cane*, for example 7–13, 22–9 (on Radcliffe).

[26] Accession no. X124. On Halford, see Munk, *Life of Sir Henry Halford*; on Lawrence, see Albinson et al., *Thomas Lawrence*, and Garlick, *Sir Thomas Lawrence*. Lawrence was president of the Royal Academy of Arts between 1820 and 1830, while Halford was president of the college between 1820 and 1844.

[27] On the Royal Society, see Hunter, *Establishing the New Science*; Hunter with Bennett, *Image of Restoration Science*; Boas Hall, *All Scientists Now*.

[28] On Sloane there is Delbourgo, *Collecting the World*; see ch. 7 for the creation of the British Museum.

[29] 'Work' is not a straightforward concept. See Barringer, *Men*. Note the subtitle with its emphasis on 'labour', from which professionals generally sought to distance themselves. Scenes of everyday life sometimes include the activities by which people earn their living. While photography in principle made depictions of work easier to produce, most medical photographs are posed and do not depict work as such; see Fox and Lawrence, *Photographing Medicine*. These points make the paintings by the American artist Thomas Eakins, *The Gross Clinic* (1875) and *The Agnew Clinic* (1889), all the more remarkable.

Professions could be identified by clothing and other aspects of their physical appearance. In the case of physicians, a wig functioned in this way over the long eighteenth century. Sober attire and a cane might complete the picture. Satirical prints usefully reveal what visual clues spectators needed to enable them to identify a figure as a physician, if a caption was absent. Sometimes prints showed physicians in the context of patients, in their homes, for instance.[30] Formal portraits of specific physicians did not include such details, however, generally showing the individual in an interior setting, a study for instance, sometimes evoked by a table and chair, with perhaps some reading matter. The college has displayed such works for centuries, offering a visual repertoire that helped mould professional identity. The social status associated with physic is implicit in these portraits, or rather the aspiration to be considered gentlemanly and learned is. One issue here is the distinction between manual and mental activities – the former being more closely associated with surgery and the latter with learned medicine.[31] Thus visual culture is suffused with assumptions about work and social position shared between sitters and artists certainly, as well as by general audiences. These are carried in the case of oils on canvas by the size of the depiction and by the amount of the subject's body that is included – full-length likenesses suggested higher rank, and artists might adopt a 'grand manner' approach, similar to portraits of royal personages and aristocrats.[32]

One historiographical challenge is how to give life to portraits that easily seem to our eyes rather staid, even indistinguishable from one another. Some such similarities had strategic value in terms of representing an occupation as 'safe', morally upright and respectable – traits that were highly valued by those who dealt with diseased and dead bodies. Professional men were generally shown indoors and soberly attired. Any given oil painting would have a limited number of viewers, even if in institutional locations they became familiar to key peer groups. Derivative prints were a crucial way in which wider audiences were reached, especially in the case of physician writers, such as Richard Blackmore (1653–1729), Samuel Garth (1659–1718/9) and Mark Akenside (1721–70), who were fellows of the college.[33] But prints have not generally been displayed on the walls of venerable institutions. They were nonetheless highly collectable, available at a range of prices, and provide historians with a vivid sense of how the medium was disseminated. Thus images of prominent individuals associated with the college had lives far beyond its walls. As a result, one facet of its visual culture was widely distributed. The common practice of

---

[30] For example Jordanova, *Nature Displayed*, 76, 77.
[31] Lawrence, 'Medical Minds', explores the contrasting imagery, stereotypes and prejudice elicited by physicians and surgeons.
[32] Wilton, *Swagger Portrait*.
[33] Jordanova, *Physicians*, 28–9, 38.

putting institutional affiliation beside the sitter's name on a print suggests that 'FRCP' was readily recognized.[34]

What is largely unspoken in the visual culture of the college is the intimate access physicians had to the bodies of their patients, their anatomical activities and in some cases their experimental researches. However, two notable works in the college's collections do broach these themes, if somewhat indirectly. The first is probably the most celebrated work of art in the collections. Entitled *William Hunter at the Royal Academy*, it was painted around 1772 by Johan Zoffany (1733–1810). This dark, oval painting set in a substantial gold frame shows Hunter (1718–83) with a skeleton and two models in a similar posture, one an écorché and the other perfectly alive, with the anatomist, helped by an assistant, expounding on their bodies to a male audience, most of whom are paying attention (Plate 5).[35] Hunter's expertise is displayed to academicians and to viewers, and it concerns the human body. There is no direct allusion to treating patients, although Hunter was well known in London for his medical and anatomical activities by this time. Recognized as an influential educator of aspiring medical practitioners, Hunter was also a voracious collector. In 1769 he had become professor of anatomy at the recently founded Royal Academy. Both Zoffany and Hunter had royal connections and shared a commitment to the exact imitation of nature. This work came into the college's collections in 1825, part of the gift from Sophia, the widow of Hunter's nephew and heir, the noted physician Matthew Baillie. Here we can see multiple connections springing from a single item of visual culture. But things are not entirely straightforward. William Hunter had trained as a surgeon, becoming a physician only later in 1750, and was never a fellow of the college, only a licentiate from 1756. His participation in protests against the college in the 1750s suggests he was not its unequivocal admirer.[36] This well-known treasure turns out to have associations with the institution that are rooted indirectly in kinship rather than the direct participation of a fellow.

There is another way in which this picture can be approached – as performance, both literally and metaphorically. William Hunter is giving a lecture on a platform that is dramatically lit, and the models also participate as performers; arguably we can include the skeleton in that term. The human frame is on active display to a highly specific audience. Hunter is also performing his professorial role in the still-young academy, presided over by his friend Sir Joshua Reynolds, holding an ear trumpet in the centre of this painting. Indeed, the Royal Academy itself is on display. But none of this would be visible to eighteenth-century and later spectators without Zoffany, a master of theatrical

---

[34] Jordanova, *Physicians*.
[35] On Zoffany, see Postle, *Johan Zoffany*; Webster, *Johan Zoffany*; and on this painting, 222–3 (Postle) and 396–7 (Webster).
[36] Clark, *History*, vol. 2, ch. 28, details issues around the status of licentiates.

portraiture, representing it.[37] He in turn is performing as an artist, revealing his talent, skills and labour. Zoffany excelled at portraying groups; here he was acting as a mediator of aspects of the academy's collective identity, and alluding to the intricate connections between artistic and medical communities. Group portraiture is a significant sub-genre.[38] It requires exceptional artistic skills, and a recent example in the college is visually cumbersome and unconvincing.[39] In fact Zoffany depicted the Royal Academy of Arts in two paintings, both of which include William Hunter.[40] Artistic quality is certainly playing a role. It is perfectly legitimate for historians to comment on this aspect of visual culture; indeed they need to be able to make value judgements that are well informed.

Zoffany's group portrait may usefully be compared with another performative work in the college's collections, painted some seventy years later – *William Harvey Demonstrating to Charles I the Circulation of the Blood from the Heart of a Deer* (Plate 6). This picture, purchased in 1869, also alludes to 'work' and reveals another facet of visual culture, since it is a mid-nineteenth-century painting of an imagined seventeenth-century scene involving William Harvey and Charles I. It cannot be called a portrait, strictly speaking, although it draws upon known portrayals of both the main figures. Rather it is part of a fashion for recreations of key historical moments that is characteristic of the time.[41] Robert Hannah (1812–1909) exhibited his work at the Royal Academy and painted another such historical scene – *Master Isaac Newton in his Garden at Woolsthorpe, in the Autumn of 1665*, in the collections of the Royal Institution, London. In making this purchase, the college revealed its interest, which continues to this day, in extending the collections. Perhaps this is partly explained by considering precisely what Harvey is doing in the picture. A deer lies on a table and Harvey holds its heart in his hand, demonstrating his circulation theory to the king. *De Motu Cordis* was dedicated to Charles, and its experimental approach was taken to be emblematic of the 'new science'.[42] In buying Hannah's picture, then, the college was not adding to authentic materials associated with an illustrious forbear but acquiring a work that celebrated his intellectual achievements more than 200 years after they occurred. It is difficult to determine the extent to which viewers perceive the picture as a nineteenth-century invention or interpret it as a 'portrait'. For later generations, Harvey was feted as a champion of experimental physiology

---

[37] Webster, *Johan Zoffany*, and Postle, *Johan Zoffany*, both discuss his theatrical scenes.
[38] Allsdorf, *Fellow Men*, is a particularly stimulating discussion of the depiction of groups. See also West, *Portraiture*, ch. 4, and Retford, *Conversation Piece*.
[39] Raymond Piper, *Comitia*, 1968, accession no. X169, which depicts the AGM of the college.
[40] Hunter also appeared in Zoffany's 1771 painting *The Portraits of the Academicians of the Royal Academy*; see Postle, *Johan Zoffany*, 218–9, and Webster, *Johan Zoffany*, 255–7. On the Royal Academy there is Hoock, *King's Artists*; and on Hunter, Campbell and Flis, *William Hunter*.
[41] Bann et al., *Painting History*, and Strong, *Painting the Past*.
[42] Harvey, *Circulation*, 1–2.

rather than as a medical practitioner, and the references to experiment are perfectly explicit in Hannah's canvas.

Silences and ceremonies

There is a paradox here. The college exists to serve a specific occupation, that of physician, which has been represented as a learned profession. Yet the work, the labour, that physicians undertake is more or less absent from its visual culture. It is alluded to quite lightly in the coat of arms, which shows a task physicians frequently undertook: taking a pulse – a practice that can be shown without any breach of decorum. Otherwise the day-to-day business of physic rarely figures in visual culture. Maybe this is precisely the point – that the actual *work* of being a physician is played down in favour of more general and generic characteristics of learning, knowledge, benevolence and, in some cases, experiment.

An integrative visual history considers what cannot be or is not present in visual culture, as well as what is. While it is difficult to be certain about such matters, our interpretations need to consider decorum, conventions and habit, as well as social hierarchies and the labile status of specific occupations. Inside institutions there are bound to be power structures, reinforced in this case by processions and the wearing of gowns (Figure 15), and by the presence of such items in paintings, prints and photographs.[43] At the same time, such an organization is inculcating its values in new cohorts of practitioners. At any particular moment the college contains physicians from a number of generations. This feature facilitates the transmission of ideas and information, that is, of traditions and institutional knowledge. Visual culture is part and parcel of these processes. At the Annual Dinner to celebrate William Harvey, which follows an Oration in his name, he is remembered collectively and portraits of him act as mnemonics. Most participants will have seen them many times before in the foyer and the Dorchester Library, for example. There is always a risk that an institution's visual culture becomes wallpaper, something that is just there and treated as merely decorative. Ceremonial events demand participants' attention, pulling its visual culture into sharper focus.

Visual culture in an institutional setting, then, serves to connect members to its past, to affirm continuities between past and present, and implicitly, the future. Through ceremonies and collecting forms of memory are cultivated.[44]

---

[43] For example, Margaret Turner-Warwick, the first woman president, was painted by David Poole in 1992 wearing her robes. See Jordanova, *Physicians*, 80. Many other portraits in the collection show sitters in robes. Robes themselves are on display in the Treasures Room and can be glimpsed in the virtual tour of the building – another visual manifestation of the college's identity that emphasizes its potential as a meeting place: https://www.rcpevents.co.uk/virtual-venue-tour, accessed 23 June 2019.

[44] Memory is now a hot topic in historical research and has been for some time; see Cubitt, *History and Memory*, and Tumblety, *Memory and History*, for introductions. In terms of the

Plates

Plate 1 Letter of defamation against John III of Bavaria issued by John III of Nassau-Dillenburg, c. 1419–21, painted paper, 26 × 42 cm (10 × 16.1 in.). Hessisches Hauptstaatsarchiv, Wiesbaden, Abt. 170, 1026 (artwork in the public domain; photograph reproduced with permission from Hessisches Hauptstaatsarchiv).

Plate 2 Letter of defamation against Louis of Hesse, 1438, watercoloured pen drawing on paper, 35.5 × 21.5 cm (13.7 × 8.3 in.). Institut für Stadtgeschichte, Frankfurt am Main, Reichssachen I, 3605, fol. 4 (artwork in the public domain; photograph reproduced with permission).

Plate 3 Christoph Weiditz, 'This is also an Indian, a Nobleman of their kind', and 'This is also the Indian manner, how they have brought wood jugs with them out of which they drink', from the 'Trachtenbuch', 1530–40, pen and gouache, gold and silver leaf, 15 × 20 cm (6 × 7⅞ in.). Germanisches Nationalmuseum, Nuremberg, Hs 22474 (artwork in the public domain; photograph provided by Historic Images/Alamy Stock Photo).

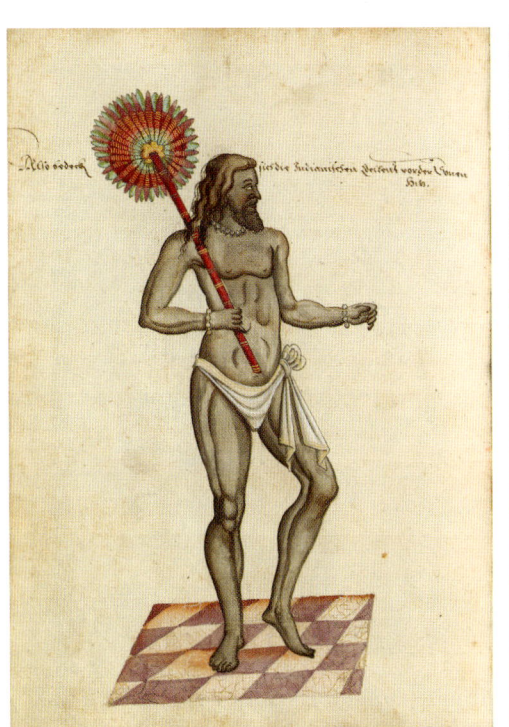 

Plate 4 'Indian Nobleman' and 'Indian Woman', from 'Kostüme der Männer und Frauen in Augsburg und Nürnberg, Deutschland, Europa, Orient und Afrika', fourth quarter of the sixteenth century, watercolour on paper, 30 × 20 cm (11⅞ × 7⅞ in.). Bayerische Staatsbibliothek, Munich, Cod.icon. 341 (artwork in the public domain; photograph © Bayerische Staatsbibliothek).

Plate 5 Johan Zoffany, *William Hunter at the Royal Academy*, 1770–2, oil on canvas, 77.4 × 103.5 cm (30½ × 40¾ in.). Royal College of Physicians, London, X142.

Plate 6 Robert Hannah, *William Harvey Demonstrating to Charles I the Circulation of the Blood from the Heart of a Deer*, 1848, oil on canvas, 80.6 × 91.4 cm (31¾ × 36 in.). Royal College of Physicians, X141.

Plate 7 Robert Edge Pine, *John Wilkes*, 1768, oil on canvas, 127 × 101.6 cm (50 × 40 in.). Parliamentary Art Collection, London, WOA 2935 (artwork in the public domain; photograph © Parliamentary Art Collection, WOA 2935, www.parliament.uk/art).

Plate 8 Johan Zoffany, *Mary Wilkes; John Wilkes*, exhibited 1782, oil on canvas, 126.4 × 100.3 cm (49⅞ in. × 39½ in.). National Portrait Gallery, London, NPG6133 (artwork in the public domain; UKPhoto © Stefano Baldini/Bridgeman Images).

Plate 9 *Bauten der Arbeit und des Verkehrs*, 2nd imprint, 1926, front dust-jacket. The colour palette, typeface, and layout (including the position of the image and the borders) are immediately recognisable elements of the brand identity of the *Blaue Bücher* series of low-cost, mass circulation photographic books published by the Langewiesche publishing house.

Figure 15 A procession is making its way up the staircase: the president in his robes with their gold decoration is preceded by a member of the college staff carrying the highly decorated ceremonial mace, a symbol of authority commonly used by institutions that are intensely aware of their history and significance.

Two projects undertaken by fellows illustrate the point, showing how helpful it is to make collecting and collections central to visual histories.[45]

Collecting practices

The collecting practices of prominent fellows such as Hans Sloane and Richard Mead have been receiving increased attention in recent scholarship. They both sought out objects that resonated with their values and networks, including

---

use of visual evidence this has been most evident in writings on memorials and monuments, for example Young, *Texture of Memory*.

[45] Thinking about professional institutions in terms of their collections is essential. So far, there are useful descriptions, such as Robinson, *Royal Society*, and Davenport et al., *Royal College*. The history of collecting is emerging as a significant historical field; see, for example, the *Journal of the History of Collections*, founded in 1989.

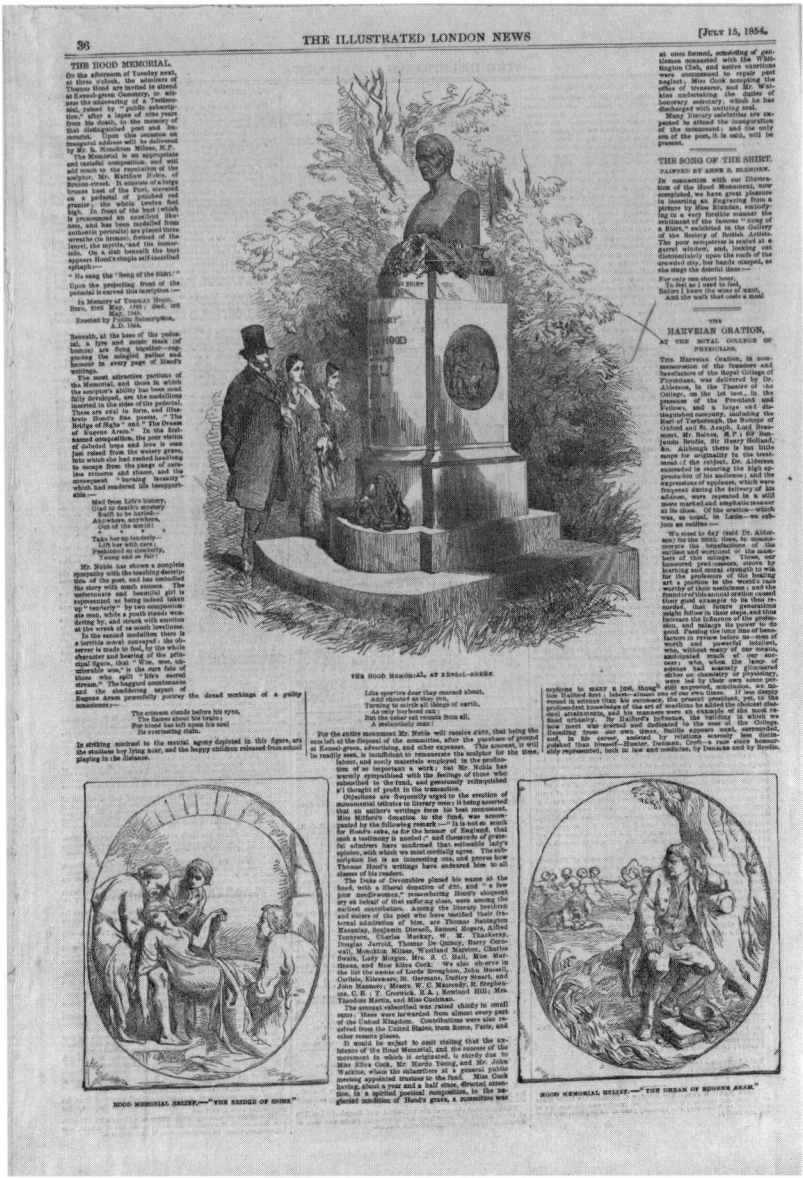

Figure 16 Cuttings in the scrapbook Frederick Farre compiled while writing his history of the Royal College of Physicians (MS-FarrF 2245). It reveals that the *Illustrated London News*, first published in 1842 and the world's first illustrated weekly news magazine, took an interest in the college's affairs. The magazine was widely read, with the images proving a particular draw.

Figure 16 (*Continued*)

portraits of people who shared their institutional and intellectual affiliations. They were also omnivorous, amassing huge collections of books, coins, medals and prints, as well as paintings that spoke to their broad interests. In later generations there is evidence of energetic collecting that has a tighter connection to the college itself.

Take the example of Frederick John Farre (1804–86), who compiled a history of the college towards the end of his life. Farre's father and brother were also fellows of the college, to which he was strongly attached.[46] Although the work was never published, and was criticized by some of his colleagues, it remains an invaluable source, especially what is known as his 'scrapbook' of fifty-nine leaves, disassembled and then rebound recently, into which he pasted maps, prints, articles from the *Illustrated London News*, pictures from books and so on (Figure 16). The manuscript and scrapbook are dated 1883, and they constitute a detailed evocation of the college by a participant. Or rather they present one vision of it. Farre paid attention to symbolic objects, such as the Caduceaus, the book of statues, the Seal and the Mace, and to the buildings the college inhabited.[47] Photographs from the 1860s, for example, depict the Warwick Lane site after the college had moved to Pall Mall. Floor plans are also included. It would be possible to describe the album in terms of portraiture – in order to generate a 'likeness' of the college, Farre amassed as many items as possible to give it life. He ranged widely, revealing how visual associations operated. A telling instance of this is his inclusion of the last print in William Hogarth's *Four Stages of Cruelty* (1751). A handwritten note explains that it represents the Cutlerian Theatre in Warwick Lane, and he attempted to identify specific figures in Hogarth's image. This work has been considered more hostile to surgeons than to physicians, although Hogarth was no doubt content to tilt at an establishment body that was embroiled in controversies.[48]

Farre's labour of love in writing, cutting and pasting bears comparison with the work of another fellow, Arnold Chaplin (1864–1944) and his wife, Margaret Douie Chaplin (1859–1936), during the First World War. In order to grasp their extra-illustration project it is necessary to consider the contributions made by William Munk (1816–98), a contemporary of the Farre brothers, who became a fellow of the college in 1854 and Harveian Librarian three years later – an office he held until his death. Munk is most famous for his biographical work, and especially his *Roll of the Royal College of Physicians of London*.[49] He also wrote the lives of Sir Henry Halford and John Ayrton Paris, both of whom presided over the college. The *Roll* was not illustrated, but Arnold and Margaret Chaplin cut up the second edition in three volumes of 1878 and sought out as many portrait prints as possible to accompany the biographies. These, together with the printed pages, were then inserted in mounts and the

---

[46] His father was John Richard Farre, and his brother was Arthur Farre; full details are on Munk's Roll (see note 3, above).

[47] Thompson, *Curiosities*; for the different buildings, see the histories cited in note 4, above.

[48] The print in Farre's album is *The Reward of Cruelty*, the last in the series *Four Stages of Cruelty*, 1751. On Hogarth's print, see Bindman, *Hogarth*, 142–7, and Uglow, *Hogarth*, 500–6. Both associate the print with surgeons. The 'official' histories by Clark, Cooke and Briggs set out the controversies.

[49] The two editions published in Munk's lifetime may be found in the bibliography, while the online edition is kept up to date.

whole rebound, again in three volumes, and presented to the college. Whereas Farre seems to have assembled a rich and diverse array of visual materials relating to the college, the Chaplins systematically focused on portraits of fellows, who appear in Munk's volumes in chronological order. Through the prints and their labours they re-experienced the historical sequence lying at the heart of an institution. Their handwritten preface made clear the close affinities they experienced in the process even if, as they admit, they were drawn more to some figures than to others.[50]

In both these cases visual culture was integral to extended engagement with an institution; the images themselves were valuable and interesting to those who collected them, but the processes involved are equally significant, precisely because they betoken attentive ways of looking, to which the Chaplins' preface bears eloquent testimony.

Conclusions

When an institution has been in existence for 500 years, its visual culture is inevitably heterogeneous. Some specific artefacts have had continued relevance and potency for much of that time, while others have shorter institutional lives. Given the devastating fire in which so much was lost, images of founding fathers had to be recreated, as happened when a portrait of the first president, Thomas Linacre (c. 1460–1524), was copied in 1810.[51] The portraits in oil and portrait busts are just the most obvious manifestations of institutional identity, and they are given pride of place in the current building, as they were in earlier ones. But they are simply the tip of a huge iceberg, where, with various levels of intention, the college creates, shapes and reproduces itself. In this case 'visual culture' can be a form of history making. Portraits are commissioned of contemporary presidents in order to provide a sense of the past for future physicians and visitors to the building. The college is clearly a brand, both in terms of its commercial activities and its medical functions. It continues to inculcate affection and interest in a range of audiences by visual means and is assisted in this project by Lasdun's iconic building. Above all it is the visual and material ensemble constituting 'the Royal College of Physicians of London', which suggests how vital the visual lives of institutions are and therefore how they help historians reconstruct accounts of the past that can be said to be visual histories.

---

[50] Jordanova, *Physicians*, discusses the Chaplins' project; for the preface, see 98, 96–102. On extra-illustration, see Peltz, *Facing the Text*.

[51] For the copy (accession no. X58), see Jordanova, *Physicians*, 101, and on Linacre himself, Madison et al., *Essays on the Life*.

4

Making an exhibition of himself: John Wilkes through visual sources

Jonathan Conlin

In a 1988 review article the renowned historian of science Roy Porter noted how far historians had come in their understanding of the relationship between 'oral' and 'literate' cultures. 'Orality' had ceased to be identified with a 'primitive' mindset. The 'coming of print' was no longer viewed as the triumph of modernity. The study of spoken and written sources had come to be seen not only as complementary but as inextricably linked. Dialogue had made historians of both camps better students of the past. Rather than questioning the merit of close reading of written sources, 'oral history' had provided new tools that made such reading more productive.

He noted that unfortunately this process had yet to occur when it came to historians' use of visual signs.

> Would there were schools of 'visual history' paralleling 'oral history'! For if historians have become more sensitive to juxtaposing what people said against what they read, we still have a long way to go in 'seeing' what people saw, and in interpreting the significance of visual signs. ... Heraldic devices, inn signs, funeral effigies, wall posters, heads on coins, and so forth – how should these be 'read'? How far should the historian see them as primarily ornamental, merely duplicating, at most reinforcing, the information and sentiments which people derived from other sources, above all from the spoken and printed word? Or were they integral and special to the processes of creating and conveying the wider sign-systems of former times?[1]

Porter's review article was inspired by a flurry of publications which sought to mine eighteenth-century Britain's rich output of graphic satires (woodcuts, engravings, etchings and mezzotints) in the service of well-established sub-disciplines of political, legal and religious history, as well as a less familiar *histoire des mentalités* and cultural history.

This chapter provides a case study in how historians can see as well as read and hear the past. It focuses on images of one man, John Wilkes (1725–97), an important figure in the social and constitutional history of Britain, who also had a strong following in Britain's North American colonies and France. To

---

[1] Porter, 'Seeing the Past', 186–7.

some contemporaries, Wilkes was a dangerous demagogue; others accepted Wilkes's invitation to identify with him as a loyal subject standing up to the despotism of King George III's ministers. Historians' views of Wilkes have ranged almost as widely. It is nonetheless clear that Wilkes's heyday (1764–72) coincided with a dramatic increase in the volume and variety of visual images of all kinds, as well as in the volume and variety of people who created, criticized, copied, adapted, edited, displayed and occasionally destroyed them. Here we will focus on four examples: the number '45' chalked on the shoes of the Austrian ambassador, a fine portrait mezzotint, an ephemeral advertisement for a tobacco merchant and an oil painting.

Sadly, the ambassador's shoes do not survive and were probably wiped clean of chalk within hours of their marking. Thanks to a set of public institutions (museums, the internet) and technologies (personal computing, broadband), however, the other three can be viewed for free, either in person, at the British Museum and National Portrait Gallery (London), or via their websites. Contrary to widely held opinion, anyone, not just professors of art history, can email the British Museum's Department of Prints and Drawings requesting an appointment, travel to Bloomsbury, fill in a call slip and wait for the originals to be brought out of store.[2] For most of us, these objects are more likely to appear as arrangements of pixels on a screen; search engines allow one simply to enter the phrase 'John Wilkes' and be presented with thumbnails of hundreds of objects (medals, punch bowls and teapots, as well as prints).

As with other technologies, there is a price to be paid for speed and convenience. Viewed on a MacBook screen, the oil portrait discussed below is four inches tall; the same painting on an iPhone is just two. The same technology which transmits an image of the painting not only changes the colour but also resizes it to fit whatever screen we happen to be viewing. The term 'window' implies that we are seeing things as they are, when in reality, any sense of scale is entirely lost. Yet it is surely significant that, whereas the oil painting is life-size, the tobacco advertisement measures only 7 by 6 cm. Materiality is lost as well: both that of the medium and what art historians call the support. The painting is oil on (linen) canvas, the '45' was chalk on leather, the prints are ink impressed onto paper. Craft and artistry, too, are less evident.

Although we pride ourselves on our supposed fluency in the language of images, as historians we are failing to notice important technology-based distinctions between images of old objects. Such distinctions may appear 'connoisseurial', recondite matters for art experts. Yet if we dismiss them we risk committing serious historical errors. We attribute the same historical

[2] Knowledge of how to make such arrangements is limited to those with the time and a certain familiarity with how such institutions work (what Bourdieu calls 'cultural capital'). In this regard, 'free access' is never quite what it seems. This is equally true of online access: broadband and the capital required to buy a computer are not distributed equally across even the wealthiest nations, while much of the world's population is without either. Bourdieu, *Distinction*.

significance to the oil painting as we do to the engraving, even though the former was a one-off commissioned by Wilkes himself, while the latter was one of around 500 impressions taken from the same copper plate, produced by an artist appealing to a far larger audience. Sitting side by side on our screens, all objects are made to appear the same size: yet an ardent Wilkite could have wallpapered a room with such engravings for less than the price that one of Wilkes's portraitists charged for a full-length oil painting in 1763 (£20, or approx. £2,600 in today's money).[3] We need to learn about earlier technologies of artistic production, reproduction and reception before we can begin to 'see the past' in the way Porter wanted us to. But first we need to know a bit more about why Wilkes is of interest to historians in the first place.

Whose liberties?

Almost all eighteenth-century Britons looked down condescendingly on their fellow Europeans as pitiable victims of despotism, who had supposedly sacrificed their self-respect as well as their rights to property and self-expression to the greater glory of absolute monarchs and the Roman Catholic Church. The sixteenth-century Reformation and the Glorious Revolution of 1688 were hailed as having set Britons free from this fealty to priests and kings. Much fuss was made of the 'rights of free Englishmen', using language which we associate with nineteenth- and twentieth-century campaigns for universal suffrage. Rather than milestones on the road to a liberal utopia located in the future, however, these freedoms were perceived as an inheritance.[4] Liberties were there to be restored, not declared. 'Innovation', like 'enthusiasm', was a pejorative term.

Britons felt that the parliament sitting in Westminster was theirs, enshrining many of their freedoms, even if only around 3 per cent of them could vote in parliamentary elections. Almost nobody held that parliament was there to represent men, let alone women. Parliament was there to represent 'interests', not individuals: the 'landed' interest (large landowners, overwhelmingly aristocrats), but also other, commercial ones, including those deriving their profits from outside the British Isles. Manchester, like the wider British Empire, was represented by mill-owners and merchants who sat in Westminster as MPs for constituencies in other, often quite distant parts of the United Kingdom. These men bought their way into parliament through one of the many 'rotten

---

[3] The £20 figure dates from 1763. The Wilkes portrait, of course, contains two full-length figures, so the artist probably charged more. Postle, *Johan Zoffany*, 194. Conversion is based on the RPI engine at https://www.measuringworth.com.

[4] Pocock, *Ancient Constitution*, 234.

boroughs' – constituencies which had been important cities in medieval times, but which were now populated by a few sheep, and whose 'electorate' was entirely under the control of the local landowner (at each election, the landowners sold the seat to the highest bidder).

Although it seems corrupt by today's standards, most contemporaries felt that this system ensured that 'the sense of the people' was embodied in parliament, which formed one (but by no means the only) channel by which that 'sense' was conveyed to their monarch, who ruled as 'King in parliament', choosing his ministers from among parliament's leading men.[5] The king controlled the Royal Navy and the rest of the armed forces. He had extensive patronage powers, that is, influence derived from his ability to appoint individuals to salaried offices in church as well as state. By European standards, however, his powers were tightly circumscribed by parliament, which controlled how taxes were raised and spent. Back in 1701, parliament had laid down that no member of the royal family who was also a member of the Roman Catholic Church could reign.

This decision resulted in Stuart claimants to the throne (those descended from James II) being passed over in favour of more distant relations, from the safely Protestant Hanoverian branch of the same family. George I duly took the throne in 1714, followed by his son George II in 1727. The Stuarts did not take this lying down. Their claims were supported, off and on, by various European powers, as a way of meddling in British affairs. In 1715 and 1745, this meddling took the form of helping Stuart claimants in their attempts to take the British throne by force. In 1745 Prince Charles Edward Stuart landed in Scotland, rallied the clans and marched south, coming perilously close to London before bad intelligence led him to pause and retreat, leading to bloody defeat at the Battle of Culloden in 1746. These events sowed lasting suspicion between Scotland and England, which Wilkes did much to exploit.[6]

Upon taking the throne in 1760 King George III sought to draw a line under these and other historical conflicts dividing his English, Scottish, Welsh and Irish subjects, declaring that he 'gloried in the name of Briton'. At the same time, however, he sought more of a say over his choice of ministers, appointing his former tutor, John Stuart, third Earl of Bute, to lead his cabinet. Early in his reign George III faced the task of negotiating the peace that would end the Seven Years' War, as well as finding new ways of servicing the massive debts left behind by this intercontinental conflict. There was little indication that these questions would end up blowing up in the king's face, making the 1760s into the pivotal decade of the eighteenth century. A good deal of the credit for this belongs to John Wilkes.

---

[5] See Wilson, *Sense of the People*; Melton, *Rise of the Public*, 19–44.
[6] See Colley, 'John Wilkes and Englishness', in *Britons*, 105–16.

Wilkes and the historians

Politics before Wilkes was an aristocratic ballet in which the 'outs' (the Opposition) toyed with a range of 'Country' or 'Patriotic' rhetoric just long enough to evict the 'ins' (the government), taking their proper place at the feeding trough of public office.[7] Parties were organized around wealthy landowners, not ideologies or manifestoes. Born with a strabismus (vulgarly called a squint) and a prognathous jaw (an extended chin), the second son of a Clerkenwell distiller, John Wilkes owed his entree to politics not to birth but to his education and considerable wit, which the wealthy Pitt family employed in support of their 'Patriot' cause from the late 1750s onwards.[8] Unlike other hacks, such as Edmund Burke, who wrote for the Rockingham Whigs, Wilkes was an enthusiastic member of that hedonistic coven of aristocrats, sex workers and hangers-on known as the Hell-Fire Club, whose satanic rites and orgies continue to fascinate historians.[9] Alongside his journalism, therefore, Wilkes also supplied his patrons with pornography, such as *An Essay on Woman*, a satire on the Roman Catholic poet Alexander Pope.

According to Wilkes's weekly paper, *The North Briton*, Bute (a Scot) was in league with the defeated French, in cahoots with the pretender and in bed with King George's mother, Augusta, Princess Dowager of Wales. Bute was supposedly encouraging his royal master to abuse his powers. So far, so boorish. Yet it soon became clear that Wilkes's gift for writing combined with his striking appearance and self-confidence could be *too* effective, threatening to change the structures of power rather than simply turning the wheel of political fortune so as to favour one set of aristocrats over another. As far as Bute's government was concerned, the forty-fifth issue of *The North Briton* (23 April 1763) went too far, and a warrant was issued for the arrest of 'the Authors, Printers & Publishers of a Seditious, & Treasonable Paper, intitled, The North Briton, Number 45'.[10] Wilkes fought back, challenging the legality of such 'general warrants', which did not name the party or parties to be detained. As Harry Dickinson notes, 'Wilkes showed great skill in bringing fundamental issues before a mass audience and in opening up political debate to the people at large.'[11] His skill as a self-promoter enabled him to present his trial as a test case for the impugned rights of all freeborn Englishmen.

Despite his unprecedented success in this endeavour, discretion led him to seek temporary exile in France in 1764. Declared an outlaw in his absence and feted by the *philosophe* salons of Paris, Wilkes would return in 1768 and

---

[7] Here the seminal study remains Namier, *Structure of Politics*.
[8] The authoritative biography of Wilkes is Thomas, *John Wilkes*. For a more thematic approach, see Sainsbury, *John Wilkes*.
[9] See Lord, *Hell-Fire Clubs*, chs 5 and 6.
[10] Nobbe, *North Briton*, 214.
[11] Dickinson, *Liberty and Property*, 210.

win election as one of the MPs for Middlesex before turning himself in to the authorities. Imprisonment in the Tower of London and King's Bench as well as repeated attempts by the House of Commons to declare his election invalid only burnished his martyr's crown. This made him the focus of a nationwide petitioning campaign in defence of civil liberties, as well as the hero of 'Wilkes and Liberty' mobs that rampaged through London. Free speech, privacy and now freedom of election seemed to be at threat as much from parliament as from 'ministerial despots'.

Wilkes would eventually take his seat in parliament and even become Lord Mayor of London in 1775. Although his radical days were behind him, in 1771 and 1776 he would defend the right of printers to publish parliamentary debates and give the first speech in favour of franchise extension delivered in the eighteenth-century House of Commons.[12] Such interventions led historians such as Herbert Butterfield to see in Wilkite agitation an 'apprehension of the great forces that were beginning to be manifest in the world', one which ought to 'give pause to those who study "the structure of politics"' (a dig at Lewis Namier's rival school of historical thought).[13] While the Marxist historian Edward Thompson refused to take Wilkite mobs as evidence of the awakening of a self-conscious working class, historians such as John Brewer have been more confident in associating Wilkes with a rising 'middling rank' that sought to reshape politics and the image of the nation itself.[14]

Since the 'cultural turn' of the 1990s this association of Wilkes with a 'middling rank' has been linked to earlier claims by John Brewer and others that Wilkes served as catalyst for a commodification of politics, with Wilkite imagery and political theatre supposedly drawing new audiences to participate in political debates.[15] The fact that production of engraved political satires peaked in 1762–3 and again in 1768–9 (both periods of Wilkite activity) could be cited in support of this.[16] More recently some of these optimistic accounts have in turn been challenged by print scholars.[17] As these revolutions in the interpretation of Wilkes and the Wilkite movement over more than fifty years indicate, this debate is one which is likely to continue.

The stakes are high. Wilkes seems to straddle a threshold separating an oligarchic *ancien régime* organized around birth, caste and clientage and a more

---

[12] Royle and Walvin, *English Radicals*, 26; Rea, *English Press*, 204–10; Christie, *Wilkes, Wyvill and Reform*, 63–7.
[13] Butterfield, *George III and the Historians*, 292–3.
[14] Thompson, *English Working Class*, 70. Compare Dickinson, 'Radicals and Reformers', 13; Brewer, 'Wilkites and the Law', 138.
[15] Brewer, *Popular Politics*, 174; Brewer, 'Commercialisation and Politics'.
[16] Donald, *Age of Caricature*, 212, n. 45.
[17] Nicholson, 'Consumers and Spectators'.

democratic modernity of aspiration, participation, mobility and exchange. Visual sources have much to contribute to our exploration of these themes.

'Damn you, I'll mark you!'

One evening in March 1768 the Austrian ambassador to the Court of St James (that is, to Britain) was returning home when his carriage encountered a Wilkite roadblock. Wilkes's supporters were celebrating Wilkes's election as MP for the county of Middlesex. After being forced to stop, the carriage's passengers were accosted and instructed to shout 'Wilkes and Liberty!' Their coachmen, who sat in front outside driving the horses, and footmen, who clung to the back, were given blue 'favours' or ribbons, and instructed to display them prominently – blue was Wilkes's colour. Given that carriages were expensive and relatively rare, this intervention was targeting the nobility, perhaps out of a concern that they did not share the widespread joy. Houses in Westminster's fashionable squares were similarly instructed to place candles in all their windows. Those who disobeyed had their windows smashed.

His Excellency the Ambassador probably did not speak English. Nor did he need to. French was the language of the European nobility and the diplomatic corps. Whether he failed to comprehend what was being demanded of him or simply refused to comply will never be known. His behaviour was certainly perceived as a refusal. Arms reached through his carriage doors and lifted him out, holding him upside down long enough to chalk '45' on the soles of his shoes. He was then posted back into his carriage and allowed to continue on his way.[18] The event was a remarkable breach of the protections His Majesty King George III solemnly undertook to extend to his fellow rulers' representatives governed by *le droit de gens* – a branch of law with its own established principles and authorities.[19] A diplomat was the embodiment of his king or emperor: an insult offered to him was an insult to his royal master, a diplomatic incident.

'45' stood for 'Number 45', a reference to the *North Briton* issue which led to Wilkes's original prosecution. It also referred to 'the forty-five', that is the 1745 Jacobite Rising – a play on 'the Scottish minister' (the despised Bute) and his supposed plot to bring back the Roman Catholic Stuarts. The cipher was chalked up everywhere in March 1768: on doors, shutters, gateposts and walls. A magistrate attempting to disperse crowds was accosted in a fashion similar to the ambassador. 'Damn you, I'll mark you,' the unidentified Wilkite is reported as saying, 'and accordingly he did mark [the magistrate] with large

---

[18] Brewer, *Party Ideology*, 186; Gilmour, *Riots, Risings and Revolution*, 335.
[19] Vattel, *Droit de gens*.

figures no. 45 on the cape of his Coat'.[20] Wilkite crowds paraded behind a boot suspended on a tall pole (boot = Bute), often exhibited together with a petticoat (to refer to Bute's supposed lover, Augusta). Once a crowd of sufficient size and ardour had formed, these objects would be ceremonially burned.[21]

Even in the aristocratic suburb of Twickenham the collector and connoisseur Horace Walpole feared for his beloved villa, Strawberry Hill. He inscribed 'talismans of number 45' on his gateposts, as a protection against mob attack. As he recognized, there was something almost magical about this cipher: to use semiotic terms, the sign's power seemed disproportionate to its signifier.[22] Nor was it a cipher limited to the lowly mob. The mob could hardly afford to buy '45'-themed jewellery, such as the '45' badge made of gold preserved in the British Museum (Figure 17). At first glance the marking of the ambassador appears ridiculous – the marking of the magistrate's cloak is at least visible to others, in a way that the ambassador's soles were not.

It is the act of marking, it appears, rather than the mark itself, which is important: a form of street theatre comparable to those discussed by Thompson in his book *Customs in Common*. The parading of petticoats might be linked to the skimmington rides used to mock henpecked or cuckolded husbands. Or perhaps the marking of the unmarked is a case of mob action 'making right',

Figure 17 Badge in the form of number '45', c. 1763, gold, length 2.5 cm (1 in.). British Museum, London, 2003,0331.3 (artwork in the public domain; photograph © The Trustees of the British Museum).

---

[20] Cited in Brewer, *Party Ideology*, 189.
[21] Donald, *Age of Caricature*, 55.
[22] Walpole to Montagu, 26 March 1769, in Walpole, *Correspondence*, vol. 10, 274.

similar to the enforced sales of grain at 'fair' prices.[23] Consideration of these most ephemeral and gnomic of signs suggests a note of caution before we assume that any 'commodification of politics' was top-down – a case of elites training their inferiors to read a new set of symbols. It suggests that the use of boots and petticoats in satirical prints attacking Bute and the Princess of Wales was more than mere visual shorthand on the part of those prints' creators.

The '45' seems to be bubbling up from below, along with the shouts to 'show your lights' (to illuminate windows). As windows were otherwise only lit up in this way after great military victories or on the king's birthday, this too would have been an unsettling sight to many: the inference is that the 'mob' are declaring loyalty to 'King Wilkes' – a treasonous thought which Wilkes certainly never expressed himself.[24] Although these visual signs are so evanescent, so ephemeral as to have left no visual traces beyond the written record, they clearly influenced how all other Wilkite imagery was produced and consumed in the period. Diana Donald is surely correct when she argues that such 'Wilkite hieroglyphics' which 'can easily appear to be a form of cultural recidivism', should in fact be considered as 'the products of an authentic popular culture which has to be understood by its own lights'.[25]

From portrait ...

In 1768 Robert Edge Pine produced the earliest surviving portrait in oil of Wilkes, now in the collection of the Palace of Westminster (Plate 7). As with all works of art, it is important to ask how such an item was produced, at what cost in time and money, and who paid. The higher the cost in time and money, the more likely a work was produced on commission: that is, that the artist knew in advance that they would be reimbursed for their time, materials and skill. Then as now, portraits in oil were time-consuming to produce. The 'sitter books' of established artists such as Joshua Reynolds indicate that three or more sessions of an hour and a half were required.[26] Less renowned artists and humbler sitters probably managed with one sitting, reusing stock poses and costumes and leaving all but the hands and faces to apprentices or other painters who worked in the same studio. John Singleton Copley sometimes painted the heads on a separate canvas, which was subsequently slotted into a canvas depicting the rest of the body and background.

---

[23] Thompson, *Customs in Common*, ch. 3. This chapter was originally published in 1971.
[24] The earliest instance of such illumination noted by the historian of such displays dates from 1716, on the occasion of George I's birthday. Doderer-Winkler, *Magnificent Entertainments*, 119.
[25] Donald, *Age of Caricature*, 50.
[26] For a discussion, see Pointon, *Hanging the Head*, 36–52.

Portraits were almost always commissioned by the sitter or his or her immediate family, often to celebrate an important milestone such as a marriage. Depending on one's budget, one could be depicted at full-length (standing), half-length (seated, from the head down to just below the knees) or three-quarter length (waist up, sometimes without any hands visible). Portraits were painted onto linen cloth stretched over a wooden frame (a stretcher). Like today's A3 and A4, the measurements of these formats were standardized and partly determined by the looms on which the linen was woven.[27] Eighteenth-century portrait painting was a trade, not a means of artistic self-expression. Only a very small elite of clients was interested in acquiring a portrait by a particular member of the profession admired for his individual artistry. Customers wanted a good likeness, not 'a Reynolds' or 'a Robert Edge Pine'.

Such commissions were the bread and butter of British painters. The Protestant Church of England rarely commissioned devotional works such as altarpieces for churches, identifying such 'Popish vanities' with the Roman Catholic Church. In Britain's case that other source of commissions, the monarchy, was also restricted, both by its limited financial resources, compared to those of other European monarchies, and suspicions that royal patronage might foster a menial, un-English culture. When George III established a Royal Academy of Arts in 1768, therefore, some, including Wilkes, interpreted it as another instance of royal overreach, rather than an attempt to make up for lost time – France's Royal Academy of painting and sculpture had been established in 1648.[28]

As members of a trade with pretensions to be a profession, to lead taste rather than merely follow fashion, British painters in the 1760s were in something of a bind. They recognized that portraiture was a private genre built in part on their clients' vanity, and yearned to practice the higher, more virtuous and public-spirited genre of history painting, which focused on depictions of virtuous acts; despite the name, these did not necessarily depict events from the distant past.[29] As the response to the establishment of the Royal Academy of Arts demonstrates, however, they were in disagreement about whether they could trust the monarchy to support them, or should fashion a new, truly 'public' audience for art through their own exhibitions and initiative.[30]

Unusually, Pine's portrait was probably not commissioned by Wilkes himself. Wilkes was rarely out of debt, and would have struggled to pay an artist to produce even a half-length portrait. Although we know little about Pine, we do know that he was heavily involved in early attempts by London-

---

[27] For examples and discussion, see Simon, 'British Portrait Painters'.
[28] Conlin, 'High Art and Low Politics', 365.
[29] Lippincott, 'Expanding on Portraiture'.
[30] Brewer, 'Cultural Production'. See also Barrell, *Political Theory*.

based painters to associate, both in order to establish an academy and to put on exhibitions.[31] Wilkes had played a small part in these activities back in 1759, chairing a meeting of painters eager to use London's Foundling Hospital (Wilkes was one of the institution's governors) as a venue in which to display their art.[32] Pine's history paintings exhibit a Wilkite disdain for royal flattery: a 1763 work depicts the eleventh-century Viking monarch Cnut on a beach facing the sea, sullenly sitting on a throne already partly submerged by the incoming tide. Legend has it that Cnut staged this deliberately to disprove the thesis of his servile entourage, who had previously assured him that the tide would not dare soak such a great king.[33] Pine clearly struggled to make a living as an artist in London, eventually moving to Bath, and then, after the American Revolution, to the United States.[34]

... to print

It is inviting to speculate that Pine's decision to paint Wilkes's portrait may reflect Pine's own political stance. We are on surer ground suggesting a commercial speculation: that the painter painted the portrait with a view to having it engraved by another artist for reproduction, just as Pine did in the case of his 'fancy portraits' of his wife posing as the Greek muse Calliope decorating a bust of the mythical bard Ossian. Although Wilkes's portrait was exhibited at a temporary exhibition of the Society of Artists in London in 1768 and 1771 (both years of Wilkite agitation), by then it had more than served its purpose by acting as the basis for hundreds of mezzotints, engravings and etchings, as well as transfers, which allowed the image to be applied to punch bowls, teacups, snuffboxes and other objects.[35]

The earliest of these works 'after Pine' was probably James Watson's 39 by 28 cm mezzotint published in March 1764 (Figure 18).[36] Unlike many of those that followed, this print is signed, acknowledges that it is based on Pine's portrait and reproduces that painting's design faithfully. Wilkes is shown at half-length, seated in fashionable attire (gold or silver braid around his coat's buttonholes), quill in hand, books and papers on the table

---

[31] Hargraves, *Candidates for Fame*, 114–6.
[32] *Public Advertiser*, 9 November 1759, cited in Whitley, *Artists*, vol. 1, 165. See also Conlin, 'High Art and Low Politics'.
[33] Sunderland, 'Mortimer, Pine'.
[34] Stewart, *Robert Edge Pine*.
[35] For one example, see the enamelled copper snuffbox manufactured in Birmingham c. 1765, British Museum, 1895,0521.21.
[36] In this context, the phrase 'after Pine' means that Watson copied or borrowed from Pine's painting.

Figure 18 James Watson after Robert Edge Pine, *John Wilkes Esqr*, 1764, mezzotint, 39 × 28 cm (15⅜ × 11 in.). British Museum, London, 1950,0520.159 (artwork in the public domain; photograph © The Trustees of the British Museum).

in front of him. His strabismus is there but by no means conspicuous. His prognathous jaw is invisible.

The title on the spine of one book and the roundel at bottom left refer to the seventeenth-century Whig political writer Algernon Sidney, who, like Wilkes, was arrested after an illegal search of his papers. Wilkes looks up to the left, in the direction of a female figure who holds a mirror and stands behind a shield decorated with a sunburst. This is not a reference to Wilkes's voracious sexual appetite but an allegorical figure representing Truth. Like the cap of liberty (also known as a Phrygian cap), such figures formed part of a complex system of signs (an iconography) whose meanings drew on a shared European heritage that ultimately looked back to Greek and Roman antiquity.

The study of iconography forms a sub-discipline of art history in and of itself. Pine's usage is rather loose; Truth's other props, or attributes, are missing. Although the Sidney references are pointed, it seems fair to assume that the allegorical figure is intended simply to suggest that Wilkes's education and character are elevated enough to make allusions to classical civilization appropriate. Not all artists shared Pine's view: when William Hogarth produced his engraving of Wilkes he included a cap of liberty, albeit satirically, drawing it as if it were a chamber pot (Figure 19). Pine's portrayal, however, is clearly intended to present Wilkes as a gentleman of letters; the pose and setting are similar to those found in Pine's portrait of the playwright and actor David Garrick. By directing Wilkes's gaze up to Truth, rather than out to the viewer, Pine creates the impression that we are voyeurs, observing the sitter in

Figure 19 William Hogarth, *John Wilkes Esqr*, 1763, etching with engraving, 35.2 × 23 cm (13⅞ × 9 in.). British Museum, London, Cc,2.206. (artwork in the public domain; photograph © The Trustees of the British Museum).

a private reverie, further supporting the claim that what we see is the true man, not a pose.

As was commonplace on such prints, the name of the mezzotint artist appears bottom right ('Jas. Watson fecit', Latin for 'made this') and the artist 'after' whose work it is based appears bottom left ('R. E. Pine pinxt', abbreviation of 'pinxit', Latin for 'painted this'). Were this a print after a drawing, we might expect to read 'Jas. Watson. sculp.' or 'sculpsit' (Latin for 'carved this') and 'R. E. Pine del.' or 'delineavit' (Latin for 'drew this'). Invented in Germany in the mid-seventeenth century and subsequently perfected in Britain, mezzotint was a printmaking medium admired for its ability to produce subtle shifts in tone ('mezzotinto' is Italian for 'halftone') and velvety blacks in an almost painterly manner. In copperplate, for example, the engraver has to incise an ever-tighter grid or web of hatched lines into the copper plate with the burin, a small chisel, in order to achieve darker shades. A consistent grey or dark background, therefore, was impossible to achieve. In mezzotint the artist usually began with an artificially roughened plate, which would produce an evenly dark print if left unworked. Instead of making marks with the burin which would fill with black ink and leave a dark line when printed, Watson and most other mezzotinters worked 'from dark to white', that is, burnishing the abrasions from the plate only where lighter tones were required.[37]

Prices are sometimes given on eighteenth-century British prints, following the pre-decimal system of pounds, shillings and pence: twelve pence (the abbreviation for pence was 'd.') in a shilling (s.), twenty shillings in a pound (L). Watson's print does not give a price, but a contemporary newspaper advertisement gives it as five shillings (£33 in 2015 prices), which was at the higher end of the range for engravings. This reflected Watson's high reputation as the leading mezzotint engraver of his age. The same announcement also notes that the print 'done by Mr Watson from an original portrait painted by Mr Pine' had already been pirated, and warned anyone selling pirated copies that they would be prosecuted for copyright infringement.[38] Several pirated mezzotints by three different artists exist in the British Museum's collection, suggesting that this warning was little heeded – and that demand for this image was high.[39]

Among the many other prints that borrowed from Pine's portrait (or, more likely, from Watson's print after Pine's painting) is an etching with engraving (c. 1768) by a German, Johann Oswald Berndt, in which Pine's figure of Wilkes is relocated to King's Bench Prison, where Wilkes was incarcerated in

---

[37] For an illustrated discussion of this and other printmaking techniques, see Griffiths, *Prints and Printmaking*.
[38] *Public Advertiser*, 31 March 1764.
[39] A mezzotint published after Pine's portrait by Robert Sayer in 1768 includes more up-to-date props. British Museum, 1902,1011.7366.

1768.⁴⁰ As Berndt's print demonstrates, the market for prints in this period was international: unlike paintings, prints were easily sent through the post. Berndt could have produced this engraving for the English market. But the fact that the inscription identifying Wilkes as 'erwählter Ritter der Grafschaft Middlesex in Kinges Bench Prison' ('elected Knight of the Shire for Middlesex in King's Bench Prison') is in German clearly indicates a German-speaking audience. Here again, study of prints leads us to consider entirely new questions, such as Wilkes's broader European fame. While we know something of Wilkes's reception during his French exile, prints such as Berndt's suggest a broader public who had read about Wilkes in newspapers and were willing to pay good money to find out what he looked like. Indeed, several other German publishers produced portrait prints of Wilkes. What did Wilkes mean to the people who admired such depictions? How did it colour their view of Britain, and of themselves?

In addressing sources like Watson's mezzotint, therefore, we are quickly pulled in a number of directions: back, as it were, to the portrait painting, to the artist and the sitter who may or may not have commissioned him, but also forwards, to other printmakers who adapted Watson and Pine's work, as well as the publishers and printsellers who may have commissioned *them* to engrave and burnish plates from which those publishers clearly expected to make a healthy profit. Although print scholars and curators have discussed such questions for some time, historians have tended not to listen. As well as suggesting new questions which we as historians had probably not thought of before, such a study of this one print's context allows us to begin to situate it within a system of genres and media as well as markets. Rather than simply seeing a cross-eyed man in funny clothes clutching a feather while ogling a naked woman, we can begin to see in the print clues about its purpose, register and audience. Watson's print is not satirical; it adopted a high register and aimed at a well-to-do, educated audience, one which was not restricted to London or even the British Isles.

'Only try it'

Thanks to his strabismus, Wilkes was easily recognizable. Indeed, as Shearer West has noted, the way in which the strabismus was employed as a visual shorthand for Wilkes by Wilkites as well as by hostile caricaturists like Hogarth allowed prints of Wilkes to combine an 'emblematical' approach, in which the aforementioned '45', boots and petticoats all played their part, with a newer

---

⁴⁰ Johann Oswald Berndt after Robert Edge Pine, *John Wilkes*, etching with engraving, 1760–87, British Museum, 1864,0813.365.

Figure 20 William Sharp, trade card for Cotterell, tobacconist, c. 1764, etching with engraving, 7.3 × 6.3 cm (2⅞ × 2½ in.). British Museum, London, 1853,1210.439 (artwork in the public domain; photograph © The Trustees of the British Museum).

'caricatural' approach.[41] His notoriety made him a brand which a London tobacco merchant named Cotterell, of Crown Street, Soho, appropriated to promote his own business. The sharp outlines and fine detail of Cotterell's palm-sized trade card, printed by William Sharp, indicate a copper engraving (Figure 20). The curlicues of the cartouche framing the text and Wilkes have a Frenchified rococo elegance. Even without the fashionable London address it would be evident that Cotterell is addressing a fashionable clientele. The fact that Wilkes's face could be used to sell Virginia tobacco and 'fine snuff' (powdered tobacco – a pinch was placed on the back of a thumb and snorted) suggests at the very least that Wilkes, for all his associations with rabble-rousing demagoguery and licentiousness, was not anathema to the polite world of Soho, in the way that, say, Lord Lovat, who was also charged with treasonous activities, incarcerated in the Tower of London, and executed in 1747, would have been.

---

[41] West, 'Wilkes's Squint'.

Such trade cards served a function similar to today's business cards, as well as being attached to deliveries and product samples sent to clients. They straddle those 'distinctly blurred dividing lines between visual and material culture' noted by the editors of this volume. This card has tears at four corners, suggesting that it was initially glued onto a box or parcel, then removed, perhaps by a Victorian collector (the card entered the British Museum in 1853). The portrait is based on Pine's portrait. Like today's scholars scouring the internet rather than visiting the British Museum, Sharp (who specialized in trade cards) almost certainly did not view the painting. A long chain of reproductions separates the card from the 'original', therefore, to the extent that it seems unhelpful even to speak of this portrait being 'after Pine'. Cotterell himself may have never heard of Pine. He may not have been a strong Wilkite. The motto 'Only try it' is rather direct for a trade card, which normally appealed to would-be clients in politer terms. Perhaps Wilkes was chosen not only for his celebrity, as opposed to his 'fame', in the sense of exemplary virtue, but because his forceful character went well with Cotterell's forthright instruction to 'Just do it', as the sportswear company Nike would put it, in 1988.

As an instance of John Brewer's 'commodification of politics', therefore, this print is almost *too* commodified. Rather than indicative of a groundswell of middling or more popular participation in debates over vice and virtue, royal and parliamentary prerogative and the rights of the subject, this image of Wilkes points to little more than a shallow celebrity.[42] The phrase 'Wilkes and Liberty' seems hollowed out or diluted when placed on an advertisement below the aggressive phrase 'Only try it.' Wilkes's head, the '45' cipher and motto here serve simply to differentiate Cotterell's shop from the other tobacconists in the neighbourhood of Soho Square.

We know from other trade cards that the devices depicted usually matched those portrayed on the shop signs which were suspended from the establishment's façade, many drawn from heraldry and myth: blue boars, angels, green men, red lions, white horses, black kings and so on. This bestiary is familiar today only from village pubs but ran rampant in the streets of Georgian London, providing location markers to help navigation before the advent of proper street signage and house numbering. Letters, for example, might be addressed to someone 'at the angel', or 'by the half-moon', or even 'beyond the world's end', followed by the name of a street or square. Cotterell may well have sold his snuff 'at the sign of Wilkes'.

This was fame of a sort: this accolade was usually reserved to crowned heads ('The King of Prussia' was a popular sign), military heroes (such as Admiral Edward Vernon, who captured Porto Bello in what is now Panama in 1739) or a handful of familiar fictional characters (such as Roger de Coverley, one of

---

[42] For celebrity, see Postle, *Joshua Reynolds*.

the regular coffee-shop visitors whose discussions formed the focus of Joseph Addison's weekly periodical *The Spectator*, published 1711–4). As an artistic genre, however, shop signs like trade cards were so low as to be almost off the scale entirely. Had Cotterell's trade card been offered to the British Museum in 1753 (the year the Museum was founded), therefore, it would have been refused. A century later, trade cards had become collectable artefacts. Amateur collectors, not professional historians, made such cards collectable: as the introduction notes, 'the past is not solely the domain of historians'.

Back in the eighteenth century, an aesthetically 'low' genre could sometimes attract sustained if ironic attention from those willing to challenge convention. In 1762 a 'Society of Sign Painters' (in reality, a group of wits led by the hack writer Bonnell Thornton) exhibited a collection of London shop signs as if they were high art, complete with entry charges and a printed catalogue.[43] Such ironic yanking of mundane advertising images from a consumer context into that of high art had never been seen before, and would not be seen again until the pop art movement, which occurred 200 years later. Eighteenth-century British visual culture was far from backward. On the contrary it was sophisticated, self-aware and playful.

A Conversation

Like Robert Edge Pine, the German-born painter Johan Zoffany travelled long distances in search of work. In May 1779 he returned from an extended visit to India, where he had painted local notables and staff of the East India Company. When Horace Walpole visited Zoffany's studio in November, *Mary Wilkes; John Wilkes* (Plate 8) was well under way.[44] Walpole joked that the prominent willow tree looked more like a palm or other tropical tree than anything found growing in Britain, which could have been a jibe at Zoffany for failing to re-acclimatize or a roundabout way of implying that depicting Wilkes as a doting father 'squinting tenderly at his daughter' was equally out of place.[45] Yet the presence of Zoffany's dog Roma at Wilkes's feet suggests an easy relationship between painter and sitters. The painting was exhibited at the Royal Academy's annual exhibition in London's Somerset House in 1782.

As the introduction to this volume notes, such 'institutional settings' as the annual Royal Academy show are 'particularly rich' contexts in which to explore the visual. It was conventional for portraits to be exhibited at the academy without the sitters' names, and so *Mary Wilkes; John Wilkes* was given the

---

[43] Conlin, 'Signpainters' Exhibition'.
[44] Webster, *Johan Zoffany*, 618–9.
[45] Cited in Sainsbury, *John Wilkes*, 27.

title *A Conversation* in the catalogue of the 1782 exhibition.[46] Visitors to the exhibition enjoyed themselves attempting to recognize the sitters, a game at which only those from the social elite or *beau monde* (French: 'beautiful world') could truly excel.[47] There would have been few prizes, however, for recognizing Wilkes. His strabismus is gently flattered by having him glance sharply up and to his right, one of the few positions in which both eyes would (almost) align. Yet this is not a comfortable or elegant posture.

By casting the left side of Wilkes's face into half shadow, Zoffany emphasizes the outline of his prognathous jaw. Hogarth's print had exploited this to suggest a leering devilry; Wilkes's witty response was to express wonder at an artist bothering to 'caricature what Nature had already caricatured'.[48] Although forthright, Zoffany's handling is not insensitive: he recognizes that facial deformities such as Wilkes's short-circuit the conventional relationship between human passions and facial expressions, making a loving smile into a lopsided leer, for example. Hence he gives Wilkes a neutral expression. Wilkes's lower position, inclined posture (leg crossed towards Mary) and hand do the work of showing Wilkes's abiding love and respect for his daughter, shown in his decision to make her his Lady Mayoress during his London mayoralty (1775).

Highlighted against the dark blue of Wilkes's coat sleeve, the pair's clasped hands are placed at the centre of the painting. The decision to show Mary with her left glove held in her gloved right hand only draws more attention to the closeness of their relationship: whether at his request or by some unspoken accord she has bared the hand her father holds. The gesture felicitously draws attention to her fashionable dress and to her responsiveness to her own virtuous passions – 'sensibility' in eighteenth-century parlance. While her father is oblivious to anyone but her, she looks out at us, unfazed. She has not been 'caught out'. She is not about to blush, tug her left hand away and pull her glove back on. The dress, setting and arrangement of figures and gazes in Zoffany's painting are a carefully staged performance of 'natural' sentiments as well as wealth. Mary's private and her public selves are in harmony: she is fashionable but not fake. She is not ashamed of her father or their relationship.

Considering Wilkes's reputation for womanizing, considering the fact that, at the time the painting was produced, his estranged wife (Mary's mother) was still alive, *A Conversation* is a triumph of its genre, the so-called conversation piece, which emerged in British painting in the 1720s. Borrowing from decidedly uncouth and low-status depictions of Dutch peasants carousing in rustic taverns, painters such as Hogarth created a new type of group portrait in

---

[46] Postle, *Johan Zoffany*, 257.
[47] For exhibitions, see Solkin, *Art on the Line*. For the *beau monde*, see Greig, *Beau Monde*.
[48] As Rauser has shown, this caricature backfired. See Rauser, 'Embodied Liberty'.

which middling and elite families were depicted enjoying their own company in naturalistic settings, furnished with accoutrements whose design was elegant rather than extravagant.

Upon his arrival in London in the 1760s Zoffany had brought new 'spirit' and 'invention' to the genre; its former stiffness was exemplified by its main practitioner in the 1740s, Arthur Devis.[49] In the 1760s Zoffany's patrons included the royal family and the third Earl of Bute. It is a sign of just how respectable Wilkes had become in later years that he and his daughter joined this select group of patrons two decades later. More importantly, it shows that men from very different social backgrounds (middling and royal) shared a set of conventions governing not only the technical aspects of portrait painting but also fashion, deportment, manners and the virtue of displaying certain passions deemed to be 'natural'. As Kate Retford notes, paintings such as *Mary Wilkes; John Wilkes* demonstrate that 'the private was not in tension with the public ... the paternal relationship could be exploited to make public statements'.[50]

Conclusion

This case study of John Wilkes and eighteenth-century British visual culture has far from exhausted its subject, particularly when it comes to print culture. Easy to transport and reproduce, frequently adapted and pirated, heavily marketed through newspapers and printshops and available at a price to suit every pocket (some, such as our trade card, were given away free), prints were everywhere in late-eighteenth-century Britain. Prints even appear in other prints. Printed satires show portrait engravings of Wilkes roughly stuck up in outhouses and carefully framed behind glass on tubby aldermen's dining room walls.[51] Publishers and artists thrived on the fad for Grangerization, that is, for extra-illustrating: inserting prints of famous men and women into historical texts.[52] Prints were also cut up and glued onto walls or folding screens then used as room dividers. Aristocrats and royals even had dedicated print rooms in which to show off their collections.[53] Although Grangerization fell from favour in the 1820s, specialized print dealers continued to serve the needs of print collectors. This market was lively enough to experience periods of irrational exuberance, or bubbles, such as that which saw mezzotint

---

[49] Retford, *Conversation Piece*, 16–7.
[50] Retford, *Art of Domestic Life*, 147.
[51] For display in an outhouse, see Anon., *The Congress or the Necessary Politicians*, etching, 1775, British Museum, J, 1.79. For a more respectful display of a Wilkes portrait print, see P. L. Dumesnil le jeune, *Sr. Epicure Guzzle Enjoying His Bottle after Dinner*, mezzotint, 1773, British Museum, 2010,7081.361.
[52] Peltz, *Facing the Text*, 1–47; Pointon, *Hanging the Head*, 55–78.
[53] Heard, 'Print Room'.

engravings after Reynolds and Gainsborough portraits reach high prices in the early 1900s.[54]

This print-centred hive of production and consumption provides further information on how contemporaries viewed Wilkes. A toilet wall is clearly not a place of respect. It also invites further questions, such as the historical legacy of Wilkes in the nineteenth century and beyond. Although the MP Francis Burdett toyed with Wilkite allusions after his critique of the Peterloo Massacre led to his arrest for seditious libel in 1820, it is striking how little use nineteenth-century middle-class or working-class reformers made of Wilkite iconography. Why was this?[55] What might it suggest about aforementioned claims (dating back to Butterfield) that Wilkite activity laid the foundation for the 1832 Reform Act and other reform legislation?

In the thirty years since Porter's plea for 'schools of "visual history"' historians, print curators and art historians have tackled many of the 'visual signs' he referred to, including signs themselves. We have become more sensitive to 'juxtaposing what people said against what they read' and begun to explore how apparently new or modern phenomena such as Wilksism employed 'the wider sign-systems of former times'. A strong tendency to view visual sources as illustrating arguments provoked by textual sources and to analyse those visual sources using tools of textual analysis persists, however.

It would be foolish to claim that the images discussed here merely duplicated discourses that might just as easily, if not more easily, be recovered using textual sources. On the contrary, our discussion of the chalk '45' leads us to hesitate before concluding that Wilkite political culture was simply a case of the commodification of elite political discourse: instead we seem to be seeing an elite political discourse trickling down to a middling rank even as a vulgar performative tradition of visual signs bubbles up from below. The use of Wilkes as a branding device by shopkeepers who may or may not have held Wilkite sympathies suggests the emergence of a recognizably modern consumer culture, one in which moralistic terms such as 'fame' (good) and 'notoriety' (bad) are superseded by a more neutral 'celebrity'. Wilkes's decision to have himself depicted by Zoffany as doting father, at full-length for a double portrait subsequently displayed in the Royal Academy, suggests a deliberate attempt to manipulate a private and sentimental relationship for the purposes of repairing a public image sullied by vice and vulgar politicking, similar to Georgiana Duchess of Devonshire's decision to have herself painted by Joshua Reynolds as loving mother, dandling a daughter on her knee, shortly after her scandalous support of Charles James Fox's 1784 Middlesex election campaign.

---

[54] O'Connell, 'Taste for Mezzotints'.
[55] Perhaps the priapic scurrility of Wilksism offended against that early nineteenth-century 'age of cant' (associated with the rise of Evangelicalism) which Gatrell sees as succeeding a late Georgian 'age of cunt'. Gatrell, *City of Laughter*, 452.

Polly's stance and dress further demonstrate how such sophisticated images embraced fashionable display and the performance of sincere sensibility at one and the same time.

Whenever we address such images it is vital to pay attention to the ways in which changing technologies of production, reproduction and consumption determined those images' social and geographical reach. The rewards of addressing visual sources, in terms of an enriched understanding of Wilkes, popular politics and eighteenth-century British society and culture generally, more than make up for the time spent learning to appreciate those same sources as something more substantial than unmediated images of equal significance.

5

Writing the history of the photographic book: Architecture in Weimar Germany

J. J. Long

As long ago as 1988, Hayden White argued that 'we are inclined to use pictures primarily as "illustrations" of the predications made in our verbally written discourse'.[1] Here is Peter Burke making the same point over a decade later: 'When they do use images, historians tend to treat them as mere illustrations, reproducing them in their books without comment. In cases in which the images are discussed in the text, this evidence is often used to illustrate conclusions that the author has already reached by other means, rather than to give new answers or to ask new questions.'[2] And in a very recent essay, Elizabeth Edwards writes, '[Photographs] are left with little to do but illustrate conclusions reached by other means.'[3] As these three quotations suggest (and the same points recur in very similar forms elsewhere, too), over the last thirty years it has become almost a reflex for commentators on historians' use of photographs and other images to note the ongoing primacy of the verbal in historical practice – at the level of both preferred sources and historians' chosen modes of representation, argument and dissemination. This chapter attempts to address the above objections to conventional historical practice by writing visual history in two ways: it writes the history of the visual and it writes history on the basis of the visual. In other words, it suggests a history of visual forms in the Weimar Republic, while also demonstrating the centrality of the visual to broader debates in interwar German society. The visual is thus both an object of study and a source. The chapter takes as its central focus the photographic book, and in particular architectural photobooks from 1920s Germany. In so doing, it expands the notion of the visual beyond the image to encompass typography, layout and graphic design, and even paper quality. From the perspective of the photobook, writing visual history requires an interdisciplinary mode of engagement that is attentive to all of the photobook's constitutive elements, while accounting for the emergence and significance of the photobook in its own time. What follows attempts to address these entwined questions.

---

[1] White, 'Historiography and Historiophoty', 1194.
[2] Burke, *Eyewitnessing*, 10.
[3] Edwards, 'Photography and the Business of Doing History'.

The Weimar Republic and the architectural photographic book

The Weimar Republic in Germany spanned the fourteen years between the end of the First World War in late 1918 and the naming of Adolf Hitler (1889–1945) as chancellor of Germany in January 1933. It is generally seen as a period of profound paradox, in that the extraordinary level of cultural innovation and vibrancy that we associate with the short life of the republic took place against a backdrop of periodic economic crisis and persistent political turmoil.[4] Weimar Germany has often been interpreted teleologically, that is, as a period best understood in light of its own end in the establishment of the Nazi dictatorship. Recent historiography on Weimar, however, has dwelt less on crisis than on the opportunities for change that went hand in hand with the political instability of its early years in particular. The realms of possibility opened up by the establishment of a democratic state on German soil were considerable, and included the introduction of universal suffrage, enhanced rights for women and workers, the abolition of censorship and concomitant rights to free speech.[5]

While the guarantee of freedom of speech was not always upheld by the Weimar Republic's largely conservative judiciary, it nevertheless created the conditions for a flourishing of public culture. A further contributory factor in this regard was printing technology: the halftone process, a means of reproducing photographs quickly and cheaply within the same printing block as the surrounding text, had been invented as early as 1880, and had been widely deployed in news periodicals since around 1900. In 1920s Germany, halftones facilitated not just the massive expansion of the illustrated periodical press, but the emergence of the photographic book as an article of both elite and mass consumption. The range of subjects presented in photographic books was vast, encompassing natural history, ethnography, topography, industry, transport, portraiture, current affairs, international relations, the First World War, sport and physical culture, technology, fashion, celebrities, graphic and product design, dance, art, sculpture and architecture.[6]

The diversity of subjects and audiences addressed by the Weimar photobook means that a purely art-historical approach is inadequate. A well-known history by Martin Parr and Gerry Badger, for example, defines the photobook as the work of a single auteur, and stresses a rather vague notion of 'artistic quality' as an essential characteristic belonging to a putative canon of photobook

---

[4] Detlev Peukert's book *The Weimar Republic: The Crisis of Classical Modernity* is the key reference point here. Daniel Magilow invokes the trope of crisis in his pioneering study of Weimar Republic photographic books, *The Photography of Crisis*.
[5] Many of these themes are taken up in Canning, Barndt and McGuire, *Weimar Publics, Weimar Subjects*. For a general history of Europe that stresses that the period between 1919 to 1933 needs to be understood in terms of the war just gone rather than the war to come, see Steiner, *Lights That Failed*.
[6] This list is not exhaustive. For a sense of the sheer scale and diversity of photobook publishing in the Weimar Republic, see Heiting and Jaeger, *Autopsie*.

masterpieces.[7] At the same time, their account disregards function, conditions of production or reception, and conceptual or formal design, telling us very little about the significance of the photobook as a cultural phenomenon.

Architectural photobooks are a particularly fruitful field of study if we are to explore precisely this significance, for several reasons. They are, first of all, complex visual objects, even by the already complex standards of the photobook in general. Architectural photography is a form of 'representation to the second degree', as Claire Zimmerman puts it: she argues that modern architecture aimed to 'provide adequate sites for the images of a society to appear in and through its buildings'.[8] So if buildings are in some sense representations of an imagined social order, photographs are the depiction in two-dimensional form of a three-dimensional representation. Photography is then integrated with other visual aspects of the book, which challenges us to think about what, precisely, we are writing the history of: architecture? the book? photography? typography? Writing the visual history of the photobook means doing justice to all these aspects. But it also means understanding the specific role played by the photobook in the Weimar Republic. Weimar Germany was home to many of the architects whose theoretical work and realized projects were central to the development of architectural modernism: Ludwig Mies van der Rohe (1886–1969), Walter Gropius (1883–1969), Erich Mendelsohn (1887–1953), Bruno Taut (1880–1938), and Adolf Meyer (1881–1929), among others. The kind of architecture they practised developed in dialogue with photography; indeed, it can be seen as 'photographic architecture', as 'technological changes to the building industry joined with alterations to the visual language of contemporary society to produce a new set of expectations for buildings'.[9] Photography was also a salient means of disseminating and popularizing new architectural ideas, which was particularly significant in Germany, where a politically charged debate raged about the architectural style appropriate to the German nation. As Barbara Miller Lane has shown in her classic study of interwar German architecture, architectural modernism was a product of war and revolution, embodying a rejection of the past and a vision of a new society. Conservative critics and architects bemoaned the internationalism of this approach: in their eyes, it was a rootless architectural style, born of anonymous urban modernity, divorced from tradition, potentially bolshevist in its homogenizing tendencies and alien to the German spirit.[10]

The debate between modernists and traditionalists played itself out in visual form. It was not only that polemical books and articles included photographic illustrations but that the argument was conducted at various levels of visual

[7] Parr and Badger, *Photobook*, 8.
[8] Zimmerman, *Photographic Architecture*, 8.
[9] Ibid., 26.
[10] Lane, *Architecture and Politics*.

signification. Far from being an optional adjunct to verbal argumentation, then, the visual dimensions of Weimar photographic books were central to their meaning and power. In order to understand how the visual worked in this way, it is useful to understand it as a kind of discourse.

The visual discourse of architectural photobooks

In an essay that I quote at the start of this chapter, Hayden White argues that 'imagistic evidence' is 'a discourse in its own right and capable of telling us things about its referents that are ... different from what can be told in verbal discourse'.[11] The notion of discourse in the humanities and social sciences is most closely associated with the work of Michel Foucault (1926–84). His book *The Archaeology of Knowledge* investigates the circumstances under which specific utterances come to be taken seriously or taken to be true at a given period. Foucault is concerned with the ways in which knowledge about the world is produced, and how that knowledge shapes action. White, who is incidentally a distinguished scholar of Foucault, seems to be working within a Foucauldian framework, in that he implies that 'imagistic evidence' is a question of what images might tell us about their referent collectively. This collective cannot be the totality of images, however; a degree of differentiation is required, and it is here that we can borrow from Foucault in order to specify the kinds of regularities that constitute images as discourse. Foucault's account of discourse in *The Archaeology of Knowledge* is relational. Discursive formations are defined not by a common object, a unified form or style, shared concepts or a common theme but rather by the relationships between these four things: 'Whenever, between objects, types of statement, concepts, or thematic choices, one can define a regularity (an order, correlations, positions and functionings, transformations), we will say ... that we are dealing with a discursive formation.'[12] In defining 'imagistic discourse', the regularity of the relationship between 'object' and 'type of statement' is central. Taking the notion of the object first of all, images refer to objects in very different ways from the written language that is Foucault's concern, because they refer at least in part by means of likeness. It thus becomes possible to group images according to the thing they depict. Architectural photography, for example, does not include studio portraiture, food photography or Alpine landscapes. All this gives us, of course, is a content-based image corpus rather than a discourse. So we need to add 'type of statement' as a co-constitutive factor in the formation of imagistic discourse. For our purposes, the type of statement is a question of medium first

---

[11] White, 'Historiography and Historiophoty', 1193.
[12] Foucault, *Archaeology*, 41.

of all: Photography is a result of chemical transformations brought about by the action of light that has been focused by a lens onto a substrate coated with photosensitive salts. Optically, photographs are organized according to the laws of single-point monocular perspective. Combined with the chemical aspect of the photographic process, this produces images that possess a particularly powerful reality effect. But the 'type of statement' is also a question of form. There are specific regularities of form, including viewpoint, lighting, cropping, framing, distance and depth of field, that constitute the discourse of 'architectural photography'. Not all photographs of buildings qualify for inclusion. At the same time, 'imagistic discourse' is not monolithic. While we might establish regularities in the relationship between object and form that determine the discourse of architectural photography, individual manifestations will inflect this discourse in various ways. The concept of discourse thus establishes rules within which individual contributions to that discourse become intelligible as such, and transformations of knowledge can take place.

The challenge posed by the photographic book is that its visual dimensions are multifaceted: at the level of the image, photography of buildings is often complemented by photographs of models, ground plans and elevations, construction diagrams, detail sketches, and axonometric and other projections of buildings and settlements. Furthermore, while typography and layout determine the visual appearance of any book, many photobooks deployed variations on the so-called New Typography, and text-image relations are central to their functioning.[13] While such things as layout and typography would not normally be considered as 'discursive' in a Foucauldian sense, a comprehensive visual analysis of photobooks allows regularities to emerge and the knowledge-producing functions of supposedly ancillary aspects of book design to become visible.

In the remainder of this chapter I describe and account for the visual discourse operative in two photographic books, before concluding with some thoughts about the role of the visual in history, with 'history' being understood in the dual sense of past events or phenomena and representations of the past.

Architectural photobooks

The Weimar Republic was awash with architectural photobooks, which became, in Roland Jaeger's words, a means not just of reporting on but of mediating and interpreting modern architecture for the public.[14] For reasons

---

[13] Jaeger, 'Vom Neuen zum nationalsozialistischen Bauen', 378.
[14] Ibid. Jaeger's article, together with its companion pieces, gives a good overview of the scale of photobook production relating to modern architecture in particular. See also Stamm, 'Moderne, vornehme Massenartikel'.

of space, I concentrate here on just two publications. The first is *Bauten der Arbeit und des Verkehrs aus deutscher Gegenwart* (Contemporary German Industrial and Transport Architecture, 1925). Edited by the art historian Walter Müller-Wulckow (1886–1964), it was the first of a three-volume set devoted to modern architecture in the highly successful photobook series *Die Blauen Bücher* (The Blue Books).[15] The second is *Ein Versuchshaus des Bauhauses in Weimar* (An Experimental House by the Bauhaus in Weimar, 1925), volume 3 in the intermittent series of *Bauhausbücher* (Bauhaus Books), of which fourteen appeared between 1923 and 1929. It was put together ('zusammengestellt' is the word used on the title page, for good reason, as we will see) by Adolf Meyer, who was also responsible for the typography. Their differences are notable: the *Blaue Bücher* cost 2.20 Reichsmark (RM) or RM3.30 in the case of the thicker *Sonderbände* (special volumes), and they were produced in initial print runs of between 13,000 and 20,000. By 1929, the third printing of *Bauten der Arbeit und des Verkehrs* had taken the print run to 50,000.[16] By contrast, the *Versuchshaus des Bauhauses* was produced in a print run of 2,300,[17] and, if priced similarly to other Bauhaus Books, cost RM40 in hardback.[18] Despite the aim for popular appeal, which crops up in several letters addressed by László Moholy-Nagy (1895–1946) to potential contributors to the series,[19] the pricing and print run nevertheless militated against mass sales, given that average net wages in 1925 were about RM30 per week, rising to just under RM38 per week by 1928.[20]

Bauten der Arbeit und des Verkehrs

Bound in Langewiesche's trademark deep navy blue embossed card, *Bauten der Arbeit und des Verkehrs* also has a stiff paper dust-jacket with the book's title and a crudely reproduced photograph of Stuttgart's main station (Plate 9). Thick dark grey bars frame a navy panel within which the title emerges in Langewiesche's house font and in the colour of natural paper, and this simple layout makes the book immediately recognizable as belonging to the series of *Blaue Bücher*, even without the series title in small majuscules beneath the

---

[15] The other volumes were devoted to public and community buildings: *Bauten der Gemeinschaft aus deutscher Gegenwart*, and domestic architecture: *Wohnbauten und Siedlungen aus deutscher Gegenwart*. Unless otherwise stated, all translations are my own.
[16] Stamm, 'Moderne, vornehme Massenartikel', 176–7.
[17] See Albert Langen Verlag to Moholy-Nagy, 24 April 1925, responding to the latter's request for a quotation for publishing the first six volumes of the Bauhaus Books.
[18] This can be deduced from correspondence; see for example Gropius to Schaedel, 30 July 1925.
[19] See for example Moholy-Nagy to Stamm, 9 September 1925: 'The only condition would be that your book deals with a problem that is of real interest to every single person' ('ein jeden menschen interessierendes problem behandelt').
[20] Bry assisted by Boschan, *Wages in Germany*, 58.

photograph.²¹ And this visual identity continues once the book is opened: each page is framed by a thin broken line – a feature that had been sporadically used before the First World War, and became a consistent element of Langewiesche's book design from the 1920s. Each halftone image occupies a page to itself and is set off from the page by a very narrow black line, while both the introductory text and the image captions are set in traditional German Gothic type, or *Fraktur* – all further hallmarks of the *Blaue Bücher*. At a purely visual level, then, *Bauten der Arbeit und des Verkehrs* is a rich artefact even before we begin to consider the images themselves or the content of the textual material. Karl Robert Langewiesche (1874–1931) had begun his career as a bookseller, and understood well the value of brand identity. The visuality of *Bauten der Arbeit und des Verkehrs* ensured that it became associated with a series whose previous architectural titles included *Deutsche Dome des Mittelalters* (German Cathedrals of the Middle Ages), *Deutsche Burgen und feste Schlösser* (German Castles) and *Tore, Türme und Brunnen aus deutscher Vergangenheit* (City Gates, Towers and Fountains from Germany's Past).²² The emphasis throughout these and other Langewiesche volumes is on Germany's past: it is a publishing programme with a distinctly nationalist and conservative orientation, and this carries through into the use of *Fraktur* (another signifier of 'Germanness' and 'pastness') and, indeed, into the ornamentation both on the embossed cover, which is reminiscent of the pre-First World War applied arts movements, and on the pages themselves: Müller-Wulckow, for example, found the broken line staid and argued (unsuccessfully) for its replacement with a more dynamic framing line.²³

As noted in the introduction, typeface, layout, paper and the use of colour are themselves signifying elements in book design, blurring the boundaries between visual and material culture. We do not need to know that Karl Robert Langewiesche's personal politics were conservative and nationalist in order to understand the visual discourse of *Bauten der Arbeit und des Verkehrs*: its intertextual references to the visual forms of past publications within and beyond the *Blaue Bücher* series allows the regularity of the books' visual features to emerge, and these constitute in themselves a discourse of past Germanness, independent of the content of the textual material and prior to an encounter with the photographic images.²⁴

---

[21] For reasons I cannot elaborate here, the Langewiesche house font is distinctive and highly unusual within the history of typography.

[22] These titles, together with their sizeable print runs of over 100,000 copies, are listed on p. 2 of *Bauten der Arbeit und des Verkehrs*.

[23] Stamm, 'Moderne, vornehme Massenartikel', 178.

[24] The only visual concession to the contemporary nature of the subject matter is the additional captioning, in very small roman type, hugging the broken line in the lower part of the page and including the construction date of the building depicted and a brief evaluative commentary. In most Langewiesche titles, even these supplementary captions are in *Fraktur*.

The photographs themselves are entirely characteristic of the day. Architectural photography had been a recognized professional subfield since the 1910s, its practitioners supplying monographic publications and periodicals that dealt with both modern and historic buildings.[25] Literature from the early twentieth century set out the aesthetic conventions governing the production of architectural photographs.[26] But the formal properties of the images encode specific kinds of knowledge, and excavating these will help establish the discursive properties of the genre.

The first is the treatment of people. In general, the inclusion of people was determined by the photographer's purpose: they were omitted if the purpose was to foreground the building itself and included if the purpose was to emphasize its use. In *Bauten der Arbeit und des Verkehrs*, if people are depicted at all, they are incidental: they tend to appear in the margins, to the side, at best as *staffage* (that is, as accessory items to mark scale), more often because their presence in public spaces was unavoidable. The second is that the buildings are, wherever possible, isolated from their immediate surroundings. This is entirely consonant with late-nineteenth-century thinking on urban form: planners and preservationists alike advocated an aesthetic of *Freilegung*, or disencumberment. *Freilegung*'s adherents prioritized unimpeded visual access to individual buildings of historical importance and conceived of urban space as a visual spectacle to be consumed by a static observer rather than inhabited by a mobile embodied subject.[27] The ideology of *Freilegung* is basically photographic, reducing three-dimensional spaces to visual forms and reducing embodied habitation to ocular perception. This is precisely what photography does, as a two-dimensional visual representation, and the lack of people and the individualizing approach taken in *Bauten der Arbeit und des Verkehrs* further contributes to the constitution of architecture as spectacle.

Photography cannot directly reproduce the embodied experience of movement through space.[28] But the images in *Bauten der Arbeit und des Verkehrs* work against the medium's own tendency to portray the built environment as visual spectacle. First, the raking diagonal view is the dominant compositional principle; frontal and symmetrical views are rare. One reason for the avoidance of the frontal view is to construct a heightened sense of three dimensions by emphasizing the orthogonals that organize depth-perception within the optical regime of linear perspective. Second, and related to the above point, is lighting. The effects of light incidence are striking in many images in Müller-Wulckow's book, with oblique overhead light the norm. This allows sharp shadows to fall across the surface of buildings, highlighting window

---

[25] See Zimmerman, *Photographic Architecture*, 130.
[26] Ibid., 133. See also 136–42 for a discussion of relevant publications, notably Schmidt, *Architektur-Photographie*.
[27] See Ladd, *Urban Planning*, 116–22.
[28] Zimmerman, *Photographic Architecture*, 136–42.

mullions, piers, balustrades, eaves, roof geometry (Figure 21) and the textural qualities of glass, brick, clinker, render and stone. The three-dimensional qualities of architecture are thus emphasized once again, not as a property of the building overall this time but of its details. The haptic quality of building materials is also partially captured, heightened by oblique overhead light and sharp shadow. This emphasizes the fact – now well recognized in studies of human vision – that the senses do not function in isolation, and that vision is never 'pure'. Third, the height of framing corresponds more or less to that of a normal human viewpoint (except in the case of tall buildings, where the use of a wide-angle lens tends to produce excessive distortion of the verticals if used from ground level): there were warnings against adopting 'unnatural' viewpoints that could not be easily identified as the perspective of the casual observer. Fourth, the foreground is shallow. Finally, very few photographs of buildings deploy a shallow depth of field in order to foreground a specific plane at the expense of detail in depth. As a result of deep focus, all details within the frame are in principle accorded equal value, creating the illusion

Figure 21 'Dyeing plant of a hat factory in Luckenwalde, designed by Erich Mendelsohn and built in 1921', from *Bauten der Arbeit und des Verkehrs*, 2nd imprint, 1926, 33 (© DACS 2019). The building is set apart from its surrounding ensemble, and there are no people in view. Raking diagonal light allows sharp shadows to fall across the surface of the building, highlighting window recesses, piers, roof geometry and the texture of construction materials. Here and in Figure 22, the line surrounding the image and the setting of the main captions in *Fraktur* connote continuity with earlier German printing traditions.

that the image has come into existence without the shaping activity of the photographer. This is entirely characteristic of the documentary conventions of photography (and film). It is part of a dual rhetoric of naturalness and transparency, according to which photographs purport to correspond to natural vision as well as providing direct access to their referent rather than constituting a highly mediated form or representation. Such principles can be seen throughout *Bauten der Arbeit und des Verkehrs*, for example, in this image of a biscuit factory in Hanover (Figure 22).

These 'formal conventions' are crucial to an understanding of the discourse of architectural photography. Height of framing that corresponds to the normal eye level, raking diagonal perspective and oblique light incidence (which stress

Figure 22 'Bahlsen Biscuit Factory Administration Block, Hanover, designed by Karl Siebrecht', from *Bauten der Arbeit und des Verkehrs*, 2nd imprint, 1926, 19. Height of framing that corresponds to that of the human eye, deep focus and a relatively shallow foreground create the impression of natural vision.

three-dimensionality and tactility), the supposed 'naturalness' of deep focus and the shallow foreground (which implies contiguity between the space of the image and the space of the viewing subject) enable imaginative inhabitation of the represented space. Rather than seeing these features as forms of compensation for the loss of the embodied experience of three-dimensionality,[29] the discourse of architectural photography as it is encoded in early-twentieth-century manuals and instantiated in the pages of *Bauten der Arbeit und des Verkehrs* strives for the closest possible alignment between visual perception of the photograph and bodily experience of the built environment. Without entirely concealing its spectacular tendencies, the photographic discourse of *Bauten der Arbeit und des Verkehrs* thus humanizes the buildings it represents.

The fact that the images in *Bauten der Arbeit und des Verkehrs* conform so closely to the dominant discourse of early-twentieth-century architectural photography is of a piece with the use of *Fraktur* and the book's generally conservative visual design. Modern architecture is assimilated to a set of formal principles that were established for taking and disseminating images of older buildings. Editorial choices at the level of content play a significant role, too: most of the buildings in *Bauten der Arbeit und des Verkehrs* date from the period before 1919, and represent a slightly earlier phase of design and construction practice than the architectural cutting edge of the mid-1920s.[30] The book thus constructs a very particular kind of knowledge about what modern architecture is and how it should be received and understood. The visual discourse of *Bauten der Arbeit und des Verkehrs* makes a claim about time as well as space. It implies a history of modern architecture as continuity rather than rupture with the past.

This conclusion is reached entirely on the basis of the visual elements of *Bauten der Arbeit und des Verkehrs*. Walter Müller-Wulckow does supply an eight-page introduction to the book, although I would argue that this provides a considerably weaker framing device for an understanding of the photographs than the book's design and typography, which are encountered prior to the act of reading. Indeed, Müller-Wulckow's text can be seen to corroborate that which the book establishes by primarily visual means. He notes in his opening paragraph the continuity between the aim of the present book and that of previous publications in the series: both bear witness to 'die deutsche Art und Schönheit' ('German distinctiveness and beauty'), even if earlier books had been devoted to the past. He is critical of historicist architecture and the *Heimatbewegung* – a movement committed to localism, tradition and rural

---

[29] As does Zimmerman, ibid., 134.
[30] Even the decision to grace the cover with Paul Bonatz's design for Stuttgart main station, begun in 1914, is telling. In the third edition of the book, it was replaced by the clean, curved horizontals of the overtly modernist headquarters of the Telschow company on Berlin's Potsdamer Platz. Subsequent volumes in the *Blaue Bücher* architectural trilogy are more adventurous in terms of both the buildings depicted and their photographic forms.

preservation – for their regressive tendencies, and sees in factory design the emergence of the genuinely new in architecture: 'Why did [factory architects] succeed in producing characterful designs? Because they could not allow themselves to be towed along by a model to be emulated, but had to focus on functional organic development. In this way they arrived at a *sobriety of construction and at artistic truth*.'[31] Like other theorists of modern architecture from Adolf Loos (1870–1933) onwards, Müller-Wulckow here argues for the moral and aesthetic superiority of functional construction, thereby implicitly criticizing historicist ornamentation and imitation of past styles. But he also pre-empts accusations that modernism is mechanistic and inhuman by stressing the organic nature of functional design. Elsewhere, he argues against technological determinism: it is not that iron and concrete determine the nature of modern design but that solutions to new problems necessitate the use of new materials. The 'geistig schöpferische, formgestaltende Kraft' (spiritually creative, form-giving power), embodied in the will of the architect, remains the decisive factor, and the individualism of the artist remains the essential characteristic of German art. But beyond this, he argues, the functional design of commercial buildings is an essential means of preventing the destruction of 'cultural harmony', which industrialization and economic growth threaten to bring in their wake (6). Architecture is thus endowed with a socially integrative capacity.

Much of Müller-Wulckow's vocabulary captures abstract entities that cannot be visually represented: spirit, will, creativity, moral truth, 'Germanness'. In this sense, text and image operate in entirely different discursive registers. But they are bound together by the fact that both the visual and the philosophical-aesthetic discourse attempt to interpret modern architecture in familiar terms. Common to both is continuity with the past, and an emphasis on Germanness. I will return to the significance of this in the conclusion.

Ein Versuchshaus des Bauhauses in Weimar

Müller-Wulckow described *Bauten der Arbeit und der Verkehrs* – untranslatably – as a 'Propagandabuch für deutsche Werktüchtigkeit'. 'Propaganda' did not, at the time, mean politically manipulative discourse but was rather a synonym for advertising. 'Werktüchtigkeit' is the quality both of having practical

---

[31] *Bauten der Arbeit*, 5: 'Warum gelangen hierbei charaktervolle Gestaltungen? Weil man sich nicht ins Schlepptau der Vorbilder nehmen lassen konnte, sondern aus zweckvoll Organisches sich einstellen mußte. So gelangte man zur konstruktiven Sachlichkeit und künstlerischen Wahrheit.' My emphasis. Subsequent references to this book will be given parenthetically in the text.

competence and of being hard-working.[32] Precisely the same description might apply to *Ein Versuchshaus des Bauhauses in Weimar*, but the book functions in an entirely different way.

Compiled and designed by Adolf Meyer, the book ostensibly documents the construction of the experimental house – also known as the 'Haus am Horn' – which was designed by the Bauhaus staff and built in the summer of 1923 as part of the first major Bauhaus exhibition.[33] But there is far more going on within the photographic discourse than pure documentation. Unlike *Bauten der Arbeit und des Verkehrs*, it seeks not to represent what is already there but to make a case for a specific philosophy and practice of housing design and production. The images in general and the photographs in particular, then, have a significant amount of work to do. Taken in 1923 but first published in 1925, they constitute not just a means of legitimation for the Bauhaus in the face of external threat, as Rainer Wick contends,[34] but an all-out polemic against current building practices and in favour of housing policy and construction methods that would revolutionize the face of Germany's urban centres.

As with *Bauten der Arbeit und des Verkehrs*, the initial visual encounter with *Ein Versuchshaus des Bauhauses* is not with the photographs inside but with the cover and the typography. The contrast with the Müller-Wulckow volume could not be more striking. In red upper-case sans serif letters (known to typographers as 'grotesques') on a white background, the title of the book is printed above a photograph depicting the eponymous house from a low angle, the wide-angle lens giving the impression that the building is set in a large enclosure whose wrought-iron gate dominates the foreground and partially impedes the view of the house itself. Beneath the image is a large, red number three, aligned with the right-hand margin of the image, and beneath that is the word 'Bauhausbücher' (Bauhaus Books) in the same typeface as the title but this time in black. The use of grotesques, the combination of red and black inks, and the complete absence of decoration are all visual signals of self-consciously modern design and would have been understood as such by readers in the 1920s.[35] This continues once the book is opened: the typography in general is characterized by grotesques in different sizes and thicknesses, asymmetrical layout, shifts between justified, left and right alignment, thick horizontal and vertical bars, large dots, and vertical as well as horizontal text. At a purely visual

---

[32] Circular from Müller-Wulckow to German architects, March 1916, quoted in Stamm, 'Moderne, vornehme Massenartikel', 175.
[33] See Winkler, *Bauhaus, Moderne in Weimar*, 32–8, for an account of the building's history.
[34] See Wick, 'Mythos Bauhaus-Fotografie', 19.
[35] The dominance of red and black, as well as the combination of type and photography in graphic design, can be seen in another photobook: Rasch and Rasch, *Gefesselter Blick* (The Captive Gaze). This is a kind of *summa* of 1920s commercial graphic design, bringing together manifestoes and examples by many of Europe's most prominent artists, including El Lissitzky, Jan Tschichold, Paul Schuitema, Hans Richter and John Heartfield.

level, then, the typography of *Ein Versuchshaus des Bauhauses* foregrounds the book's modern, experimental nature.

Whereas *Bauten der Arbeit und des Verkehrs* contains only photographs of buildings, an immediately striking feature of *Ein Versuchshaus des Bauhauses* is the sheer variety of the pictorial material. The first images printed inside the book are not photographs but drawings by Walter Gropius that demonstrate ways in which a set of basic three-dimensional cuboid forms can be differentially assembled in order to produce a variety of house designs.[36] Facing them are three ground plans that show the same principle at work but in horizontal section rather than exterior dimetric projection (9). On the following double-page spread are two photographs showing a card model of serially produced houses, which correspond to the earlier drawings (10–1). The reader then encounters plans, vertical sections and elevations for a circular house designed by Karl Fieger (12) and a photograph of several card models of serially produced houses (14), displayed to demonstrate once again the variations in exterior form achieved by varying the distribution of uniform prefabricated units. It was not unusual for architectural photobooks to include plans: the companion volumes to *Bauten der Arbeit und des Verkehrs* do so, for example. But they are normally plans of completed structures, whereas the plans in *Ein Versuchshaus des Bauhauses* are for buildings that have not yet been constructed.[37] The exploded views, projections and photographs of models are images of a yet unrealized future of domestic architecture.

The next section of the book includes the ground-floor plan (16) and a double-page spread that reprints the ground-floor plan to reduced scale and includes also the cellar plan, a vertical section, site plan and three elevations (20–1). In between is a photograph of the house taken from the same angle as the cover image but in full-page close-up and sharply lit from the right so as to plunge the left elevation into deep shadow (18). The subsequent pages depict a set of houses in ground plan and axonometric projections from above, showing how the basic design can be modified by changing the positions of the basic modules from which the Haus am Horn was constructed, and even joining them together into a terrace (22–3).

There is more to this than mere variety. The photographs in *Bauten der Arbeit und des Verkehrs* are presented paratactically: although there is a loose attempt to establish morphological similarities between different building types, their sequence is largely unimportant, and photographs could be added or subtracted without substantively changing the book's photographic discourse. The arrangement of images in the first part of *Ein Versuchshaus des Bauhauses*,

---

[36] Meyer, *Versuchshaus*, 8. All subsequent references to this book will be given parenthetically in the text.
[37] Plans, elevations and artists' impressions of unbuilt architecture were, of course, widespread in the architectural periodical press, then as now. But they were less common in photographic books.

Figure 23 Bathroom fittings in the experimental house designed by the Bauhaus in 1923, from Adolf Meyer (ed.), *Ein Versuchshaus des Bauhauses in Weimar*, 1925, 46–7 (© Bauhaus-Archiv Berlin). The emphasis on verticality in the images is emphasized by the horizontal text that accompanies them. Photographic optics produces perfect alignment of vertical planes and design elements, while large windows and mirror glass create an impression of light and air. The rooms are shown to embody the hygiene principle.

on the other hand, follows a clear narrative trajectory that moves from plans and axonometric projections through card models to the finished building. The inclusion of the photograph is important, because it represents the incarnation of the principles established in paper form. In other words, it shows that the future potential of architecture has already been achieved, in prototype, by the Bauhaus. In effect, it claims that the future has arrived. Like the visual discourse

WASCHTISCH IM BAD

Figure 23 (*Continued*)

of *Bauten der Arbeit und des Verkehrs*, the visual discourse of the Bauhaus book ultimately presents an argument about architectural history, one that stresses not continuity with the past, but a radical break, by means of which a utopian future of mass housing can be realized *now*, in the Germany of 1925.

Turning our attention to the main body of images, there are certain features whose regularity of occurrence implies a degree of discursive stability. First, the images strongly emphasize clean lines and planes, with all perpendiculars perfectly aligned; see, for example, the legs of the washstand on the left with the waste pipe beneath or the alignment of the fixtures above the washhand basin on the right (Figure 23). These features are embodiments of the modernist functional aesthetic that rejects ornamentation. Plans reproduced on page 20 show the room height at 2.5 m, which is low by the standards of late-nineteenth-century and early-twentieth-century tenements against which the Bauhaus theorists were reacting. But these and other images seek to compensate for this by the framing, which is characterized by strong verticals, and by the fact that there is no upward limit to the represented space.[38] This is a flagrant breach of convention; indeed, Hans Schmidt's manual *Die Architektur-Photographie* (Architectural Photography, 1902) insists on the inclusion of wall-ceiling joints, and sees the absence of such from the image as 'uncommonly disturbing'.[39] The highly polished reflective surfaces foreground the light, airy nature of the space, with the large windows included in the scene – if only through their reflection in a large mirror. This is hygiene in action: light and air, and smooth clean surfaces unencumbered by the messy accoutrements of human activity, such as curtains, towels, toothbrushes and so on. Hygiene is also one implication of the technology on display in this new form of dwelling, the other being convenience: the huge radiator and the electric light switches and fluorescent tubes relegate coal and oil to the basement, while the lever for raising and lowering the plug means that clean hands need not be plunged into dirty water.[40]

But of course there is more to this spread than just the images; the captions, too, play a significant role in guiding the reception of the photographs. This is always the case. Indeed, for commentators from Walter Benjamin to Roland Barthes and beyond, the anchoring of photographic meaning by the caption is key to making the photograph politically useful (in Benjamin's case) and comprehensible as a semiotic object (in Barthes's case).[41] Captions in *Ein Versuchshaus des Bauhauses*, however, are no straightforward matter. Throughout the main picture sections of the book, there is a typographic division of labour that is encoded in purely visual terms: typeface and orientation are key, as are the relationships between text and image. Horizontal captions in bold grotesque type identify the room and the fitters, while the upper-case vertical captions in serif font work in conjunction with the framing and aspect ratio of the images themselves to stress verticality – irrespective of image content. The vertical captions note the materials and the firms responsible for supplying them. In this particular case, they register the prevalence of crystal glass in the mirrors, and translucent alabaster glass as a material for sinks and wall tiles, as well as naming the firm that produced them. This fulfils at least three functions. First, it once again foregrounds hygiene as a goal and consequence of modern construction, thereby, second, demonstrating the value

---

[38] See for example 40, 50, 51, 53, 57, 63.
[39] Schmidt, *Architektur-Photographie*, 65, quoted in Zimmerman, *Photographic Architecture*, 137.
[40] For a discussion of hygiene and domestic architecture in Weimar, see Ward, *Weimar Surfaces*, 80–1.
[41] See Benjamin, 'Author as Producer', 24, and Barthes, 'Photographic Message', 25–6.

of mass-produced materials and third, it is an advertisement for the firms concerned (as a payback for their assistance in constructing the *Versuchshaus* at a time when hyperinflation was ravaging the German economy).

There is another aspect of the photography in *Ein Versuchshaus* that I would like to highlight: its tendency to mimic constructivist art. In these two pages, space is represented by sets of regular geometric forms (Figures 24, 25). Of course, the impression of three-dimensional space cannot be entirely eradicated, for two main reasons. First, the very purpose of the book is to demonstrate the advantages of modern methods of house construction, so the nature of the represented space is of necessity three-dimensional. Second, photographic optics, which operate according to the laws of linear perspective, combine with ingrained viewing conventions to create the illusion of three dimensions on a flat plane. But within these limitations, space is represented as far as possible as a montage of regular polygons extended into three dimensions, with the occasional circle where this cannot be avoided.[42] The photographs thus show the house to be a *combinatoire* of heterogeneous elements rather than an artisanally produced organic totality. In so doing, they offer a visual correspondence both to Gropius's recipe for mass-produced modular housing as outlined in his introductory essay (5–13) and to the other textual apparatus that lists the firms and individuals who contributed to the finished product.

The constructivist moment is further underlined by Adolf Meyer's typography. Text is divided into functional blocks, separated by font size and type, sometimes with vertical text, asymmetrical organization and the integration of company logos into the page picture. This clearly differentiates between the title, supplier and a commentary extolling the virtues of the material and product (Figure 26). Within a few years, Jan Tschichold (1902–74) was to formalize and refine much of the typographical innovation of the Bauhaus and others, claiming that the 'New Typography' was different from everything that had gone before because it sought to derive typographical appearance from the function of the text itself.[43] While Meyer's typography might not embody the virtues of clarity that Tschichold insisted on in his theoretical and design work, it *is* functionally organized. More importantly, though, it foregrounds the constructed nature of the artefact, which is assembled from diverse sources rather than being the creation of a single writing subject.

It is here that the narrative ordering of the photographs in the second part of *Ein Versuchshaus* becomes relevant: like the rest of the text, the finished house, which is pictured from the outside at the very end of the book, is shown to be

---

[42] Cf. Siegfried S. Giedion's remark that the Dutch De Stijl movement, which had a significant influence on the Bauhaus, involved a rediscovery of the value of the plane in visual art and its projection onto building design, in 'Das Bauhaus und seine Zeit', 21.

[43] Tschichold, *Die neue Tyopgraphie*, 68: 'die Erscheinungsform aus den Funktionen des Textes zu entwickeln'.

Figure 24 Living room and study area in the experimental house designed by the Bauhaus in 1923, from Adolf Meyer (ed.), *Ein Versuchshaus des Bauhauses in Weimar*, 1925, 67 (© Bauhaus-Archiv Berlin). Here and in Figure 25, the planar surface of the photograph is composed largely of polygonal shapes whose juxtaposition and superimposition recall constructivist art.

the result of an accumulation of the numerous individual components pictured in the previous pages.

Before concluding, I would make one further observation: there is, throughout the book, a meticulous documentation of who was responsible for all aspects of production, not only of the *Versuchshaus* as a building but of *Ein Versuchshaus des Bauhauses* as a book: on page 4, Georg Muche (1895–1987) and the Architecture Section of the Bauhaus are identified as the architects, under the leadership of Adolf Meyer and Walter March (1898–1969); construction and interior finishing are undertaken with the assistance of German industry, the firm of Adolf Sommerfeld and the Bauhaus workshops; Adolf Meyer is named as the typographer, and the typesetter and printer are also identified. There is an inventory of those responsible for various highly specific aspects of the interior design, and a list of the firms and individuals who participated in

Figure 25 Dining room in the experimental house designed by the Bauhaus in 1923, from Adolf Meyer (ed.), *Ein Versuchshaus des Bauhauses in Weimar*, 1925, 70 (© Bauhaus-Archiv Berlin).

the interior fit. Throughout, the manufacturers of products and appliances are named. And yet, the photographs are anonymous. In the context of a book that is desperately keen to identify authorship and provenance, the failure to name the photographer clearly signals the primacy of the photographed object over the image, as though the image were a self-generating and entirely transparent mode of representation. As I hope to have shown in this short analysis of the book, photography is in fact by no means simply a transparent window onto the Bauhaus world; on the contrary, it is a discourse that constructs knowledge about time ('the future is here') as well as space (the domestic realm should be one of light and air, hygiene, geometric abstraction) in very specific ways. And yet the book seeks to naturalize the knowledge-producing power of the photographic discourse by failing to acknowledge the mediated nature of photographic representation. Whereas in *Bauten der Arbeit und des Verkehrs* photographic transparency is achieved by the images' own formal properties, in *Ein Versuchshaus des Bauhauses* it emerges as a result of text-image relations.

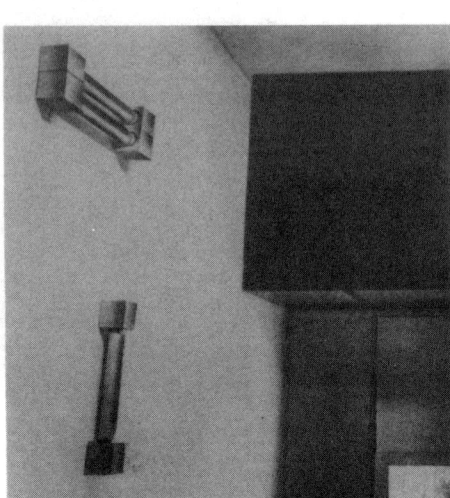

Figure 26 Electrical installations in the experimental house designed by the Bauhaus in 1923, from Adolf Meyer (ed.), *Ein Versuchshaus des Bauhauses in Weimar*, 1925, 58–9 (© Bauhaus-Archiv Berlin). Text is divided into functional blocks, using different typefaces and font sizes, and mixing upper-case and lower-case text, some of which is printed vertically rather than horizontally. This typographical experimentation is typical of the book as a whole.

Concluding remarks

In the foregoing discussion, I have identified, on the basis of a modified Foucauldian understanding of discourse, the regularities of object and 'type of statement' that characterize the visual discourse of two architectural photobooks from 1920s Germany. I have argued that we cannot reduce 'the visual' to 'the image', and that layout and typography themselves construct knowledge about the world prior to any engagement with the content of the texts. In the books discussed here, the combination of typography, extratextual design features and photographs makes statements about modern architecture and its relationship to the past and to the German nation. In the case of *Bauten der Arbeit und des Verkehrs*, a case is made for the habitability of modern buildings, and for the continuity and compatibility of modern architecture with German tradition. *Ein Versuchshaus des Bauhauses*, on the other hand, is unconcerned with questions of the nation. (The only mention of Germany occurs in the context of the cooperation of 'German industry' in the realization of the Haus am Horn project: Germany here is important only for its technocratic prowess, not as a repository of tradition or national spirit.) Rather than continuity with the German past, the book's visual discourse claims that the future – as represented by universally applicable modular housing – has already arrived in the form of the experimental house. It is a future characterized not by cosy inhabitability but by hygiene, technological convenience and serial production. These conclusions are reached on the basis of visual discourse analysis alone.

Returning to the question of writing visual history, there are several conclusions that can be drawn from this. The first is that discourse allows us to write the history of visual forms without reducing the visual to the image, and without merely reproducing conventional histories of stylistic evolution, according to which, for example, photographic pictorialism gave way to avant-garde formal experimentation or decorative type gave way to functional typography. Indeed, the books belie such constructions of linear progress: there is nothing especially innovative about the photography in *Ein Versuchshaus des Bauhauses*, and as Robert Kinross argues, the exaggerated use of bars, dots and the combination of different fonts have distinctly decorative effects: a kind of rebirth of ornamentation from the spirit of functionalism.[44] Understanding historical changes in the form of the photobook requires a consideration of all visual aspects of the publications, and in particular their interrelationships. In other words, it requires an understanding of the overall visual discourse of the artefact.

This understanding of visual discourse also allows historians to move away from the assumption that the primary value of photographs as historical sources is their representation of how things actually were. As I have shown, there is nothing

---

[44] Kinross, *Unjustified Texts*, 248.

transparent or natural about the photographs reproduced in the two books I have discussed; they are, on the contrary, coded, conventionalized and deployed strategically to make specific arguments about modern architecture. We misread photography entirely if we use it simply as empirical evidence of past states. In a lucid introduction to discourse analysis, Gillian Rose notes that discourse 'is a particular knowledge about the world which shapes how the world is understood *and how things are done in it*'.[45] This is a crucial point. Florence Grant and Ludmilla Jordanova argue in the introduction that visual materials and their contexts exist in a dynamic reciprocal relationship. Writing visual history from the perspective of discourse allows us to understand this relationship in terms of the effects that representations and other visual forms have in the world. These effects do not have to be direct: Bruno Latour notes that between the extremes of 'determining' human action and acting as a mere backdrop to it, objects perform all sorts of functions: they 'authorize, allow, afford, encourage, permit, suggest, influence, block, render possible, forbid, and so on'.[46] In the Weimar Republic, visual artefacts such as architectural photobooks enabled forms of interaction, dissemination and reception that could not have happened in the same way if they had not existed. As noted in the first paragraph of this book, cultural change and political conflict are shaped rather than being simply represented in the visual register. In Weimar Germany, visual culture became the primary means of staging the debate between the defenders and detractors of modern architecture. And the stakes of this debate were high, for on their outcomes hung the awarding of commissions, which in turn determined the trajectory of individual careers, the shape of cities and the living conditions of many thousands. Writing visual history in terms of discourse allows us, ultimately, to begin to understand this far-reaching agency of visual forms.

---

[45] Rose, *Visual Methodologies*, 142. My emphasis. This chimes with work in visual culture studies, anthropology and sociology, where scholars have sought to understand the agency of objects and artefacts. See for example Edwards, *Raw Histories*; Gell, *Art and Agency*; Latour, *Reassembling the Social*; and Mitchell, *What Pictures Want*.
[46] Latour, *Reassembling the Social*, 72.

6

The picture magazine: *Life* and the limits of photography

Melissa Renn

While *Life* magazine's reputation in the field of photojournalism has led many to equate 'picture magazine' with the photographic essay and black-and-white documentary photographs, the premise of its editors was that all things visual were pictures.[1] Indeed, *Life* magazine promised to show its readers the world in pictures, not just in photographs, and the editors conceived of the 'picture magazine' much more broadly than has been acknowledged.[2] As Daniel Longwell (1899–1968), one of the founding editors of *Life* described, 'From the very first *Life* toyed with the idea of assigning artists to do graphic stories, much as a cameraman might be assigned.'[3] Thus from its founding in 1936 to its end as a weekly publication in 1972, *Life* commissioned thousands of works from a wide range of artists, illustrators and designers on an array of topics, from Hollywood and American history to baseball and Dante. Looking

---

This chapter draws from my essay 'From Life: Tom Lea and the World War II Art of *Life* Magazine', in the exhibition catalogue by Adair Margo and Melissa Renn, *Tom Lea, 'Life' Magazine, and World War II* (El Paso, 2016), published in conjunction with an exhibition organized by the Tom Lea Institute with the National Museum of the Pacific War and The National World War II Museum. Thank you to Ludmilla Jordanova and Florence Grant for the opportunity to publish this work in another context, to Jennifer Watts for connecting us, and to Evelyn Rosenthal for her insightful edits. For their help with my research, thank you to Adair Margo; Brendan M. Greeley, Jr; Renée Klish; Sarah Forgey, US Army Center of Military History; Rick Watson, Richard Workman, Linda Briscoe Myers and Peter Mears at the Harry Ransom Center, The University of Texas at Austin; Claudia Rivers, Special Collections, The University of Texas at El Paso Library; Michelle Villa, El Paso Museum of Art; Jean Henry, Archives, National Gallery of Art, Washington, DC; Marisa Bourgoin, Archives of American Art, Smithsonian Institution; James Moske, The Metropolitan Museum of Art Archives; Bob Ellis, Henry G. Fulmer, Brian J. Cuthrell and Graham Duncan, South Caroliniana Library, University of South Carolina; and Tara C. Craig and staff, Rare Book and Manuscript Library, Butler Library, Columbia University.

[1] *Life*'s articles reached millions of Americans. Its first press run in 1936 of 466,000 sold out immediately, and by 1939, it had a circulation of more than two million. In 1960 it had a circulation of approximately six million. These statistics, as Erika Doss has noted, do not include its 'passalong' rate of four to five people per issue, so 'each issue reached as many as forty million people'. See Doss, 'Looking at *Life*'. The magazine's numbers remained high throughout the 1950s and 1960s, until, in the 1970s, television surpassed it. For a study of *Life*'s audience, see Baughman, 'Who Read *Life*?'.

[2] As Daniel Longwell stated, 'May I put the place of art in LIFE as simply as I can ... pictures and art are the same thing. Let us not get into aesthetics or semantics.' Longwell to Heiskell, 15 October 1948.

[3] Longwell to Saint, 24 April 1968.

at the magazine's patronage during the Second World War as a case study, this chapter will show how *Life*'s collaborations with artists and designers not only added variety and depth to its weekly reports on the war but also, in many cases, resulted from the limitations of photography.[4]

Life's war artist-correspondents

On 1 September 1939, the day Adolf Hitler invaded Poland, Time Inc. circulation director Pierrepont Prentice wrote to *Life* magazine's managing editor John Shaw Billings:

> It is eighty years since the Civil War, but everybody still remembers the Civil War drawings in *Harper's* and *Leslie's Weekly*. It is twenty-five years since the World War, but everybody still remembers the war drawings in the *Illustrated London* weeklies, and I sincerely hope that we are not so set in our devotion to the camera that we won't put a staff of first class illustrators to work right away drawing the war news.[5]

Billings, along with the other editors at *Life*, clearly agreed with Prentice. By early 1941 the magazine, led by Daniel Longwell, had commissioned seven American artists to depict national defence preparations for a special 'Defense Issue'.[6] Longwell, associate editor Edward K. Thompson (1907–96) and editorial associate John Field went to Washington to arrange inspection tours with the Army Public Relations Office. Once approved, *Life* swiftly sent its artists to sites nationwide. The resulting story for the 7 July 1941 issue contained 'more pages in color than … ever before printed in a single issue' and was one of *Life*'s largest art-related features to date.[7]

In late summer 1941, when Longwell wanted to cover developments in the North Atlantic and 'couldn't get a photographer into Argentia [in Newfoundland]', he persuaded the US Navy to allow Tom Lea (1907–2001) to paint the North Atlantic Patrol.[8] With that assignment, Tom Lea became *Life*'s first official war artist-correspondent and, according to Longwell, 'that started the war artists'.[9]

---

[4] Many of *Life*'s editors were active in the American art world: Henry R. Luce was an art collector and a trustee of both the Metropolitan Museum of Art and Museum of Modern Art; Daniel Longwell was an art collector, and both trustee and director of the American Federation of Arts in the 1950s; and Margit Varga had studied art at the Art Students League and National Academy of Design and exhibited regularly at the ACA Gallery and Midtown Galleries in New York.

[5] '*Life* Collection of War Art', [1].

[6] 'Defense Paintings'.

[7] 'Arming of America'. *Life*'s ability to print colour reproductions of works of art for a weekly magazine was made possible by key advances in printing processes invented in 1934 by R. R. Donnelley and Sons, the Chicago firm that printed *Time* magazine. For more, see Renn, '*Life* in Color'.

[8] Sugarman, 'Transcript of Interview of Daniel Longwell', 24.

[9] Ibid.

Modelled in part on American nineteenth-century magazines and illustrated newspapers that hired artists to paint and draw life during wartime on both the battlefields and home fronts,[10] as well as on twentieth-century British precedents,[11] *Life*'s war art commissions constituted its largest patronage project. The magazine sent artists all over the world to sketch, paint and record every aspect of the Second World War, from preparations at home to battles abroad, from beach landings and aerial raids to the experiences of soldiers and civilians.[12]

Covering the war was central to *Life*'s mission. From its inaugural issue the magazine had positioned itself on the front lines; indeed, Henry R. Luce (1898–1967) promised in his 1936 prospectus that *Life*'s readers would 'eyewitness great events'.[13] Early on editors and staff members recognized the need for both written and visual documentation of the Second World War, and from the outset the editors envisioned both photographic and painted images of the war as essential to their reporting.

The commissioning of paintings during the war stemmed partly from necessity, especially during the early years of the Second World War. Artists were often permitted access to certain areas where photography was banned on account of wartime restrictions. This was because, as *Life* art editor Margit Varga (1908–2005) explained, an artist 'could omit censorable material from his canvas and still produce an effective picture – which a photographer could not do'.[14] Adm. A. J. Hepburn, who had allowed Tom Lea to paint the North Atlantic Patrol for *Life*, remarked on the camera's limitations during war:

> The modern camera, in spite of its great scope and versatility, has definite limitations, particularly during night actions, in foul weather, or for battles which take place over wide expanses of sea and sky. These phases of warfare, however, may be depicted by an artist, who not only can capture the dramatic intensity

---

[10] During the Civil War, for example, Winslow Homer worked as a correspondent-illustrator for *Harper's Weekly*, and during the Spanish-American War, Frederic Remington worked as a war correspondent for William Randolph Hearst's *New York Journal*.

[11] *Life*'s editors were aware of British precedents, most notably the War Artists' Advisory Committee headed by Sir Kenneth Clark. They were also influenced by their viewing of the 1941 exhibition *Britain at War* at the Museum of Modern Art, which showed work by British artists from both the First World War and the Second World War. See Wheeler, *Britain at War*. The exhibition even inspired *Life* editor Margit Varga to write an essay on the topic. See Varga, 'Britain Mobilizes Her Artists'.

[12] The artists were George Biddle, Henry Billings, Julien Binford, Aaron Bohrod, Alexander Brook, Tom Craig, Floyd Davis, Gladys Rockmore Davis, Anton Otto Fischer, David Fredenthal, Peter Hurd, Joe Jones, Reuben Kadish, Lucien Labaudt, Edward Laning, Tom Lea, Carlos Lopez, Reginald Marsh, Fletcher Martin, Frank Mechau, Barse Miller, Bruce Mitchell, Bernard Perlin, Ogden Pleissner, Henry Varnum Poor, Edna Reindel, Paul Sample, Millard Sheets, Byron Thomas and James Turnbull.

[13] Long before Pearl Harbor, and even prior to *Life*'s appearance as a weekly picture magazine, Time Inc. recognized both the reportorial and financial value of war. In 1935 Longwell, then Luce's special assistant at *Time*, wrote to Luce that 'a war, any sort of war, is going to be natural promotion', and he even encouraged Luce to speed up the release of the newly planned picture magazine – that is, *Life* – in order to capitalize on Italy's predicted attack on Ethiopia. As quoted in Wainwright, *Great American Magazine*, 121.

[14] Varga, '*Life*'s Art Program', 120.

of an action and put it on canvas, but also, by proper use of his skill, can make scenes and activity more vivid and poignant, stressing and integrating essential elements and omitting unimportant details.[15]

Thus *Life*'s war artists could paint or sketch what a camera could not capture because of military restrictions, technical limitations and environmental challenges. They could also do so *in colour*. As Daniel Longwell explained, 'When the war broke out, those of us who got around the country at the various training camps realized color had to be used. ... One of the things to remember about the war artists was that Eastman had not yet developed fast color film and the color film procedure was too slow to report the war in action.'[16]

Life's wartime commissions from artists were an essential supplement to its photographic coverage. In the view of *Life*'s editors, the combination of paintings, drawings, photographs and text did more than just provide a more thorough account of the war; it also distinguished *Life*'s reportage from that of its peers and competitors. As editor Edward K. Thompson later reflected, '[Other publications] didn't have the graphic approach which put our readers right at the ringside. ... You've heard scores of people say that LIFE outdid the newspapers in reporting the war.'[17]

Life and the War Department

Likely inspired by *Life*'s great success with its wartime commissions, in November 1942, Lt. Gen. Brehon Somervell issued a directive requesting that the US Army form its own group of artists to cover the war. In early 1943 assistant secretary of war John J. McCloy organized the War Department Art Advisory Committee, designating artist George Biddle as its chair. The committee included artist Henry Varnum Poor and writer John Steinbeck, as well as David Finley of the National Gallery of Art, Reeves Lewenthal of the Associated American Artists and Edward B. Rowan of the Public Buildings Administration. Upon receipt of this news, Daniel Longwell immediately contacted Henry Luce expressing concern about what would happen to *Life*'s programme.

> On research, I discovered today that a Directive from the Secretary of War has set up a committee consisting of Henry Varnum Poor, David Finley, George Biddle and Ed Rowan to carry out a project of sending civilian artists out as War Correspondents. ... This is exactly the scheme that we have been following for the past two years ... and now we have the spectacle of the War Department with

---

[15] Hepburn, 'Introduction'.
[16] Longwell to Saint, 24 April 1968.
[17] Thompson to Longwell, 19 June 1946, 2. Emphasis in original.

unlimited funds competing against private industry – and, indeed, in the case of Fletcher Martin, we have them competing for personnel.[18]

Longwell's fears were short-lived, however, as was the government's programme.[19] Although only $125,000 out of a $71.5 billion budget was allocated for the programme, its funding was still challenged. Some in Congress supported the proposal, including A. Willis Robertson of Virginia, who argued, 'We can take photographs of what happens in Europe … [but] it takes the vision and artistic skill of the artists to bring us the inspiration which only an artist can put down on canvas.' Others, such as Congressman Joe Starnes of Alabama, dismissed the project as a 'piece of foolishness'.[20] In the end the war programme was cut, and in June 1943, when the war bill was passed, forty-two artists lost their positions. As soon as Longwell heard the news, he immediately went to see McCloy and offered to employ all the civilian artists who had formerly been working for the War Department. Out of the nineteen applicable civilians, seventeen, including Biddle and Poor, decided to join the magazine's ranks, and *Life* was once more in command of the largest group of war artist-correspondents in the United States.

Life around the world

With renewed vigour, *Life* enlarged its programme, sending artists to every corner of the globe. Artist-correspondents continued to paint both battles abroad and war preparations at home. For example, *Life* had Edward Laning paint the Santa Fe Railroad's role in the war effort and commissioned Julien Binford to paint the busy port of New York Harbor.[21] Edna Reindel depicted war preparations on the home front, painting women welding and riveting airplanes at the Lockheed Aircraft plant in California.[22]

Life allowed its war artists great latitude, asking only that they paint what they saw, in the style they deemed most appropriate to the subject. The artists rendered their experiences in a variety of styles and media, and each artist offered a unique and personal record of the war. Bernard Perlin, who went to Greece with the first allied troops, made graphite sketches and vibrant oil paintings of Greek life under German occupation.[23] Millard Sheets, on assignment in

[18] Longwell to Luce, 18 February 1943, 2–3.
[19] For more on the art produced by the Armed Forces during the Second World War, see Crane, *Art in the Armed Forces*; Baldwin, *Navy at War*; and Klish, 'Art of the American Soldier'.
[20] As quoted in Lanker and Newnham, *They Drew Fire*, 7.
[21] See 'Santa Fe at War' and 'New York Harbor'.
[22] 'Women at War'. For more on Reindel's work for *Life*, see Speck, *Beyond the Battlefield*.
[23] A selection of his pencil sketches, along with a personal account of his experience in Greece as an artist-correspondent, was published in *Life* in 1944. See Perlin, 'Liberation Will Find the Greeks Are Ready'. Some of his paintings were reproduced a year later in 'Aegean Actions'.

India, painted stark, expressionist images of suffering and the starving poor he encountered.[24] Peter Hurd painted tempera portraits of US airmen stationed in England, and in 1944 travelled with Air Transport Command to Puerto Rico, Trinidad, British Guiana (now Guyana), Brazil, Africa and India.[25] Many of the artist-correspondents focused on the architectural destruction resulting from war: Fletcher Martin painted surrealistic scenes of the ruins in North Africa; Tom Craig painted the bombed abbey at Monte Cassino in Italy; and Edward Laning drew the destruction of bridges and buildings in Florence.[26] Others focused on military actions, including those taking place at night, which would have been difficult with a camera. In December 1943 David Fredenthal accompanied a marine unit on a night landing on a Japanese-occupied island in the South Pacific, which he documented in expressive drawings and paintings.[27] The following year Fredenthal went to Yugoslavia to cover Tito's partisans, and was the first to depict the Russian army in Yugoslavia, at a time when neither allied reporters nor photographers were allowed access to the Russian front.[28]

Life published the work of its artist-correspondents both as part of its regular war reports and in special issues. In 1943 the magazine printed a thirty-six-page colour portfolio of war paintings by six American artists who had been sent to fronts worldwide, with a commentary by John Hersey.[29] Two years later *Life* produced another twenty-five-page full-colour article highlighting the range of work done by its war artists for its 30 April 1945 issue.[30] *Life* published not only the artists' paintings but also, in some cases, their personal accounts, as well as pages from their sketchbooks. For instance, Aaron Bohrod and Byron Thomas were initially sent to England to paint London and the surrounding areas in wartime; six days after the 1944 Normandy invasion, the two hitchhiked their way across England and through France to the battle site at Omaha Beach. *Life* reproduced sketchbook pages documenting that journey in the 9 October 1944 issue.[31]

The dangers of their assignments prompted many of the war artists to keep lengthy journals and sketchbooks to record their thoughts and impressions quickly, so that they could create finished paintings when on safer ground, often back in their studios upon their return home. Tom Lea, for example, recounted the origins of his painting *Death of the Wasp*. In 1942, while aboard the USS *Hornet*, he witnessed the attack on the USS *Wasp*. Struck by three torpedoes

---

[24] See 'Bengal Famine'; Sheets, 'Attack on Bamboo Hill'; 'India'; and 'Indian Village'.
[25] See 'Peter Hurd'. Some of his sketches from the 1944 assignment were published in the magazine. See 'Speaking of Pictures'. For more on Hurd's work for *Life*, see Renn, '"Enduring Record"'.
[26] See 'North Africa' and 'Italy'. Laning's drawings were also exhibited in 1945 at Midtown Galleries in New York. See Gruskin, *War in Italy by Edward Laning*. For more on these depictions of architectural destruction, see Renn, 'Fine Arts under Fire'.
[27] 'Night Landing on New Britain'.
[28] See 'Russian Soldiers'.
[29] Hersey, 'Experience by Battle'.
[30] '*Life*'s Artists Record a World at War'.
[31] 'Two Artists Hitchhiked to Normandy'.

fired from a Japanese submarine, the *Wasp* caught fire. Lea quickly grabbed a 'stub pencil' and sketched the scene. He later wrote about the experience: 'I had a dog-eared fliers' chart of the Solomons folded in my shirt pocket. On the back of the sweat-damp chart, with a shaky hand I made a sketch-diagram of *Wasp* dying, and wrote notations about the light and the color. As if I might forget.'[32] In this sketch Lea meticulously recorded the shape of the clouds, the colour of the sky and sea, and the position of the sun.[33] Upon returning to his studio he created a painting of the event, which was published in *Life*'s pages in 1943.[34]

Many readers were moved by Lea's rendering of the sinking ship. Allen Grover, vice president of Time Inc., for instance, wrote Henry Luce about how the painting captured aspects of the event not possible with a camera. In Grover's view, although the photograph was a 'kind of instant truth', it needed to be supplemented 'by that distilled, considered truth which only the artists can put into a picture'. He continued, 'Some might say ... that the sky was not that particular shade of blue the day the *Wasp* went down,' but 'Tom Lea has painted the very essence of that dreadful September afternoon and has given us an unforgettable image of an unforgettable moment in our history. It cannot be fairly said that a photograph would do the same thing.'[35]

War from another angle

The limitations of the camera in documenting the war are also exemplified in *Life*'s collaborations with industrial designer Norman Bel Geddes (1893–1958). In 1942, *Life*'s art director Worthen Paxton approached Bel Geddes and commissioned him to design models for a story on the Battle of the Coral Sea.[36] These three-dimensional models were designed specifically to be photographed and then reproduced in the magazine, in order to illustrate various war manoeuvres, battles and military strategies. Although the models were photographed in black and white, 'they [were] built in full color, grading from bright tones in foreground to gray in background to emphasize perspective'.[37] The models were well received. As one reader wrote to *Life*: 'The remarkable

---

[32] Lea, *Picture Gallery*, 64.
[33] Lea recorded the events both in pictures and in words. His moving account of the sinking of the *Wasp*, as well as his experiences aboard the *Hornet*, can be found in Lea, *Picture Gallery*, 59–74.
[34] 'Sinking of *Wasp*'.
[35] Grover to Luce, 23 November 1960.
[36] 'Coral Sea'. Paxton had previously collaborated with Bel Geddes on General Motors' corporate exhibition *Futurama* for the 1939 New York World's Fair. *Life* also promoted *Futurama* in its pages. See '*Life* Goes to Futurama'. For more on Bel Geddes's wartime work, see Cogdell, 'Theater of War'.
[37] Museum of Modern Art, *Norman Bel Geddes*, n.p.

models ... deserve the highest praise. Their excellent craftsmanship, scale and accuracy, assisted by exceptionally good photography, give an impression of striking and uncanny realism. Even better than pictures of the actual scenes, which in many cases would be impossible, they show the physical surroundings, the action and the strategy involved in our most important military and naval engagements.'[38]

Bel Geddes continued to make models for a number of stories in *Life*, including one on how the Russians took Orel. The article described: 'On these pages *Life* uses models by Norman Bel Geddes to show as no actual pictures could possibly show, what these tactics are and why they were so significantly successful in the battle for Orel.'[39] Bel Geddes also did models for a 1943 article on the Sicily invasion.[40] The works garnered even more attention when the Museum of Modern Art exhibited them a year later. The exhibition *Norman Bel Geddes: War Maneuver Models Created for 'Life' Magazine*, which ran from 26 January to 5 March 1944, showcased Bel Geddes's three-dimensional topographic maps (at the scale of one to one hundred inches) of the various theatres of war.[41] One of the most popular was the model of an invading army coming up against a river defence line. From a specially constructed runway, visitors could look down on it from above, replicating the experience of viewing the site from the air. *Life* saw such models as transcending the limitations of photography. Other models in the exhibition represented battle formations and tactical operations. Pages from the exhibition catalogue show the various views one could encounter at the exhibit, from the experience of the three-dimensional model itself to the photographed model in a two-dimensional wall panel.

The exhibition catalogue also documented the making of the models, and at one point during the exhibition, the Museum of Modern Art brought in Bel Geddes's employees to demonstrate the making of a model for museum visitors. The exhibition catalogue text even likened the construction of these simulated models to the actual process of preparing for war: 'The building of this fleet began shortly before the United States entered the war. A miniature shipbuilding race was begun in Bel Geddes's shop to complete all of the models before the real Navies met in battle.'[42]

Bel Geddes's models of war manoeuvres were commissioned due in part to the limitations of aerial photography at the time. With these models, *Life* could photograph what was impossible to capture with a camera, as the text of the exhibition catalogue explained: 'Actual photographs of carrier task forces never show any more than picture above. At best only two or three ships are

[38] Hudson, letter to the editors.
[39] 'How the Russians Took Orel'.
[40] 'Sicily Invasion Goes Well'.
[41] See also Maffei, *Norman Bel Geddes*, ch. 7, and Grischkowsky, 'FOUND!'.
[42] Museum of Modern Art, *Norman Bel Geddes*, n.p. Such models were also used by the military. For more, see Roberts, *Norman Bel Geddes*.

within field of one picture. Drawings or models are necessary to show complete formations.'[43] The models could show strategic plans, maps and conflicts at sea as well as night attacks and battles during storms. As the catalogue text stated, they 'have added an extra dimension to pictorial reporting. By recreating large or small parts of the sea and the earth's surface in miniature they have made it possible for the camera to take positions which would normally be highly unusual or impossible.'[44]

Life's war art exhibitions

Life also exhibited the work of its artist-correspondents in travelling exhibitions, beginning in 1943. War Art, which opened 20 June 1943, at the National Gallery of Art in Washington, included 122 paintings, watercolours and drawings made in US battle zones by nine of *Life*'s war artists: Henry Billings, Aaron Bohrod, Floyd Davis, Peter Hurd, Edward Laning, Tom Lea, Fletcher Martin, Barse Miller and Paul Sample. While many of the paintings by the artist-correspondents in the exhibition focused on wartime preparations, civilian experiences, architectural destruction and soldiers during downtime between battles, Lea was one of the few to paint the carnage resulting from combat, and his works were the only ones in the exhibition that showed 'a shot being fired'.[45] Lea's *Blood on the Deck* of 1942, which depicts two corpsmen kneeling over a dead sailor lying on a flight deck in a pool of blood, was not only one of the most graphic pictures in the exhibition but also one of the earliest images of dead soldiers to pass naval censorship.[46] In fact, the painting was shown at the National Gallery and was published in colour in the pages of *Life* prior to the magazine's publication of George Strock's now famous 1943 black-and-white photograph *Dead GIs on Buna Beach, New Guinea*, which showed three dead American soldiers on a South Pacific beach.[47]

In the foreword to the *War Art* exhibition's accompanying catalogue, the Metropolitan's director, Francis Henry Taylor, compared the work by *Life*'s artists to history paintings such as Benjamin West's 1770 *Death of General Wolfe* and Emanuel Leutze's 1851 *Washington Crossing the Delaware*. What distinguished *Life*'s war art from those examples, Taylor argued, was that artists like West and Leutze 'were seldom eyewitnesses to the scenes they depicted.

---

[43] Museum of Modern Art, *Norman Bel Geddes*, n.p.
[44] Ibid.
[45] Lea to Dobie, 20 June 1943.
[46] Just as with any film sent back from the fronts by staff photographers, the work of *Life*'s artist-correspondents required review and approval by the Office of War Information.
[47] *Life* printed a colour reproduction of Lea's *Blood on the Deck* on p. 47 in its report '*Hornet*'s Last Day'. *Life* published George Strock's photograph with an editorial over a month later. See 'Three Americans'.

Instead, their works were painted out of the fragments of recollection here, the word of an eyewitness there, and a liberal dash of romantic imagination from somewhere else'. In contrast, *Life*'s artist-reporters had 'observe[d] history in the raw'.[48] The exhibition also had record attendance; over 26,000 people visited the show when it was at the Metropolitan Museum of Art.[49]

While the exhibition was a success with the public, it elicited a range of reactions from critics and artists. *New York Times* critic Edward Alden Jewell initially doubted that painters could 'compete with the camera', but after seeing the exhibition his opinion was 'tellingly reshaped'. He wrote, 'The exhibition as a whole is impressive. It contains much fine and serious work by American artists who have been provided with every opportunity to observe their material at close range, often intimately. It is the intimate, personal, penetratingly perceptive touch, indeed, that is equipped to furnish a chapter that would be missing were the camera exclusively relied upon. This manifests preponderantly on the human side.'[50] An editor at *Art Digest* wrote that the works on display 'make a thrilling story … one more real than words, reproductions, [and] news photographs',[51] and singled out Hurd's depiction of a tail gunner and Lea's painting of the *Hornet* as especially powerful. In the *New Yorker* Robert M. Coates likewise lauded *Life* for recording the war in paint, writing, 'It's a good thing for us all too that *Life* undertook the job, for as things have turned out, if it hadn't done so we would now have practically no artistic record of the fighting so far.' Coates continued: 'The great work of the show is that its actual reporting of wartime scenes … is both accurate and plausible.'[52] In contrast, Jerome Mellquist, a critic at *The Nation*, labelled the artists 'feeble recorders', and argued that the war art on view at the Metropolitan had 'little, all too little of war's calamity, grief, heroism, humor, depth and generosity'; he further criticized the institution for displaying the work.[53]

Some artists also disliked the exhibition. In 1944 a group of artists, each of whom for different reasons had not gone to the fronts, protested the Metropolitan Museum of Art's showing by mounting an exhibition of their own. *We Challenge War Art*, organized by artist Fernando Puma (1915–55), opened at his gallery on West 57th Street in New York.[54] In the exhibition catalogue Puma wrote, 'There are in essence only two important reasons why

---

[48] Taylor, 'Foreword'.
[49] '*Life* Collection of War Art', 5.
[50] Jewell, 'War Art'.
[51] [Riley], 'Pictorial Reporting'.
[52] Coates, 'Art Galleries'.
[53] Mellquist, 'Feeble War Art'.
[54] Reviews and clippings of Puma's exhibition are in the Fernando Puma Papers at the Archives of American Art, Smithsonian Institution. In 1944 the exhibition travelled to the San Francisco Museum of Modern Art and was shown, under the title *We Challenge War Art: An Emotional, Not Pictorial, Record of Wartime, with Works of Weber, Grosz, Puma, Gropper, Lipton, Thall and Groth*, alongside the exhibition *Art of the Armed Forces: Pictorial Record of Wartime Experience by Men in the Armed Forces* from 1 January to 30 January 1944. See

artists should be sent to the war fronts. First, that the paintings would bear records in pictorial history, history that the camera could not capture. Second, that the paintings would express an artist's psychological or philosophical reaction or comment on war. Both of these aspects were sadly lacking at the Metropolitan.'[55] Believing that the exhibition should 'not be left unchallenged', Puma along with William Gropper, George Grosz, John Groth, Seymour Lipton, Victor Thall and Max Weber created their own works expressly for this exhibition, to show an alternative view of the war. In the text of the exhibition brochure, Puma claimed that the work his gallery was showing could 'bring the pathos, the martyrdom, the horror, the overwhelming power of the action on the different war fronts closer to us here than anything that was accomplished in the *Life* Magazine exhibition'. The artists saw their exhibition not as an 'anti-war show' but as an 'exhibition illustrating the menace and horror which our heroic soldiers are facing in the fight, illustrating the true stature of their martyrdom in this struggle for universal freedom'.[56]

As soon as *Life* got wind of the exhibition, it published a spread on Puma's show. *Life* reported, 'Mr. Puma believes that these pictures are better than the painting records done by LIFE war artist correspondents at the front because they express the "psychological or philosophical reaction" of the artists to the war.' The magazine photographed the rebel artists with their paintings and reproduced in colour George Grosz's expressive *I Was Always Present*, Puma's *They Will Not Conquer* and William Gropper's *Pearl Harbor*, among other works. The article concluded by asking readers to 'judge the issue for themselves'.[57] Many replied, with some thanking *Life* for the 'provocative art stor[y]', while others were appalled that those who did not go to the fronts would attempt to paint what they had not experienced. Another reader argued in favour of Puma's exhibition, writing that 'the paintings in Mr. Puma's exhibition are much more powerful and telling than the work of LIFE's war-artist correspondents'. *Life* even conducted its own informal poll of art critics, art history professors and museum directors, and printed the most common responses, concluding that 'it all depends on the man behind the brush'.[58]

Life continued to exhibit its commissions at venues coast to coast, during the war and after. In 1945 the magazine collaborated with the US Treasury to organize an exhibition as part of an effort to stimulate the sale of war bonds. *The War against Japan: Paintings and Drawings by American Artists* featured over 100 paintings depicting the war in the Pacific, from New Guinea

'We Challenge War Art' and 'Art of the Armed Forces', San Francisco Museum of Modern Art Exhibition Records.
[55] Puma, *We Challenge War Art*, n.p.
[56] Ibid. Puma's critique especially dismisses *Life*'s Second World War commissions from Reuben Kadish, Tom Lea, David Fredenthal and Millard Sheets, all of whom created works variously showing the destruction, suffering and psychological damage resulting from war.
[57] 'Studio War Art'.
[58] Letters to the editors, 3 July 1944.

to Okinawa, and showed work by artists in the US Army, Navy and Marine Corps, as well as paintings produced by Aaron Bohrod, David Fredenthal and Paul Sample for the magazine. Like the previous *Life* war art exhibitions, this too opened at the National Gallery and travelled to the Metropolitan Museum of Art before touring the United States.[59]

In 1945–6 the American Federation of Arts circulated the exhibition *New War Art*, which featured paintings by *Life* war artists Julien Binford, Aaron Bohrod, Floyd Davis, Fletcher Martin, Ogden Pleissner and Byron Thomas.[60] Though this exhibition, like the other war art exhibitions of the period, was generally well received, not all in the art world were fans. Critic and curator Katharine Kuh, for example, criticized both *Life* and the Art Institute of Chicago for presenting what she viewed as a propagandistic exhibition, and for showing paintings that were 'completely factual but largely lacking in quality, imagination or intensity.'[61] Critiques such as Kuh's and Puma's seem to miss or disregard the point of the commissions. *Life*'s artists were hired as correspondents, to record what they saw, in the manner they felt suited the subject best. They were dispatched as artist-reporters, and they took their charge seriously. As Tom Lea would later write regarding his wartime work for *Life*, 'I want to make it clear that I did not report hearsay; I did not imagine, or fake, or improvise; I did not cuddle up with personal emotion, moral notion, or political opinion about War with a capital-W. I reported in pictures what I saw with my own two eyes, wide open.'[62]

A record of war

In just five years, *Life*'s war artists produced over one thousand paintings, drawings and watercolours, hundreds of which were reproduced in its pages both during and after the war. By mid-1944 *Life* had published approximately 160 reproductions of the 678 oils, watercolours and sketches that had been done up to that time, and a total of 467 by May 1946, bringing this diverse body of work to millions of people, many of whom would likely not have had the opportunity to see them in person.[63] Although interacting with such reproductions on the printed page of a magazine is profoundly different from experiencing an original work of art in person in a gallery or museum, the

---

[59] 'Press Release', 4 July 1945. See also *War against Japan*.
[60] *Life's New War Art Exhibition*.
[61] Kuh also wrote that *Life*'s war pictures 'did not constitute a war art of serious stature. It is unfortunate but not surprising that the slick-paper magazines specialized heavily all during the war in a patriotic type of bastard art which should have been labeled news illustration'. See Kuh, 'The War and the Visual Arts', 399–400.
[62] Lea, *Southwest*, n.p.
[63] These statistics are given in '*Life* Collection of War Art', 5.

images nonetheless provoked powerful reactions from many readers. For example, two images by Tom Lea of the 1944 Battle at Peleliu – *Marines Call It That Two Thousand Yard Stare* and *The Price*—elicited particularly strong responses when they were published in the 11 June 1945 issue.[64] While some praised the magazine for printing such brutal 'realism' and the 'stark reality' of war, others were appalled by the 'gruesome pictures'.[65] Three members of the US Navy wrote a letter to *Life* defending *The Price*, which shows a mortally wounded Marine taking his last steps.

> Why such a picture? ... Need we be reminded that our shipmates are giving their lives in this, the greatest struggle for survival that the world has ever known? The picture of the gallant marine who took his 'Last Step' on Peleliu is the most depressing I have ever seen. Need they, the millions who have loved ones giving their blood in this the most cruel of wars, be reminded of how another's most beloved has given his? Yes, gentlemen. We have had a taste of how our countrymen have lived. We have had 18 months overseas and feel that we are in a position to write thusly.[66]

In his Peleliu paintings Lea captured the horror of war. He returned to the United States deeply affected by what he experienced, and felt it was his duty to record what he had witnessed. He wrote, 'I am trying to paint precisely and exactly and absolutely truly what I saw with my own two eyes. Nothing else. These are to be literal pictures, to be taken literally. Few painters have ever seen such things, and certainly none I know of has painted them.'[67]

The collection of war art remained at *Life* until 1960, when it was given to the Department of Defense by editor-in-chief Henry R. Luce in a ceremony at the Pentagon.[68] The multitude of works commissioned by *Life* during the war constitute an invaluable archive of the Second World War and reveal that the scepticism surrounding the evidentiary nature of photography continued well into the twentieth century.[69] Indeed, *Life* hired artists to paint the war not only for variety but also to lend credibility to its pictorial reporting. As Roy Larsen, a director at *Time*, observed, 'Strangely enough ... despite the fantastic success

---

[64] These two paintings were reproduced in 'Peleliu'.
[65] Letters to the editors, 2 July 1945.
[66] Adams, Evans and Good, letter to the editors, 2 July 1945.
[67] Lea to Dobie, 30 October 1944.
[68] This was the result of Longwell's incredible persistence, long after he retired, to ensure that the collection remained a unit and that it would be donated to the military as originally intended. The *Life* Collection of World War II Art is now at the US Army Center of Military History, Fort Belvoir, VA. The gift was also celebrated in *Life*'s weekly pages. See 'Rich Gift of War Art'.
[69] As Elizabeth Edwards has shown, doubts about the objectivity of photography have existed since the nineteenth century: 'Photography might not have been a particularly new medium by 1870, but its evidential efficacy was still under negotiation.' Edwards, 'Photographic Uncertainties', 184. *Life*'s editors were keenly aware that the photograph, like all other pictures, could be constructed and manipulated. See, for example, Glenn Willumson's discussion of W. Eugene Smith's manipulation of prints in Willumson, *W. Eugene Smith and the Photographic Essay*, ch. 6. On the constructed aspect of news photographs and editorial processes, see also Gervais, 'Reaching beyond the Index'.

of *Life* and other picture magazines, news photography is not a respectable profession, and the photograph is not considered to be a complete and accurate medium for the reproduction of news and general information.'[70]

Well versed in photography, *Life*'s editors likewise knew its limitations. From their perspective, paintings, drawings, photographs and text together could provide a more complete picture of the war. As Daniel Longwell concluded, 'Although we covered the war with our cameras better than any other illustrated magazine had ever covered the war, it was our painters who added the extra 10% that made the show truly notable.'[71] Some of *Life*'s artist-correspondents concurred. One of the artists, Fletcher Martin, even argued that paintings were more personal, and perhaps – at least in terms of the subjective, emotional experience of war – more accurate than photographs. He wrote:

> The painter can make a more personal statement than the camera. His record can be stronger than the camera's because he can eliminate unnecessary detail and concentrate on the significant. Some of my work that digressed frankly from actuality met the approval of the fighting men themselves. They responded to it and said I'd got the feel of the action. That was the acid test.[72]

To *Life*'s editors and artists, a painting, sketch or three-dimensional model offered different views of the war, and could do what a photograph could not. Clearly, *Life* aimed to present the world in pictures, and the magazine's wartime commissions were both a vital part of that mission and essential to its reporting on the war. As Henry Luce articulated in an early version of his prospectus for the magazine: 'It proposes to be the biggest picture show on earth ... [and] takes for its field not all the news but all the news which now and hereafter can be seen; and <u>of these seen events it proposes to be the complete and reliable record</u>.'[73] *Life*'s varied commissions were not only central to the editors' vision for the picture magazine but also counter the prevailing narrative of the modernist faith in the objectivity of photography in the twentieth century.[74]

---

[70] Quoted in Wainwright, *Great American Magazine*, 136.
[71] Longwell to Luce, 9 January 1948.
[72] Martin, 'Press Release'.
[73] Luce, *Prospectus for SHOW-BOOK*. Emphasis in original. One of the early proposed names for the magazine was *Show-Book*.
[74] Mia Fineman, for instance, has summarized the cycles of 'credulity and skepticism toward the photographic image' in four phases: '1) a positivist faith in the photograph as a direct transcription of nature, first voiced by the medium's inventors and extending into the 1850s; 2) an increased awareness of photographs as crafted artifacts, originating in the late 1860s and holding sway until the turn of the century; 3) a renewed confidence in the ideal of authenticity and documentary truth, emerging in the early twentieth century and continuing through the 1970s; and 4) a pervasive skepticism about photographic truth that arose in tandem with postmodernism and digital manipulation in the 1980s and that persists today'. Fineman, *Faking It*, 19.

Concepts

This section is designed to draw readers' attention to a limited number of 'keywords', to use Raymond Williams's term. Williams selected words that do a disproportionate amount of cultural work, often because they are ambiguous, emotionally charged and politically loaded, like 'art' for example. He used his training as a literary critic, and the concerns that arose from his embrace of Marxian traditions, to probe in brief, dense entries the changing meanings and usages of his chosen terms. In subsequent decades other publications have addressed significant concepts and ideas in a dictionary format. The Critical Terms series is a good example, and the volume on art history (Nelson and Shiff, 2003) is relevant here. The short discussions that follow are intended to provide an introduction to concepts that are frequently used, often without an appreciation of how complex and labile they are. Historians benefit from being aware of the history of the main ideas they use, the intellectual traditions with which they are associated and the resonances that they carry in both specialist use and everyday life. Accounts of such important notions are bound to vary; they resist neat definition, hence it is worth consulting a variety of sources and bringing a critical perspective to bear upon them. For example, a reworking of *Keywords* (Bennett et al., 2005) provides an opportunity to make comparisons with Williams's project, first published in 1976.

Agency

Agency is the word we use to express the ways in which objects and human beings can have effects on social relationships, since individual responses to visual materials occur within a wider relational framework. When dealing with visual materials, it is essential to ask about the agents involved in their production, distribution, use and representation. More than this, when value is created, whether it is aesthetic, economic, emotional or social, agency is also involved. This goes far beyond artists' intentions, which are in any case tricky to discern and document. Religious imagery is capable of inspiring strong, even violent responses, as we know from the history of iconoclasm, and it seems plausible in such cases to attribute agency to the artefact in question. Reactions to any given item are likely to be diverse and are always dependent on context; some images give rise to a range of responses, even within a single individual. 'Agency' also draws attention to the division of labour in making artworks of the highest value: framers and colour makers for paintings, studio assistants for sculptural projects and all those involved in making prints. It also brings to the fore those who commission, sell and display works. It helps us guard against simplistic understandings of power, which rarely rests in a single person.

Many items of visual interest are the work of numerous, sometimes unnamed hands, hence we need a subtle sense of agency that takes account of institutions, business practices and collaborations. Advertising is an excellent example of a domain that produces visual culture where its agency is central – otherwise it would not be effective at promoting brands, commodities and ideas. Being as explicit as possible about the forms of agency involved in any given artefact assists our understanding of its production and subsequent life history and is integral to *description*, discussed below. Further, forms of agency provide a bridge into *contextualization*, since tracking people and their actions is part of provenance studies, for example.

Art

'Art' is a slippery notion. At some times it and its cognates are used to refer to any kind of cultural production, and at others they denote specifically the visual arts. 'Art' also implies standards. Despite commonplace disparagements of contemporary art, anything cannot count as 'art'. Indeed there are many gatekeepers around this concept – museums, galleries, auction houses, critics and art historians, for instance. The notion of a canon is relevant here. It refers to those works deemed to form a central, valued tradition, whether in art, music or literature, to which the products of other traditions can be compared and their value determined. In practice 'art' has fluid boundaries and was used in the past more loosely to draw attention to skilful creations. At some points distinctions have been made between artists and artisans, the former bringing an intellectual dimension to their work that the latter allegedly lacked. Thus 'art' is dense with value judgements. Furthermore the status of artefacts can change. We might think of so-called 'non-Western' art, in which there has been an active trade since the nineteenth century. Many such items were not produced as 'art' but as parts of social and cultural life in settings without elaborate markets; they have later been deliberately made into artworks with exchange value. Disputes constantly arise about what is 'good' and 'bad' art, about whether certain objects are qualified to enter prestigious collections, about the neglect of art made by marginalized groups, about whether items are really worth what they fetch at auction. We may confuse expensive art with great art – again standards are at issue. These complexities have led some scholars to view the very term with scepticism, and its elaborate history certainly needs to be taken account of when using it. Yet given its long and intricate history and the manner in which it is embedded in modern institutions, it cannot be discarded. It is best thought of as an arena for debate, and the term still evokes exceptional accomplishment. The precise criteria for judging works of art vary over time and space and between individuals, inviting historical analysis.

Discourse

Those who work on texts have been keen to understand how they may be parts of larger systems or modes of thought. 'Discourse' suggests something broader and less specific than 'theory'; it indicates ways of thinking and knowing, and forms of languages that cross *genre* and *medium*. By paying attention to such questions, we can discern patterns in societies that are of interest to scholars precisely because they shape perceptions and experiences of the world. It is worth distinguishing discourse from ideology, which implies the presence of specific political interests that underpin a world view and promote it. Ideologies are likely to be in conflict with one another, and to have material concerns underpinning them. 'Discourse' can help those using visual materials to think about broader patterns, for example, linking images and texts within specific discursive formations such as imperialism and colonialism. The term 'discourse' comes from studies of the nature of language and hence fits especially neatly with the analysis of texts. An underlying assumption is that language shapes experience, and thence reality. If 'discourse' refers to broad ways of thinking, it necessarily has visual manifestations, so that illustrations of people living outside Europe could be understood as part of colonialist discourse, for example.

Genre

'Genre' refers to a way of classifying cultural productions, whether these are literary, musical or visual. In the visual arts it was common to distinguish between history painting, portraiture, landscape and so on, and place them in a hierarchy with history painting at the top and still life considerably lower down. The perceived differences between types of art derived partly from their subject matter, and partly from conventions that influenced size, the positions in which artefacts were displayed and the prestige of the work. History painting drew upon classical and religious narratives and could include depictions of the deeds of more recent powerful figures, such as rulers and military leaders. Academies of art, which came into prominence over the early modern period, construed themselves as guardians of the hierarchy of genres. A major historical shift occurred in the second half of the nineteenth century, when many artists rejected academic values and embraced self-consciously innovative forms of art practice associated with impressionism and modernism.

Viewers are aware of genres, even if they have received no formal instruction in the history of art and visual media. The use of photography in newspapers and magazines, for example, schooled readers in what to expect from documentary photography, war journalism and so on. Sometimes genres are blurred deliberately, as when documentary film is used in a fiction movie. We use genre terms in everyday life, not just by the common deployment of 'documentary' but in terms such as 'soap opera' and 'holiday snap'. Grasping generic conventions is vital for *contextualization* since they shape the relationships between makers and spectators. At the same time, the historical understanding of genres such as satire can require complex contextual knowledge of social mores, contemporary gossip and cultural references. Familiarity with established genres forms part of the basis of innovation in the arts, literature and other fields, since conventions invite people to flout them. Indeed the ways in which such rules are broken depend on both the existence and acknowledgement of generic boundaries.

Iconography

Iconography is the study of the content of works of art, especially those items that have established meanings. Some biblical figures have attributes, such as keys for St Peter, who is Heaven's gatekeeper. Similarly saints are associated with the manner of their martyrdom – St Catherine with wheels and St Sebastian with arrows. Colours also have conventional religious associations, such as blue for the Virgin Mary. Iconographers tend to focus on objects depicted, however, making the assumption that viewers shared producers' repertoires of symbols and attributes. Sometimes these were codified in emblem books and other compilations, for example, by Cesare Ripa in his *Iconologia* (first edition 1593), which went through many editions over several centuries. Interest in such conventions has waxed and waned over time. Nonetheless, historians need to be aware of these customary associations and also to grasp the history of their use, which is related to the ways in which classical and sacred texts were deployed as privileged sources for the pictorial arts.

Heraldry, which is still part of contemporary life, alerts us to continuing associations between objects and certain well-established meanings. Further, psychoanalytic traditions have engaged deeply with myths, especially classical ones, that appear capable of shedding light on human experience in general. Thus an understanding of iconography as a field and of specific associations between objects, people and traits, features or characteristics is important for historians who wish to interpret items of visual culture from sculpture, paintings and tapestries to book illustration, architectural motifs and prints. Many of these traits make more sense when their role in a narrative is grasped; hence iconography leads historians into funds of stories upon which artists and artisans in the past could draw. Iconography can also reveal the historical interests of makers, who drew upon antique sources. Sitters in portraits were sometimes given attributes that referred back to earlier times. An iconographic approach reveals the ways in which meanings could be transferred, often across many centuries.

Medium

'Medium' refers to the materials out of which something is made – stone, wood, ink, paper and so on. Being precise about the medium of any given made thing is essential, as is some grasp of how it was made – the different techniques involved in printmaking are an excellent example. Despite the apparent simplicity of a category such as 'stone' or 'wood', the idea of medium is complex and culturally specific. In certain settings, the use of particular materials conveys certain symbolic meanings. The medium of oil painting has played an especially privileged role in the development of painting as a fine art and thence in the development of art history as a discipline. Some media, such as photography, invented in the first half of the nineteenth century (various dates are given), struggle to establish themselves as worthy of being called 'art'. Much earlier, the 'new' medium of print had dramatic social, economic and political effects, so that its advent is seen to define a new historical era, thanks to what has been called 'the print revolution'. 'Medium' leads historians to reflect on *genre*, techniques, *skill*, forms of training and the economics of producing those items that invite visual attention. The plural of medium is media, and there is potential for confusion here, since now the word 'media' generally refers to TV, radio, digital products, newspapers and so on, that is to the means by which material is broadcast. Thus 'media' can refer to podcasts, blogs and tweets. 'Medium' is also used in a more specialized sense, to refer to the oil or other liquids with which pigments are mixed to produce paint.

Reception

'Reception' complements 'production' and is used to draw attention to the complex, changing responses items of visual culture provoke. It can be tracked through the reactions of critics, for example, and for more recent times through the audience research that major museums and galleries as well as media outlets undertake. It can also be considered by examining the activities of collectors and of markets. Thus it links to themes that are notoriously difficult to analyse, such as fashion and taste. Nothing is made in isolation, and artists of all kinds tend to have ideas about how their work will be received and by whom as they are working. In the case of commissioned work, the intended audience is integral to the production process. Forms of display shape visitors' reactions, hence understanding the ways in which organizations present the items they own is vital for historians. These forms are historical phenomena, thus an account of how something was displayed in the past provides important clues to the responses it elicited.

Photographic evidence, inventories, written criticism and travellers' accounts are instances of the sort of evidence historians can use to probe reception. It is clear that studying provenance can provide important clues to the nature of reception, since, for example, goods were – and still are – sometimes purchased because of their former owners, rather than for their intrinsic value, in global markets. Indeed this is a feature of current celebrity culture. Artists have frequently amassed significant collections, and on their death other artists may be keen to acquire something they had owned. These phenomena are not confined to artistic circles. In some big sales members of the public are eager to buy even a tiny artefact associated with a charismatic individual, which sheds light on the previous owner's status and 'reception'. Then there are iconic works that are reproduced many times; such patterns also shed light on reception, both of the work and of its maker. The most familiar example of this phenomenon is Leonardo Da Vinci's *Mona Lisa*, but it is also evident in the enthusiasm for versions of Claude Monet's water lily paintings. 'Reception', then, can refer to the purchase of tea towels and fridge magnets, as well as to the commentaries of critics, collectors and scholars.

Reproduction

Many examples of visual culture exist in multiple forms – a phenomenon referred to as 'reproduction'. Reproduction is often thought of in terms of copying, which suggests a particular set of relationships, defined by resemblance as well as difference (of scale or medium, for example) and also by variations in value between an 'original' and its reproductions, and among the reproductions themselves. A copy of an oil painting, using the same medium, is an obvious example and a fairly common practice over many centuries, when artists in training were encouraged to replicate works of art by acknowledged masters. Prints may be but are not necessarily reproductions. The process of casting metal is essentially reproductive, even if only one finished work is made, since the metal is poured into a mould that was, in turn, made from a preliminary model or pattern. Thinking of reproductions as translations, rather than as copies, has the benefit of highlighting the material practices and processes of decision-making involved, as well as the conventions that have governed, for example, the rendering of colourful originals in black-and-white prints.

Printed and photographic reproductions of paintings and sculpture have been fundamental to the development of art history as a discipline. Before the advent of widespread cheap travel and photography, a print was often the only form in which significant works were seen by those in distant lands. Eighteenth-century commentators wrote about the renowned sculpture of Laocoön and his sons being killed by serpents (second century BCE–first century CE) in the Vatican collections, for example, without ever having seen it at first hand and only studied it in prints. Digital media now enable exceptionally fine reproductions to be made at reasonable costs, and most museums and art galleries provide this service for works in their collections. This history speaks to the broader point that reproduction can drastically expand the social reach of works of art and visual culture; it both constitutes an act of *reception* in itself and makes versions of well-known images available to a far wider audience than would otherwise be possible.

Rhetoric

Every humanly wrought thing can be understood as making one or more points. Rhetoric is the name of a field that analyses how points are made in a persuasive manner, and hence it, together with rhetorical practices, is relevant to our understanding of visual materials. At various times in history, wigs and hats, for example, conveyed signals about their wearers – their status, the ways in which they performed decorum, their gendered qualities. All this was therefore transferred into depictions of people, with the result that a figure whose headgear was in disarray could be 'read' as morally as well as sartorially disordered. This type of rhetoric implies shared understandings and can be construed as a kind of common culture. Thus readers and viewers could be expected to recognize common tropes: themes or subjects that, through repetition, become established parts of cultural life. As we know from public speaking, rhetoric is designed to elicit specific emotions in audiences, indeed to manipulate them.

Visual materials can usefully be approached with this in mind, making us alert to visual tropes that shed light on the likely responses of spectators, or at least those the maker had in mind. Representations of the crucifixion in active Christian communities are a case in point. History painting is another clear example, where viewers are invited to perceive the narrative and to generate appropriate responses, sometimes by virtue of already being familiar with the texts upon which artists drew. Rhetoric is also useful for thinking about more recent visual culture, including photography, where iconic images often draw upon long-established modes of representation to create powerful and emotive effects. The use of photography and film in the campaigns of charitable bodies neatly illustrates the use and the *reception* of highly charged images designed to elicit donations from viewers – rhetoric in action. The cultivation of a visual identity or brand, in the context of marketing, politics or social media, can also be thought of as a form of visual rhetoric, shaping public perceptions of character and value. Through close analysis of the rhetorical effects of visual culture we are led seamlessly into their contexts of production and use by considering shared assumptions, common motifs and emotional styles.

Skill

There are many kinds of skills to be considered here, including those of makers and the rather different ones of interpreters. In the case of the former, it is necessary to grasp the forms of training that were in operation for any given occupation, such as engravers, book binders or frame makers. In these examples an apprenticeship model has been and remains relevant. Long years of practice, perhaps following some initial training with a highly skilled master, are a common pattern. The elaborate institutions that educate some other makers are relatively recent historically speaking. Debates about the respective status of art and of craft, and of artisans and artists, reveal precisely the social stakes in various kinds of skill. Change occurs when established hierarchies, with their concomitant claims about 'skill', are explicitly challenged, although default positions about 'proper' art are often deeply entrenched.

Historians need to grasp exactly what skills are involved in the production of their objects of study, including the nature of design, which is frequently hived off and treated as a separate domain both by scholars and by practitioners. The very words 'design' and 'craft' imply distinct skills from 'art', even though the practices involved may be identical. Phrases such as 'art photography' and 'wildlife photography' imply that there are different kinds of skills involved in the various forms of camera work. Underneath these issues sits the distinction between head and hand that was integral to social organization, and that persists in various forms to this day. We see how crucial 'skill' is in the common claim about contemporary art that 'a six-year-old could have done that'. Even as the art world has come to devalue certain kinds of manual ability, there continues to be a public expectation that the value of works derives in part from recognizably skilful making.

When it comes to historical interpretation it is vital to note that subtle skills are involved. This is clear in the case of connoisseurship, the epitome of refined visual attentiveness, and still necessary for the authentication and attribution of high-value items. Working with visual culture demands a range of skills, some of which are more 'technical' than others. The ability to identify different kinds of prints is an excellent example. But such skills are just a prelude to the more elaborate ones of *describing* what we see, placing images and objects in their multiple *contexts* and drawing out their historical significance in our written work. Such skills cannot be taught mechanically but grow and develop through self-aware practice.

Style

Style has been a central term in art-historical analysis. Many people are familiar with 'baroque', 'Georgian' and 'Victorian' as style terms. They can be widely applied to diverse types of artefact, from furniture to architecture and jewellery. It is common for museums to use such language, as do commercial enterprises that sell goods associated with the past. There are two issues here: one is the classification of objects and images, which is useful when making generalizations, and the other is *periodization*, since style terms can also denote historical periods. Historians need to be wary in both cases; such labels contain implicit assumptions and can be lazy ways of thinking about the past. Style is also used in another way to characterize an individual's distinctive manner of making. While this can also be a form of pigeonholing, it can equally facilitate close attention to what is characteristic of the person in question.

Although researchers may use style terms rigorously, they have to accept that such language has a vigorous life in popular culture, hence the ability to exploit popular styles for economic ends. Merchandise in Glasgow, Scotland, for example, endlessly incorporates elements from the style of Charles Rennie Mackintosh, who worked there in the late nineteenth and early twentieth centuries, and whose buildings and furniture have become iconic. 'Style' is also a staple notion when it comes to fashion. Again, it operates at more than one level. We might associate high-profile designers with a certain style – Chanel with small handbags with gold chains, for instance. Prominent designers of clothes, shoes and hats are just as likely as artists to have defining visual characteristics. But we also recognize styles that are more general and indeed characteristic of a period – the miniskirt is a prime example. Furthermore, personal style is a familiar phenomenon, especially prominent in celebrity culture, even if the person in question has a stylist.

Visual culture

'Visual culture' is a term with wide embrace, in contrast to 'art', which generally implies filters of some kind, even if their precise nature remains unspecified and hotly contested. Those who identify most strongly with visual culture studies tend to be critical of the narrowness that 'art' implies, and to advocate the study of many types of images and objects, especially modern media such as advertising, television, video and film. Such work often engages with theoretical accounts from a range of fields including the social sciences and communications. There is another inflection that can be given to visual culture that is more 'historical'. Historians search for shared threads or motifs in the cultures they examine. If an author writes about Elizabethan visual culture, for example, we understand them to be interested in a wide range of phenomena, not just painting and sculpture. We would expect to find dress and jewellery, church monuments, coins, furnishings (such as tapestries and tableware) and courtly culture included in such an account. We would also look for the more or less explicit premise that items produced at the same time are likely to possess visual similarities that are indicative of a broader cultural situation. So 'visual culture' can be taken as an invitation to bring diverse items that invite visual attention together in a single analytical frame, precisely because their coexistence and shared features can help to give coherence to historical understanding.

Practices

Writing Visual Histories shows how a self-aware approach to using visual sources in an integrative manner makes a valuable contribution to the discipline of history. We emphasize the processes and practices that undertaking historical work necessarily involves. In this section we are drawing attention to three of them. In order to share a starting point with readers of our publications, it is essential that historians describe the visual sources with which we engage. *Description* forms a bridge between artefacts and accounts and also between writers and readers. When we describe, the most salient features of an object are being pulled into focus, and the foundations for analysis are being laid. In order to develop full arguments, however, it is helpful to probe how an artefact came into being, how it was used, bought and sold, displayed and so on. We are considering its conditions of existence, and also how to explain its significance to others. These tasks may be summed up as *contextualization*, and it is always a matter of judgement what counts as context for any given historical project. These judgements are informed by wider considerations, such as theoretical predispositions and assumptions about human nature as well as by responses to other historical accounts. They are also shaped by our understanding of periods, their coherence and defining characteristics. *Periodization* – the ways in which chunks of time are named and conceptualized – shapes all historical practice. Since different aspects of the past tend to march to different beats, it is not obvious that what works for politics or economics will be fruitful for cultural or visual history. Here then are three practices of the utmost significance for historical work that takes visual sources seriously.

Description

Description can take various forms, from information presented in conventional formats in captions or exhibition labels to condition reports and technical analyses of museum objects to evocative prose and criticism. What all these forms of writing have in common is that they channel attention towards the visual and material characteristics of objects, as well as their effects and associations. They provide the means for weaving visual materials into written accounts.

Information such as the maker's name (if known), title or other designation, date of production, medium, dimensions, holding institution and identifying number enables an understanding of the object under discussion that is at once basic and substantial. Each item in this list is essential, especially when the object in question is being seen through a book illustration or digital image. Together, they provide the basis for establishing its historical, social and economic contexts, material qualities and associated processes of production, a sense of scale, and the present location and institutional setting. These aspects of description can be thought of as analogous with the documentation of a written source: they establish scholarly legitimacy and the sense that readers can access and weigh for themselves the evidence under consideration.

The use of style and period terms in description is a kind of shorthand in which multilayered perceptions can be compressed into a single word or phrase. To refer to a building as 'Georgian' or 'postmodern', for example, is to bundle together more or less specific ideas about architectural theory, aesthetics, the design and use of spaces and ornament, or ways of borrowing from the past. It is valuable in any case to identify and examine the particular elements that contribute to such often-intuitive and unexamined perceptions. Genre terms, too, convey complex information; to describe an image as 'political satire' places it in a particular relationship with a range of other images and with the social milieu and power structures of its time.

Visual artefacts can produce strong impressions that seem direct but emerge from complex qualities. The practice of description gives historians a way of interrogating their own responses, of disciplining their reactions and thus of framing questions about past meanings. Its use depends not only on skills of close observation but also on a kind of thoughtfulness and deliberation about language and its power to evoke visual experiences.

Historical descriptions of surviving visual artefacts, whether in letters or diaries, travel writing, lectures or critical essays, can offer invaluable resources for understanding how such artefacts were received and for the kind of triangulation necessary to posit ideas about the ways of seeing and modes of visual response that shaped the visual culture of a particular time and place. In other cases, only descriptions may survive and provide a kind of access to lost buildings, landscapes or objects.

In reading descriptions as well as in writing them, it is important to recognize that the person doing the describing is always situated with a partial perspective, a set of visual habits and interests, and a perhaps unstated agenda. Descriptions are necessarily selective; they play an active part in building historical arguments but are not neutral. The choices made in description partially determine, as well as enable, evaluation, analysis and narrative.

Contextualization

Context can be thought of as the set of conditions that makes possible the existence of a given piece of visual culture. It also refers to the settings, circumstances and relationships that give meaning to any particular thing. To say that a statement or image has been taken out of context can be synonymous with saying that it has been misunderstood. Thus a large part of the work that historians do in constructing accounts of the past goes towards assembling this broader picture in which meaning is thought to reside. What should be considered as the most significant contexts in any given project is largely determined by approach and by the chronological and geographical boundaries of the topic. A biography or a close study of a single object will weave a picture at a different scale, and with different priorities, from that of a cultural phenomenon over the course of a century or across a broad geographical region.

Some contextual information, such as the identity of an object's maker and its date of production, for example, is so fundamental to the identification of artefacts that we have discussed it as an aspect of *description*. In other cases, relevance is determined by the historian's choices; it is always important to be conscious of how one is making such decisions. Visual sources alone are often of ambiguous significance, and the varied contexts of making, display, reception or use are particularly relevant, since these help to establish conceptual frameworks through which an object's visual characteristics can be interpreted. The text surrounding a drawing or printed image on a page; a group of similar objects with which comparisons can be made; the sources and economic or social value of specialist materials; the setting where an artefact was displayed – who owned it, and who could view it – all of these can provide invaluable points of reference. Which ones are emphasized depends to some extent on the questions being asked and answered and on the type of history being written.

When historians contextualize visual materials in order to use them most effectively as evidence or as the focus of historical research, they are seeking larger structures of meaning that might be found in revealing patterns and connections, such as the emergence of a visual trope across a range of media; broader narratives, of which a particular case might be seen as a telling instance; or causal relationships, which might link phenomena or levels of analysis previously thought of as separate. All these contextualizing moves, and the arguments that they underpin, also operate in the context of other historical writing, with respect to which academic historians are expected to orient their own questions, research and conclusions.

Museum and gallery exhibitions do historical work in part by creating contexts for the objects on display, and thereby bringing to light the connections and differences among them, as well as producing an environment or atmosphere that can in itself be striking and persuasive. The short texts installed on gallery walls often give an indication of the historical contexts, such as places of making or the biographies of artists and their networks of association, that the selected objects bring into play. In these settings, historical contextualization is sometimes also intended to guide viewers' responses to objects that represent viewpoints, actions or systems of power recognized as disturbing or morally unacceptable. Thus context can be deployed in complex manoeuvres that seek to mitigate negative associations that objects in museum collections, or on public display, might have in the present. For example, a cast bronze monument to alumni who had served as Confederate soldiers, made by the Boston sculptor John Wilson, was erected on the Chapel Hill campus of the University of North Carolina in 1913. The monument, later known as Silent Sam, became a site of antiracist demonstrations in the 1960s, and protesters pulled it down in 2018, denouncing it as a white-supremacist symbol. The university has decided that it cannot be reinstalled, but North Carolina law prohibits the removal of monuments on public property; multiple alternatives have been deemed unworkable or unlawful. One solution proposed (but later rejected) by the university's trustees was that the statue be moved to a dedicated 'history centre' that would frame it within the context of the broader history of race at the university. This proposal was consistent with approaches taken to Confederate monuments by universities and municipalities across the American South, which indicate the perceived power of historical context in the public construction of meanings around objects of visual and material culture.

Periodization

Historians customarily divide time into segments in order to define their fields of study and to organize teaching and research. These divisions provide ways of demarcating continuity and change, and are present not only in the time spans addressed by research projects but also in the ways in which history departments in universities are organized and museum objects catalogued and displayed. Some of these units of time, such as centuries, are so familiar as to seem self-evident, although formulations like 'the long eighteenth century' in British history (usually taken to be 1688–1815) indicate some of the difficulties. Periodization makes more- or less-explicit reference to the histories of particular regions or cultures, and it should be borne in mind that the divisions that seem second nature to historians working on European topics, for example, might only bear limited relation to those most relevant for Asian or African histories.

Historical periods vary greatly in length, depending on the type of analysis that they serve. A biography or microhistory might span a single lifetime or far less; a history of social structures or human relationships with geography, in the style of the *Annales* school, might encompass several centuries. The trend towards specialization in historical disciplines has meant that, with some exceptions, the scale of periodization in historical research and writing has become smaller. At the same time, some recent work, including large-scale histories of commodities such as cod or salt, has continued to address longer time spans. In any case, periodization is a central way in which historians define the context of their materials and shape the narratives that they tell.

The names of historical periods can be more or less descriptive of a cultural or political moment; the 'eighteenth century' and the 'age of enlightenment' might refer to roughly the same time span but with very different emphasis. The sense that phenomena that are contemporary with each other share some quality of coherence or connection certainly informs the use of words such as 'baroque', which can serve equally as style terms and period terms. The pathways of such connections are often left unspoken, or expressed in metaphorical terms. Michael Baxandall's phrase 'the period eye' represents one model for specifying the ways in which visual materials (paintings in particular) were embedded within the cultures that produced them. The idea of a 'golden age' is another, in which multiple factors are thought to align in producing visual works that are exemplary of some less tangible but exceptionally generative quality of time, place and people. It is worth noting that 'modernism' and 'modern' function differently from other period terms, in that 'modernism' has a fixed chronological referent while 'modern' is a moving target that often carries implied judgements about progress and innovation.

In art history the boundaries between periods are often marked by the emergence of innovations associated with the work of 'great' artists whose influence is understood to shape their times. In fields concerned with visual matters, they can also be defined by the emergence of new media or technologies, such as oil painting, photography or film. In many historical fields, political events and wars – or the reigns of monarchs – are frequently used to mark boundaries between historical periods, even when they are not directly connected with the topic under discussion. This is in part because events such as the world wars involve whole societies and are justifiably considered major markers. But it can also indicate the existence of a hierarchy among areas of historical study that emerges in practice – politics is more significant than culture, for example – even if it is not always expressed directly.

Practicalities

In this the final section of the book we provide some practical advice to help historians working on and publishing with images. Once the basic principles have been grasped, it should be relatively straightforward, if time-consuming and potentially costly. One such principle is the need to apply for permission to reproduce both photographs of objects and the objects they depict. Note that photographs of any given artefact may be available from a number of sources, so it is worth shopping around. We advocate allowing plenty of time to sort out permissions. It is also worth negotiating with publishers about who pays for what, and asking whether they have any special arrangements with image providers.

All the comments in this section reinforce points made throughout the book about treating words and images together, for example, seeing captions as bridges between illustrations and arguments, and grasping how images make points so that they can be used as effectively as possible in our writings. Thus choosing the images for a publication and selecting their size – whole page, half page and so on – is an integral part of producing a persuasive whole, not a tedious set of tasks best outsourced to someone else. Image placement is crucial for the effectiveness of historical arguments and hence requires authors' close attention. This last part of the book, then, is also about the craft of history.

Using image databases

Museums, libraries, archives and other institutions holding visual materials are often the best resource for images of these materials. Institutions' online collections databases are usually searchable with keywords and with more refined queries. Advanced search options in the British Museum collections online, for example, include people, places, date, object type, subject, culture, period or dynasty, technique, style or school, material, ethnic group, and more. Broad searches will return more relevant results, and in searches that are intended to identify materials at the outset of a project, it's a good idea to try several different terms, getting at the research question from different directions, since cataloguing procedures and priorities vary across institutions. It is worth remembering that images may not be available for all objects in such databases and that search results may not include every relevant object in an organization's holdings.

In general, the institution that houses an object will have the most up-to-date information and photography. Some organizations provide direct downloads through their websites, for which they may charge a fee; some respond to email requests; others licence their images through services such as Artstor or Getty Images, which charge either for subscriptions to their services or per image download. Some of the images available through third-party services may be misleading about colour, for example, because they are scanned from old photographs or slides. Changes in attribution or other updates resulting from new research are more likely to be found in collections databases than on image services' websites. At the same time, some image libraries charge lower fees than holding institutions, for images of the same artefact. If you are looking for images of a particular object and nothing suitable is available online, it is worth contacting the holding institution directly. There may be photography that has not been uploaded, or it may be possible to commission new photography. Curators are extremely knowledgeable about the objects in their care, and they are usually happy to share what they know – an initial enquiry, courteously made and with plenty of lead time, can open up new possibilities for research.

Organizing permissions

If you plan to publish with images, in many cases you must get permission to do so, and this can take time and money. It is best to start the process of requesting such permissions as early as possible. Different types of images have different permission sources, and each type of use (colour or black-and-white reproduction, print or digital format, and so on) requires a specific type of permission. For works in copyright, the artist, artist's estate or publisher likely owns the rights, even if the work itself is in a museum collection. In some cases, such as the chapter by Melissa Renn in this volume, the cost of permissions for relevant images can be so high as to become prohibitive, and descriptions, perhaps in combination with links to websites where materials may be viewed but not downloaded, become a primary means of access. Photographers, image services or holding institutions may claim copyright over new photographs of works that are old enough to have passed into the public domain. Some organizations and services will provide free high-resolution images for personal, research or educational uses but require payment for permission to publish. Others require payment whatever the use. In order to acquire the appropriate type of permission, you will need to be able to supply information about how the image will appear (size; black and white or colour), the format of the publication (print, online or both), the print run and the area of distribution (within a certain country or region, or global). Any credit line supplied by a holding institution or image service must accompany the published image, either in a caption or list of photo credits. Even if you took the image you wish to publish yourself, it's important that you establish whether permission is needed to publish it.

Writing captions

We have based the format for information in captions on the guidelines provided by the College Art Association in the United States, which has also published its position on the fair use of images in academic publications. Other models for captions are available, and the main thing is that details should be as complete and as consistently presented as possible, ideally including the maker's name, a title or brief description of the object, the date, medium, dimensions, holding institution, identifying number, institutional credit line (if required), and image credit.

In the course of research, you may find that comparable information is presented in varying ways, depending on the source. For example, artists' names may have variant spellings, and middle names may be given or not. The title of a single work may change over time, or may exist in multiple versions or languages. Dating may alter or be contested. Media and supports can be described in a number of ways, and dimensions given in varying order and in imperial or metric units and so on. It is good practice to establish consistent forms for all these details, throughout the captions, text and notes of any publication. This requires editorial decisions and the selection of some standard terms and reference works. Journals and publishers often have house styles for the presentation of such information. Institutional credit lines and image credits should not be edited, but rather are presented exactly as they are given by the holding institution or image source.

Remarks in captions provide a valuable space for the kinds of detailed descriptive and contextual work that links images with accompanying prose. Although rare in art-historical writing, their use in this way creates links between levels of analysis and allows greater flexibility in framing the relationships between images and the directions taken by the main text.

Publishing with pictures

The number of pictures included in a book or article may be limited by the publisher, requiring careful prioritization in the selection of illustrations. Black-and-white images are less expensive to print than colour – a consideration that often restricts possibilities in design and production. For digital images, a minimum resolution and file size are needed for good-quality reproduction. Requests for images from institutions or image services should be made with as much information as possible on hand from the publisher, about how digital files will be reproduced and the technical requirements for doing so.

The placement and scale of images go far beyond aesthetic considerations, since they affect the way readers will perceive the materials and how they are integrated into the text. Specific notes will help guide the designer's decisions as the publication is being laid out. In proofreading it is important to consider how relationships of scale and placement are working, to check that captions and images have been matched correctly, and to ensure that the orientation of images is correct and none has been flipped inadvertently.

Conclusions

This volume contributes to a series about 'writing history'; arguably writing itself is among the most complex of historians' skills. One way of honing this skill is to read a great deal of historical writing by others, thereby developing the facility for critically evaluating it and emulating the practices that appeal most consistently. Choices in the construction of prose, decisions about examples and illustrations, the presentation of scholarly apparatus and so on concern taste and preferences that are, at once, intellectual, emotional and also aesthetic, especially when visual culture is the object of analysis.

Every piece of historical writing represents a composite of scholarly practices that ideally come together to produce an effective, persuasive ensemble. The importance of attending to both the holistic effects of such ensembles and the 'nuts and bolts' of their constituent parts has been one of our guiding principles as editors of this book. In an integrative approach to writing visual histories, even the most ostensibly logistical details – those conveyed in captions, for example – carry intellectual and ethical significance. Captions provide essential information for readers, which helps them anchor the image by appreciating its specific attributes and hints at connections with other sources and with key people. In this way they are central to the work of weaving illustrations into arguments. They are also a kind of formal documentation, like citations in notes, through which historians perform accountability to their readers and to the standards of their discipline.

In order to achieve our goals in this volume we have divided it into sections, each one contributing something distinctive. The essays, which sit at the heart of our book, reveal the ways in which six historians have set about 'writing visual histories', making their moves as explicit as possible. It is simply good practice to share both our modes of reasoning and the ways in which sources, whether verbal, visual, material or aural, have been mobilized in making claims about the past. Paying attention to modes of production, checking other accounts for confirmation, understanding digital media and their relationships with historical artefacts, and rigorously evaluating all materials used are vital. Such care comes through in writing and is assisted by conceptual and historiographical awareness, robust and imaginative contextualization, and the meticulous use of visual examples.

The other sections aim to unfold the multiple levels at which historical writing operates simultaneously, separating conceptual, rhetorical and practical threads so that each may be examined in greater depth. What historians are doing when they say they are 'writing' is a complex, multifaceted and often underexamined process. Our discussions of key practices – of description, contextualization and periodization – and of the logistics of sourcing, documenting and publishing with images aim to provide a toolkit for more self-aware practices of writing, reading and reflection. These elements were written partly in response to the essays, and partly with the intention of opening the book outwards, giving entry points into broader conversations.

One of the complexities that writing specifically visual histories presents is the array of fields that have an interest in the matter. We have been clear about the immense value to historians of interdisciplinarity, that is of genuine collaboration and exchanges between scholars whose training and situations may be markedly different, but whose interests and concerns overlap. The discipline of history touches and blends with many forms of knowledge. It is perfectly acceptable to be pragmatic and eclectic when it comes to the precise ways in which we perform interdisciplinarity. It is essential, however, to appreciate the possibilities and to grasp some of the principal features of cognate domains.

Art history, visual culture studies, communication studies and material culture studies are obvious points of reference, as are photography and film studies. Within the discipline of history itself there are many relatively new fields in which visual resources are playing a significant part – women's history, gender studies and transnational history, for example. Then in well-established areas – literary history above all – there have been visual and material turns. The discipline of history as a whole is also much more visually orientated than it was only a few years ago, and 'the visual turn' is a recognized phenomenon there too. At the same time it is important to remember that centuries ago historians used visual and material culture as ways of understanding past times. We track changes while acknowledging the rich historical cultures to which we are heirs. The fields we have just mentioned, whether young or old, have their own lineages and habits of mind; recognizing these helps historians to grasp their usefulness for any given project and to borrow and adopt from them in a responsible manner.

There is a further discipline to be taken account of, namely philosophy, since aesthetics is one of its major branches. It is striking that most historians are not especially engaged with philosophy, the obvious exception being those who write in an explicitly theoretical mode. In those cases they may well be drawing on literary, cultural and social theory as much as from philosophy as this is usually defined, although inevitably there are no watertight distinctions between these categories. However one defines 'theory', only a few of its great exponents have been historians. For those interested in visual culture, however, it is valuable to get a sense of the conceptual frameworks, the forms of argument, the ideas and debates that philosophically minded commentators have generated and deployed. They help us to undertake more rounded forms of interdisciplinary history.

One recurrent theme in this book has been 'integration': between words and images, between description, interpretation and the composition of arguments, between theoretical concerns and empirical materials, and between forms of history that have been seen as separate. The use of visual culture to understand politics, institutions and intercultural encounters are instances that come up in earlier pages. We have separated out some of the key tasks historians address for the sake of accessibility, allowing these tasks to be made explicit and receive their due, but the ultimate goal is to write history in such a way that they are fully integrated, allowing more a vivid sense of the past to emerge, which is based on careful visual analysis and considered historical understanding.

Bibliography

Archival materials

Albert Langen Verlag to László Moholy-Nagy, 24 April 1925, Bauhaus-Archiv, Gropius, Walter (1883–1969), Bauhaus-Verlag Briefwechsel, Mappe 9.

De Heere, Lucas, 'Théâtre de tous les peuples et nations de la terre avec leurs habits et ornemens divers, tant anciens que modernes', 1570/80, University of Ghent Library, HS 2466.

Ehrenspiegel des Hauses Österreich, Augsburg, 1555/59, Bayerische Staatsbibliothek, Munich, Cgm. 895.

Gropius, Walter, to Lia Schaedel, 30 July 1925, Bauhaus-Archiv, Gropius, Walter (1883–1969), Bauhaus-Verlag Briefwechsel, Mappe 11.

Grover, Allen, to Henry R. Luce, 23 November 1960, photocopy from Time Inc. Archives, *Life* War Art Files, US Army Center for Military History.

'Kostümbuch – Kopie nach dem Trachtenbuch des Christoph Weiditz', c. 1600, Bayerische Staatsbibliothek, Munich, Cod.icon. 342.

'Kostüme der Männer und Frauen in Augsburg und Nürnberg, Deutschland, Europa, Orient und Afrika', 4th quarter 16th c., Bayerische Staatsbibliothek, Munich, Cod.icon. 341.

'Kostüme und Sittenbilder des 16. Jahrhunderts aus West- und Osteuropa, Orient, der Neuen Welt und Afrika', 4th quarter 16th c., Bayerische Staatsbibliothek, Munich, Cod.icon. 361.

Lea, Tom, to J. Frank Dobie, 20 June 1943, C. L. Sonnichsen Special Collections, The University of Texas at El Paso Library.

Lea, Tom, to J. Frank Dobie, 30 October 1944, C. L. Sonnichsen Special Collections, The University of Texas at El Paso Library.

Letter of defamation against Landgrave Louis of Hesse, 1438, Institut für Stadtgeschichte, Frankfurt am Main, Reichssachen I, 3605.

'The *Life* Collection of War Art', n.d. Box 83, Daniel Longwell Papers, Columbia University Rare Book and Manuscript Library, MS 0798.

Longwell, Daniel, to Andrew Heiskell, 15 October 1948, Box 28, Daniel Longwell Papers, Columbia University Rare Book and Manuscript Library, MS 0798.

Longwell, Daniel, to Henry R. Luce, 18 February 1943, Box 29, Daniel Longwell Papers, Columbia University Rare Book and Manuscript Library, MS 0798.

Longwell, Daniel, to Henry R. Luce, 9 January 1948, Box 29, Daniel Longwell Papers, Columbia University Rare Book and Manuscript Library, MS 0798.

Longwell, Daniel, to Irene Saint, 24 April 1968, Box 80, Daniel Longwell Papers, Columbia University Rare Book and Manuscript Library, MS 0798.

Martin, Fletcher, 'Press Release', War Art Exhibition 1943 Folder, Office of the Secretary Records, The Metropolitan Museum of Art Archives.

Moholy-Nagy, László, to Mart Stamm, 9 September 1925, Bauhaus-Archiv, Gropius, Walter (1883–1969), Bauhaus-Verlag Briefwechsel, Mappe 11.

Plea and Memoranda Rolls, City of London, no. 26, 1381–3, London Metropolitan Archives, CLA/024/01/02/026, membr. 2b.

'Press Release', 4 July 1945, War against Japan Folder, Office of the Secretary Records, The Metropolitan Museum of Art Archives.

Puma, Fernando, Papers, Archives of American Art, Smithsonian Institution.

Sugarman, Celia, 'Transcript of Interview of Daniel Longwell for Time Inc.', 6 March 1958, Box 26, Daniel Longwell Papers, Columbia University Rare Book and Manuscript Library, MS 0798.
Thompson, Edward K., to Daniel Longwell, 19 June 1946, John Shaw Billings, Time-Life-Fortune Collection, South Caroliniana Library, University of South Carolina.
'Trachtenbuech / Darinen viller Volckher vnnd Nationen Klaidung', 1580, Lipperheidesche Kostümbibliothek, Berlin, Lipp Aa 20.
'We Challenge War Art' and 'Art of the Armed Forces', 1944, Box 20, Folders 2 and 3, San Francisco Museum of Modern Art Exhibition Records, SFMOMA Library and Archives, ARCH.EXH.001.
Weiditz, Christoph, 'Trachtenbuch', 1530–40, Germanisches Nationalmuseum, Nuremberg, Hs 22474.

Published sources

Abrahams, Philippa, *Beneath the Surface: The Making of Paintings* (London, 2008).
Académie des inscriptions et belles-lettres (ed.), *Ordonnances des roys de France de la troisième race*, 21 vols (Paris, 1729).
Adams, CY H. Garland, USNR, Y2/c C. Roger Evans, USNR, Y2/c Walter L. Good, USNR, Advanced Base Supply Training Unit, Norfolk Virginia, letter to the editors, *Life*, 2 July 1945, 4.
'Aegean Actions: *Life* Artist Perlin Paints the War in the Greek Sea', *Life*, 26 February 1945, 47–54.
Ailes, Adrian, 'Heraldry as Markers of Identity in the Medieval Literature: Fact or Fiction', in Catalina Gîrbea, Laurent Hablot and Raluca L. Radulescu (eds), *Marqueurs d'identité dans la littérature médiévale* (Turnhout, 2014), 181–91.
Albinson, A. Cassandra, et al., *Thomas Lawrence: Regency Power & Brilliance* (London and New Haven, 2010).
Allsdorf, Bridget, *Fellow Men: Fantin-Latour and the Problem of the Group in Nineteenth-Century French Painting* (Princeton, 2013).
'The Arming of America: Industry's Vital Effort Introduces *Life*'s Issue on National Defense', *Life*, 7 July 1941, 17.
Arnoldi, Johann von, *Miscellaneen aus der Diplomatik und Geschichte* (Marburg, 1798).
Aurell, Martin, 'Honour, Sense of', in André Vauchez (ed.), *Encyclopedia of the Middle Ages* (Oxford, 2005), 689.
Baillie, Matthew, *The Works of Matthew Baillie, M.D.*, 2 vols (London, 1825).
Baker, Malcolm, and Brenda Richardson, *A Grand Design: The Art of the Victoria and Albert Museum* (London, 1997).
Baldwin, Hanson W., *The Navy at War: Paintings and Drawings by Combat Artists* (New York, 1943).
Bale, John, 'Bale's Chronicle', in Ralph Flenley (ed.), *Six Town Chronicles of England* (Oxford, 1911), 114–52.
Bann, Stephen, et al., *Painting History: Delaroche and Lady Jane Grey* (London, 2010).
Barrell, John, *The Political Theory of Painting from Reynolds to Hazlitt* (New Haven, 1986).

Barringer, T. J., *Men at Work: Art and Labour in Victorian Britain* (New Haven and London, 2005).
Barthes, Roland, 'The Photographic Message', in Stephen Heath (ed. and trans.), *Image, Music, Text* (London, 1977), 15–31.
Bassett, Steven (ed.), *Death in Towns: Urban Responses to the Dying and the Dead* (Leicester, 1992).
Baughman, James L., 'Who Read *Life*?: The Circulation of America's Favorite Magazine', in Erika Lee Doss (ed.), *Looking at 'Life' Magazine* (Washington, DC, 2001), 41–51.
Bauten der Arbeit und des Verkehrs aus deutscher Gegenwart, 2nd imprint (Königstein im Taunus and Leipzig, 1926; 1st edition, 1925).
Bauten der Gemeinschaft aus deutscher Gegenwart (Königstein im Taunus and Leipzig, 1928).
Baxandall, Michael, *Painting and Experience in Fifteenth-Century Italy: A Primer in the Social History of Pictorial Style*, 2nd edn (Oxford and New York, 1988).
Bedos-Rezak, Brigitte, 'Medieval Identity: A Sign and a Concept', *American Historical Review*, 105/5 (2000): 1489–533.
Bedos-Rezak, Brigitte, *When Ego Was Imago: Signs of Identity in the Middle Ages* (Leiden and Boston, 2011).
Belting, Hans, *An Anthropology of Images: Picture, Medium, Body* (Princeton and Oxford, 2014).
'The Bengal Famine', *Life*, 22 November 1943, 16–20.
Benjamin, Walter, 'The Author as Producer', in Victor Burgin (ed.), *Thinking Photography* (Basingstoke, 1982), 15–31.
Benjamin, Walter, *Illuminations* (London, 1970).
Bennett, Tony, et al. (eds), *New Keywords: A Revised Vocabulary of Culture and Society* (London, 1995).
Berger, Stefan, 'Comparative History', in Stefan Berger, Heiko Feldner and Kevin Passmore (eds), *Writing History: Theory and Practice*, 2nd edn (London, 2010), 187–205.
Bindman, David, *Hogarth and His Times* (London, 1997).
Biscoglio, Frances M., 'Unspun Heroes: Iconography of the Spinning Woman in the Middle Ages', *Journal of Medieval and Renaissance Studies*, 25/2 (1995): 163–76.
Blockmans, Wim, and A. Janse (eds), *Showing Status: Representation of Social Positions in the Late Middle Ages* (Turnhout, 1999).
Boas Hall, Marie, *All Scientists Now: The Royal Society in the Nineteenth Century* (Cambridge, 1984).
Boissard, Jean-Jacques, *Habitus Variarum Orbis Gentium. Habitz de nations estranges* (Cologne, 1581).
Boone, Marc, Élodie Lecuppre-Desjardin and Jean-Pierre Sosson (eds), *Le verbe, l'image et les représentations de la société urbaine au Moyen Âge* (Antwerp, 2002).
Boorde, Andrew, and F. J. Furnivall (eds), *The Fyrst Boke of the Introduction of Knowledge Made by Andrew Borde, of Physycke Doctor: A Compendyous Regyment; Or, A Dyetary of Helth Made in Mountpyllier* (London, 1870).
Bourdieu, Pierre, *Distinction: A Social Critique of the Judgment of Taste*, trans. by Richard Nice (Cambridge, MA, 2002).
Boytsov, Mikhail A., 'Ghostly Knights: Kings' Funerals in Fourteenth-Century Europe and the Emergence of an International Style', in Joëlle Rollo-Koster (ed.), *Death in Medieval Europe: Death Scripted and Death Choreographed* (London and New York, 2017), 149–63.

Brewer, John, 'Commercialisation and Politics', in Neil McKendrick, John Brewer and J. H. Plumb (eds), *The Birth of a Consumer Society: The Commercialisation of Eighteenth-Century England* (London, 1982), 197–262.

Brewer, John, 'Cultural Production', in Brian Allen (ed.), *Towards a Modern Art World* (New Haven, 1995), 7–27.

Brewer, John, *Party Ideology and Popular Politics at the Accession of George III* (Cambridge, 1976).

Brewer, John, 'The Wilkites and the Law, 1763–74', in John Brewer and John Styles (eds), *An Ungovernable People: The English and Their Law in the Seventeenth and Eighteenth Centuries* (London, 1980), 128–71.

Bridgeman, Jane, 'The Origins of Dress History and Cesare Vecellio's "pourtraits of attire"', *Costume*, 44/1 (2010): 37–45.

Brie, Friedrich (ed.), *The Brut or The Chronicles of England*, 2 vols (London, 1906).

Briggs, Asa, *A History of the Royal College of Physicians of London: Volume Four* (Oxford, 2005).

Brunet, Jean Louis (ed.), *Songe du Vergier* (Paris, 1731).

Bry, Gerhard, assisted by Charlotte Boschan, *Wages in Germany, 1871–1945* (Princeton, 1960).

Burgin, Victor (ed.), *Thinking Photography* (London, 1982).

Burke, Peter, *Eyewitnessing: The Uses of Images as Historical Evidence* (London, 2001).

Butterfield, Herbert, *George III and the Historians* (London, 1957).

Bylebyl, Jerome, *William Harvey and His Age: The Professional and Social Context of the Discovery of the Circulation* (Baltimore and London, 1979).

Calder, Barnabas, *Denys Lasdun's Royal College of Physicians: A Monumental Act of Faith* (London, 2008).

Calvi, Giulia, 'Cultures of Space: Costume Books, Maps, and Clothing between Europe and Japan (Sixteenth through Nineteenth Centuries)', *I Tatti Studies in the Italian Renaissance*, 20/2 (2017): 331–63.

Camille, Michael, 'Before the Gaze: The Internal Senses and Late Medieval Practices of Seeing', in Robert S. Nelson (ed.), *Visuality Before and Beyond the Renaissance: Seeing as Others Saw* (Cambridge and New York, 2000), 197–223.

Campbell, Mungo, and Nathan Flis (eds), *William Hunter and the Anatomy of the Modern Museum* (New Haven, London and Glasgow, 2018).

Canning, Kathleen, Kerstin Barndt and Kristin McGuire (eds), *Weimar Publics, Weimar Subjects: Rethinking the Political Culture of Germany in the 1920s* (New York, 2010).

Caro Baroja, Julio, 'Honour and Social Status', in J. G. Peristiany (ed.), *Honour and Shame: The Values of Mediterranean Society* (London, 1965), 79–137.

Cheesman, Clive, 'Heraldry', in *The International Encyclopedia of Communication* (Malden, 2008), https://doi.org/10.1111/b.9781405131995.2008.x.

Cherry, Bridget, and Niklaus Pevsner, *London 3 North West (The Buildings of England)* (London, 1999), reprint with revisions of 1991 edition.

Cherry, John, 'Heraldry as Decoration in the Thirteenth Century', in W. Mark Ormrod (ed.), *England in the Thirteenth Century: Proceedings of the 1989 Harlaxton Symposium* (Stamford, 1991), 123–34.

Chinthapalli, Krishna, *Physicians and Global Health* (London, 2018).

Christie, Ian R., *Wilkes, Wyvill and Reform: The Parliamentary Reform Movement in British Politics, 1760–1785* (London, 1962).

Clark, Sir George, *A History of the Royal College of Physicians of London*, 2 vols (Oxford, 1964–6).

Clarke, Graham, *The Photograph* (Oxford, 1997).
Cline, Howard F., 'Hernando Cortés and the Aztec Indians in Spain', *Quarterly Journal of the Library of Congress*, 26/2 (1969): 70–90.
Coates, Robert M., 'The Art Galleries: Reports from the Front', *New Yorker*, 28 August 1943, 57.
Cockerham, William, *Medical Sociology*, 12th edn (Boston, 2012).
Cogdell, Christina, 'Theater of War', in Donald Albrecht (ed.), *Norman Bel Geddes Designs America* (New York, 2012), 316–39.
Cohen, Esther, 'Symbols of Culpability and the Universal Language of Justice: The Ritual of Public Executions in Late Medieval Europe', *History of European Ideas*, 11 (1989): 407–16.
Cohn, Samuel Kline, *Popular Protest in Late Medieval Europe: Italy, France and Flanders* (Manchester, 2004).
Colley, Linda, *Britons: Forging the Nation, 1707–1837* (London, 1992).
Collyer, Fran (ed.), *The Palgrave Handbook of Social Theory in Health, Illness, and Medicine* (Basingstoke and New York, 2015).
Compston, Alastair, *Simples and Rarities Suitable and Honourable to the College* (London, 2018).
Conlin, Jonathan, '"At the expense of the public": The 1762 Signpainters' Exhibition and the Public Sphere', *Eighteenth-Century Studies*, 36/1 (2002): 1–21.
Conlin, Jonathan, 'High Art and Low Politics: A New Perspective on John Wilkes', *Huntington Library Quarterly*, 64/3/4 (2001): 356–81.
Conrads, Marian, 'Het Theatre van Lucas d'Heere: Een kostuumhistorisch onderzoek', PhD diss., University of Utrecht, 2006.
Cook, Harold, *The Decline of the Old Medical Regime in Stuart London* (Ithaca and London, 1986).
Cooke, A. M., *A History of the Royal College of Physicians: Volume Three* (Oxford, 1972).
'Coral Sea: Norman Bel Geddes' Model Reenacts Naval Battle', *Life*, 25 May 1942, 21–5.
Corfield, P. J., *Power and the Professions in Britain, 1700–1850* (London, 1995).
Cortés, Hernán, *Letters from Mexico*, ed. and trans. by Anthony Pagden (New Haven and London, 2001).
Crane, Aimée, *Art in the Armed Forces* (New York, 1944).
Cubitt, Geoffrey, *History and Memory* (Manchester, 2007).
Cuvelier, Jean, *Chronique de Bertrand du Guesclin*, ed. by Ernest Charrière, 2 vols (Paris, 1839).
Daston, Lorraine (ed.), *Things That Talk: Object Lessons from Art and Science* (New York, 2004).
Daston, Lorraine, and Elizabeth Lunbeck (eds), *Histories of Scientific Observation* (Chicago and London, 2011).
Daston, Lorraine, and Katharine Park, *Wonders and the Order of Nature, 1150–1750* (New York, 1998).
Davenport, Geoffrey, et al. (eds), *The Royal College of Physicians and Its Collections: An Illustrated History* (London, 2001).
Davies, Surekha, *Renaissance Ethnography and the Invention of the Human: New Worlds, Maps and Monsters* (Cambridge, 2016).
Davis, Natalie Zemon, 'Women on Top', in Natalie Zemon Davis (ed.), *Society and Culture in Early Modern France: Eight Essays* (Stanford, 1975), 124–51.
Day, J. F. R., 'Buried "the King's Trew Subject": The Late Medieval English Heraldic Funeral in Decline', *Coat of Arms*, new ser., 13 (2000): 233–43.

'Defense Paintings: *Life* Recruits Major Artists', *Life*, 7 July 1941, 60–4.
Defert, Daniel, 'Un genre ethnographique profane au XVIe siècle: Les livres d'habits; Un essai d'ethno-icongraphie', in Britta Rupp-Eisenreich (ed.), *Histoires de l'anthropologie: XVIe–XIXe siècles* (Paris, 1984), 25–41.
Delbourgo, James, *Collecting the World: The Life and Curiosity of Hans Sloane* (London, 2017).
Desprez, François, *Recueil de la diversité des habits, qui sont de présent en usage, tant es pays d'Europe, Asie, Affrique & isles sauvages, le tout fait après le naturel* (Paris, 1562).
Díaz del Castillo, Bernal, *The True History of the Conquest of New Spain: Volume 4*, ed. by Genaro García and trans. by Alfred Percival Maudslay (London, 1908).
Dickinson, H. T., *Liberty and Property: Political Ideology in Eighteenth-Century Britain* (London, 1977).
Dickinson, H. T., 'Radicals and Reformers in the Age of Wilkes and Wyvill', in Jeremy Black (ed.), *British Politics and Society from Walpole to Pitt* (London, 1990), 123–46.
Digby, Anne, *Making a Medical Living: Doctors and Their Patients in the English Market for Medicine, 1720–1911* (Cambridge, 1994).
Doderer-Winkler, Melanie, *Magnificent Entertainments: Temporary Architecture for Georgian Festivals* (New Haven, 2013).
Dolphin, Erika, *Gustave Doré (1832–1883): Master of Imagination* (Paris, 2014).
Donald, Diana, *The Age of Caricature: Satirical Prints in the Reign of George III* (New Haven and London, 1996).
Doss, Erika, 'Looking at *Life*: Rethinking America's Favorite Magazine, 1936–1972', in Erika Doss (ed.), *Looking at 'Life' Magazine* (Washington, DC, 2001), 1–3.
Driver, A. H., *Catalogue of Engraved Portraits in the Royal College of Physicians of London* (London, 1952).
Droste, Magdalena, *Bauhaus 1919–1933* (Cologne, 2019).
Dumolyn, Jan, Jelle Haemers, Rafael Oliva Herrer and Vincent Challet (eds), *The Voices of the People in Late Medieval Europe: Communication and Popular Politics* (Turnhout, 2014).
Edgerton, Samuel Y., *Pictures and Punishment: Art and Criminal Prosecution during the Florentine Renaissance* (Ithaca and London, 1985).
Edwards, Elizabeth, 'Photographic Uncertainties: Between Evidence and Reassurance', *History and Anthropology*, 25/2 (2013): 171–88.
Edwards, Elizabeth, 'Photography and the Business of Doing History', in Gil Pasternak (ed.), *Handbook of Photography Studies* (London, 2020), 170–86.
Edwards, Elizabeth, *Raw Histories: Photographs, Anthropology and Museums* (Oxford, 2001).
The Family of Man (New York, 1955).
Findlen, Paula, *Possessing Nature: Museums, Collecting, and Scientific Culture in Early Modern Italy* (Berkeley and London, 1994).
Fineman, Mia, *Faking It: Manipulated Photography before Photoshop* (New Haven and London, 2012).
Foucault, Michel, *The Archaeology of Knowledge*, trans. A. M. Sheridan Smith (London, 2002; first edition, 1969).
Fox, Daniel, and Christopher Lawrence, *Photographing Medicine: Images and Power in Britain and America since 1840* (New York, 1988).
Freedberg, David, 'The Fear of Art: How Censorship Becomes Iconoclasm', *Social Research*, 83/1 (2016): 67–99.

Freedberg, David, *Iconoclasts and Their Motives* (Maarssen, 1985).
Freedberg, David, *The Power of Images: Studies in the History and Theory of Response* (Chicago, 1989).
Freind, John, *The History of Physic from the Time of Galen, to the Beginning of the Sixteenth Century, Chiefly with Regard to Practice: In a Discourse Written to Doctor Mead*, 2 vols (London, 1725–6).
Froissart, Jean, *The Chronicles of Froissart*, ed. by George Campbell Macaulay, trans. by John Bourchier Berners (London, 1899).
Froissart, Jean, *Les Chroniques de Sire Jean Froissart*, ed. by J. A. C. Buchon, 3 vols (Paris, 1836).
Froning, Richard (ed.), *Frankfurter Chroniken und annalistische Aufzeichnungen des Mittelalters* (Frankfurt am Main, 1884).
Galbraith, Vivian H. (ed.), *The Anonimalle Chronicle, 1333–1381* (Manchester, 1927).
Gameson, Richard (ed.), *The Early Medieval Bible: Its Production, Decoration, and Use* (Cambridge, 1994).
Garlick, Kenneth, *Sir Thomas Lawrence: A Complete Catalogue of the Oil Paintings* (Oxford, 1989).
Gatrell, Vic, *City of Laughter: Sex and Satire in Eighteenth-Century London* (London, 2006).
Gell, Alfred, *Art and Agency* (Cambridge, 1998).
Gervais, Thierry, 'Reaching beyond the Index: The Publication of News Photographs', in Sabine T. Kriebel and Andrés Mario Zervigón (eds), *Photography and Doubt* (London and New York, 2017), 81–101.
Giedion, Siegfried S., 'Das Bauhaus und seine Zeit', in Leonhard Reinisch (ed.), *Die Zeit ohne Eigenschaften: Eine Bilanz der zwanziger Jahre* (Stuttgart, 1961).
Gilmour, Ian, *Riots, Risings and Revolution: Governance and Violence in Eighteenth-Century England* (London, 1992).
Gittings, Clare, *Death, Burial and the Individual in Early Modern England* (London, 1984).
Götze, Ludwig, 'Ein Scheltbrief des Grafen Johann III. von Nassau-Dillenburg gegen den Herzog Johann von Bayern und Holland', *Monatsschrift für die Geschichte Westdeutschlands*, 4 (1878): 63–73.
Greig, Hannah, *The Beau Monde: Fashionable Society in Georgian London* (Oxford, 2013).
Griffiths, Antony, *The Print before Photography: An Introduction to European Printmaking, 1550–1820* (London, 2016).
Griffiths, Antony, *Prints and Printmaking: An Introduction to the History and Techniques*, 2nd edn (London, 1996).
Grischkowsky, Thomas, 'FOUND! Photographs from MoMA's 1944 *Norman Bel Geddes' War Maneuver Models* Exhibition', *Inside/Out* [blog], (25 February 2015), https://www. moma.org/explore/inside_out/2015/02/25/found-photographs-from-momas-1944-norman-bel-geddes-war-maneuver-models-exhibition/ (accessed 26 June 2019).
Groebner, Valentin, *Defaced: The Visual Culture of Violence in the Late Middle Ages* (London, 2009).
Grössinger, Christa, *Picturing Women in Late Medieval and Renaissance Art* (Manchester, 1997).
Gruskin, A. D., *War in Italy by Edward Laning* (New York, 1945).
Habich, Georg, 'Studien zur deutschen Renaissancemedaille. IV. Christoph Weiditz', *Jahrbuch der Königlich Preussischen Kunstsammlungen*, 34 (1913): 1–35.

Hablot, Laurent, 'Le bris des armes: L'iconoclasme héraldique dans la société médiévale', in Pascale Charron, Marc Gil and Ambre Vilain (eds), *La pensée du regard: Études d'histoire de l'art du Moyen Âge offertes à Christian Heck* (Turnhout, 2016), 181–91.

Hablot, Laurent, 'Emblèmes outragés, corps ravagés: L'utilisation de l'emblématique dans les châtiments à la fin du Moyen Age', in Lydie Bodiou, Véronique Mehl and Myriam Soria (eds), *Corps outragés, corps ravagés de l'Antiquité au Moyen Age* (Turnhout, 2011), 139–52.

Hablot, Laurent, 'Heraldic Imagery, Definition, and Principles', in Colum P. Hourihane (ed.), *The Routledge Companion to Medieval Iconography* (London, 2017), 386–98.

Hablot, Laurent, '"Sens dessoubz dessus": Le blason de la trahison', in Maïté Billoré and Myriam Soria (eds), *La trahison au moyen âge: De la monstruosité au crime politique* (Rennes, 2009), 331–52.

Hablot, Laurent, '"Ubi Armae Ibi Princeps": Medieval Emblematics as the Real Presence of the Prince', in Frédérique Lachaud and Michael A. Penman (eds), *Absentee Authority across Medieval Europe* (Woodbridge, 2017), 37–55.

Hakluyt, Richard, *The Original Writings of Correspondence of the Two Richard Hakluyts: Volume One*, ed. by E. G. R. Taylor (London, 1935).

Hale, David George, *The Body Politic: A Political Metaphor in Renaissance English Literature* (The Hague and Paris, 1971).

Hanson, Craig, *The English Virtuoso: Art, Medicine, and Antiquarianism in the Age of Empiricism* (Chicago and London, 2009).

Hargraves, Matthew, *Candidates for Fame: The Society of Artists of Great Britain, 1760–1791* (New Haven, 2005).

Harris, Jonathan, *Art History: The Key Concepts* (London, 2006).

Hartmann, Heiko, 'Heraldry', in Albrecht Classen (ed.), *Handbook of Medieval Studies: Terms – Methods – Trends; Volume One* (Berlin and New York, 2010), 619–24.

Harvey, Karen (ed.), *History and Material Culture: A Student's Guide to Approaching Alternative Sources*, 2nd edn (London, 2017).

Harvey, William, *The Circulation of the Blood and Other Writings* (London, 1963).

Harvey, William, *Exercitatio Anatomica de Motu Cordis et Sanguinis in Animalibus* (Frankfurt, 1628).

Harvey, William, *Opera Omnia* (London, 1766).

Haslam, Fiona, *From Hogarth to Rowlandson: Medicine in Art in Eighteenth-Century Britain* (Liverpool, 1996).

Hatt, Michael, and Charlotte Klonk, *Art History: A Critical Introduction to its Methods* (Manchester, 2006).

Haworth-Booth, Mark, *Photography: An Independent Art* (London, 1997).

Heard, Kate, 'The Print Room at Queen Charlotte's Cottage', *British Art Journal*, 13/3 (2012): 53–60.

Heiting, Manfred, and Roland Jaeger (eds), *Autopsie: Deutschsprachige Fotobücher 1918–1945*, 2 vols (Göttingen, 2012–4).

Hepburn, A. J., 'Introduction', in Hanson W. Baldwin and Griffith B. Coale (eds), *The Navy at War: Paintings and Drawings by Combat Artists* (New York, 1943), 6.

Hersey, John, 'Experience by Battle', *Life*, 27 December 1943, 48–84.

Hill Boone, Elizabeth, 'Seeking Indianness: Christoph Weiditz, the Aztecs, and Feathered Amerindians', *Colonial Latin American Review*, 26/1 (2017): 39–61.

Hills, Helen (ed.), *Rethinking the Baroque* (Farnham, 2011).

Hoock, Holger, *The King's Artists: The Royal Academy of Arts and the Politics of British Culture 1760–1840* (Oxford, 2003).
Hopkins, David, *After Modern Art: 1945–2017*, 2nd edn (Oxford, 2018).
Hori, Hikari, *Promiscuous Media: Film and Visual Culture in Imperial Japan, 1926–1945* (Ithaca, 2018).
'*Hornet*'s Last Day: Tom Lea Paints Death of a Great Carrier', *Life*, 2 August 1943, 42–9.
'How the Russians Took Orel: Models by Norman Bel Geddes Show Red Tactics in Winning Their First Big Summer Victories', *Life*, 16 August 1943, 21.
Hudson, A. Clark, letter to the editors, *Life*, 21 December 1942, 13.
Hunter, Michael, *Establishing the New Science: The Experience of the Early Royal Society* (Woodbridge, 1989).
Hunter, Michael, with Jim Bennett, *The Image of Restoration Science: The Frontispiece to Thomas Sprat's History of the Royal Society (1667)* (London, 2017).
Hupp, Otto, *Scheltbriefe und Schandbilder: Ein Rechtsbehelf aus dem 15. und 16. Jahrhundert* (Munich and Regensburg, 1930).
'India', *Life*, 30 April 1945, 60–1.
'An Indian Village: Millard Sheets Paints an Ancient Community', *Life*, 21 January 1946, 80–2.
'Italy: Two Artists Paint War and Its Wreckage', *Life*, 17 September 1945, 69–76.
Jaeger, R., 'Vom Neuen zum nationalsozialistischen Bauen: Fotoillustrierte Architekturbücher der Zwischenkriegszeit', in Manfred Heiting and Roland Jaeger (eds), *Autopsie: Deutschsprachige Fotobücher 1918–1945; Volume Two* (Göttingen, 2014), 378–409.
James, Mervyn Evans, 'English Politics and the Concept of Honour, 1485–1642', in Mervyn Evans James (ed.), *Society, Politics and Culture: Studies in Early Modern England* (Cambridge, 1986), 308–415.
Jaritz, Gerhard, 'Images', in Albrecht Classen (ed.), *Handbook of Medieval Studies: Terms – Methods – Trends; Volume Two* (Berlin and New York, 2010), 1520–3.
Jeffrey, Ian, *Photography: A Concise History* (London, 1981).
Jewell, Edward Alden, 'War Art: Weighing New Show at Metropolitan', *New York Times*, 22 August 1943.
Jones, Ann Rosalind, 'Habits, Holdings, Heterologies: Populations in Print in a 1562 Costume Book', *Yale French Studies*, 110 (2006): 92–121.
Jones, Ann Rosalind, '"Worn in Venice and throughout Italy": The Impossible Present in Cesare Vecellio's Costume Books', *Journal of Medieval and Early Modern Studies*, 39/3 (2009): 511–44.
Jones, Evan John (ed. and trans.), *Medieval Heraldry: Some Fourteenth Century Heraldic Works* (Cardiff, 1943).
Jordanova, Ludmilla, *The Look of the Past: Visual and Material Evidence in Historical Practice* (Cambridge, 2012).
Jordanova, Ludmilla, *Nature Displayed: Gender, Science and Medicine 1760–1820* (London, 1999).
Jordanova, Ludmilla, *Physicians and Their Images* (London, 2018).
Jordanova, Ludmilla, 'Portraits, People and Things: Richard Mead and Medical Identity', *History of Science*, 61 (2003): 293–313.
Jordanova, Ludmilla, 'Science, Memory and Relics in Britain', in Marco Beretta et al. (eds), *Savant Relics: Brains and Remains of Scientists* (Sagamore Beach, 2016), 157–81.
Jovita Baber, R., 'Empire, Indians, and the Negotiation for the Status of City in Tlaxcala, 1521–1550', in Susan Kellogg and Ethelia Ruiz Medrano (eds),

Negotiation within Domination: New Spain's Indian Pueblos Confront the Spanish State (Boulder, 2010), 19–44.
Keen, Maurice Hugh, *Chivalry* (New Haven, 2005).
Keynes, Geoffrey, *The Life of William Harvey* (Oxford, 1966).
Keynes, Geoffrey, *The Portraiture of William Harvey* (London, 1949).
Kinross, Robert, *Unjustified Texts: Perspectives on Typography* (London, 2002).
Klein, Bernhard, 'Oroonoko and the Mapping of Africa', in Jorge Bastos da Silva and Miguel Ramalhete Gomes (eds), *English Literature and the Disciplines of Knowledge, Early Modern to Eighteenth Century: A Trade for Light* (Leiden and Boston, 2017), 25–55.
Klish, Renée, 'Art of the American Soldier: Documenting Military History through Artists' Eyes and in Their Own Words', *U.S. Army Center of Military History* [electronic publication] (2011), http://www.history.army.mil/html/books/epubs/art_of_the_american_soldier/army_of_am_soldier.pdf (accessed 26 June 2019).
Knighton, Henry, *Chronicon Henrici Knighton, vel Cnitthon, monachi Lycestrensis*, ed. by Joseph Rawson Lumby, 2 vols (Cambridge, 1889).
Kuh, Katharine, 'The War and the Visual Arts', *Antioch Review*, 6/3 (1946): 398–409.
Kuin, Roger, 'Colours of Continuity: The Heraldic Funeral', in Nigel Ramsay (ed.), *Heralds and Heraldry in Shakespeare's England* (Donington, 2014), 166–89.
Kunzle, David, 'World Upside Down: The Iconography of a European Broadsheet Type', in Barbara A. Babcock (ed.), *The Reversible World: Symbolic Inversion in Art and Society* (Ithaca, 1978), 39–94.
Kuske, Bruno, *Quellen zur Geschichte des Kölner Handels und Verkehrs im Mittelalter*, 4 vols (Bonn, 1934).
Ladd, Brian, *Urban Planning and Social Order in Germany* (Cambridge, MA, 1990).
Lane, Anthony, 'Spike Lee Does Battle with "BlacKkKlansman"', *New Yorker* [website], 9 August 2018, https://www.newyorker.com/magazine/2018/08/20/spike-lee-does-battle-with-blackkklansman (accessed 24 January 2019).
Lane, Barbara Miller, *Architecture and Politics in Germany, 1918–1945* (Cambridge, MA, 1985; first edition, 1968).
Lanfranchi, Giovanni B., and Robert Rollinger (eds), *The Body of the King: The Staging of the Body of the Institutional Leader from Antiquity to Middle Ages in East and West* (Padua, 2016).
Lang, Beryl (ed.), *The Concept of Style*, rev. and exp. edn (Ithaca, 1987).
Lanker, Brian, and Nicole Newnham, *They Drew Fire: Combat Artists of World War II* (New York, 2000).
Latour, Bruno, *Reassembling the Social: An Introduction to Actor-Network-Theory* (Oxford, 2005).
Lawrence, Christopher, 'Medical Minds, Surgical Bodies: Corporeality and the Doctors', in Christopher Lawrence and Steven Shapin (eds), *Science Incarnate: Historical Embodiments of Natural Knowledge* (Chicago and London, 1998), 156–201.
Lea, Tom, *A Picture Gallery* (Boston, 1968).
Lea, Tom, *The Southwest: It's Where I Live* (Dallas, 1992).
Leitch, Stephanie, *Mapping Ethnography in Early Modern Germany: New Worlds in Print Culture* (Basingstoke, 2010).
Lentz, Matthias, 'Defamatory Pictures and Letters in Late Medieval Germany: The Visualisation of Disorder and Infamy', *Medieval History Journal*, 3/1 (2000): 139–60.

Lentz, Matthias, *Konflikt, Ehre, Ordnung: Untersuchungen zu den Schmähbriefen und Schandbildern des späten Mittelalters und der frühen Neuzeit (ca. 1350 bis 1600)* (Hannover, 2004).
Letters to the editors, *Life*, 3 July 1944, 3.
Letters to the editors, *Life*, 2 July 1945, 2–4.
'*Life* Goes to Futurama', *Life*, 5 June 1939, 79–85.
'*Life's* Artists Record a World at War', *Life*, 30 April 1945, 42–67.
Life's New War Art Exhibition No. 9 (Dayton, 1946).
Lippincott, Louise, 'Expanding on Portraiture: The Market, the Public, and the Hierarchy of Genres in Eighteenth-Century Britain', in Ann Bermingham and John Brewer (eds), *The Consumption of Culture, 1600–1800: Image, Object, Text* (London, 1995), 75–88.
Litten, Julian, *The English Way of Death: The Common Funeral since 1450* (London, 2002).
López de Gómara, Francisco, *Cortés: The Life of the Conqueror by His Secretary*, ed. and trans. by Lesley Byrd Simpson (Berkeley, 1964).
López de Gómara, Francisco, *Primera y segunda parte de la Historia General de las Indias con todo el descubrimiento y cosas notables que han acaecido dende que se ganaron hasta el año de 1551. Con la conquista de México de la Nueva España* (Zaragoza, 1552).
Lord, Evelyn, *The Hell-Fire Clubs: Sex, Satanism and Secret Societies* (New Haven, 2010).
Lovell, Richard, *Churchill's Doctor: A Biography of Lord Moran* (London and New York, 1992).
Luce, Henry R., *Prospectus for SHOW-BOOK* (1936).
Macmichael, William, *The Gold-Headed Cane. A Facsimile Edition of the Author's 1827 Copy Illustrated and Interleaved with his own Amendments and Additions* (London, 1968).
Madison, Francis, et al. (eds), *Essays on the Life and Work of Thomas Linacre* (Oxford, 1977).
Maffei, Nicolas P., *Norman Bel Geddes: American Design Visionary* (London, 2018).
Magilow, D., *The Photography of Crisis: The Photo Essays of Weimar Germany* (University Park, 2012).
Mancall, Peter C., *Hakluyt's Promise: An Elizabethan's Obsession for an English America* (New Haven, 2007).
Margo, Adair, and Melissa Renn, *Tom Lea, Life Magazine, and World War II* (El Paso, 2016).
Marstine, Janet (ed.), *New Museum Theory and Practice: An Introduction* (Malden and Oxford, 2006).
Martorell, Joanot, *Libre del valeros e strenu caualler Tirant lo Blanch*, ed. by Marian Aguilo y Fuster, 3 vols (Barcelona, 1873).
Martyr d'Anghiera, Peter, *De Orbe Novo: The Eight Decades of Peter Martyr D'Anghera; Volume Two*, trans. by Francis A. MacNutt (New York and London, 1912).
Massing, Jean Michel, 'Early European Images of America: The Ethnographic Approach', in Jay A. Levenson and National Gallery of Art (U.S.) (eds), *Circa 1492: Art in the Age of Exploration* (Washington, DC, New Haven and London, 1991), 515–20.
Mellinkoff, Ruth, 'Riding Backwards: Theme of Humiliation and Symbol of Evil', *Viator*, 4 (1973): 153–76.

Mellquist, Jerome, 'Feeble War Art', *Nation*, 2 October 1943, 389.
Melton, James Van Horn, *The Rise of the Public in Enlightenment Europe* (Cambridge, 2001).
Mentges, Gabriele, 'Pour une approche renouvelée des recueils de costumes de la Renaissance. Une cartographie vestimentaire de l'espace et du temps', *Apparence(s)*, 1/12 (2007), http://apparences.revues.org/104.
Merback, Mitchell B., *The Thief, the Cross and the Wheel: Pain and the Spectacle of Punishment in Medieval and Renaissance Europe* (London, 2001).
Meyer, Adolf (ed.), *Ein Versuchshaus der Bauhauses in Weimar* (Munich, 1925).
Milani, Giuliano, 'The Band and the Bag: How Defamatory Paintings Worked in Medieval Italy', in Carolin Behrmann (ed.), *Images of Shame: Infamy, Defamation and the Ethics of Oeconomia* (Berlin, 2016), 119–40.
Mills, Robert, *Suspended Animation: Pain, Pleasure and Punishment in Medieval Culture* (London, 2006).
Mirzoeff, Nicholas, *An Introduction to Visual Culture* (London and New York, 1999).
Mitchell, W. J. T., 'What Do Pictures *Really* Want?', *October*, 77 (1996): 71–82.
Mitchell, W. J. T., *What Pictures Want: The Lives and Loves of Images* (Chicago, 2005).
Mitman, Greg, and Kelley Wilder (eds), *Documenting the World: Film, Photography and the Scientific Record* (Chicago, 2016).
Molinet, Jean, *Chroniques de Jean Molinet*, ed. by J.-A. Buchon, 5 vols (Paris, 1828).
Monstrelet, Enguerrand de, *La chronique d'Enguerran de Monstrelet en deux livres avec pièces justificatives 1400–1444*, ed. by L. Douët-d'Arcq, 2 vols (Paris, 1857).
Montaigne, Michel de, *The Essays of Michel de Montaigne*, ed. and trans. by M. A. Screech (London, 1991).
Moore, Rowan, *Anatomy of a Building* (London, 2014).
Moxey, Keith P. F., *Peasants, Warriors, and Wives: Popular Imagery in the Reformation* (Chicago, 2004).
Mullett, Michael, *Popular Culture and Popular Protest in Late Medieval and Early Modern Europe* (London and New York, 1987).
Munk, William, *A Brief Account of the Circumstances Leading to and Attending the Reintombment of the Remains of Dr. William Harvey* (London, 1883).
Munk, William (ed.), *The Gold-Headed Cane* (London, 1884).
Munk, William, *The Life of Sir Henry Halford* (London, 1895).
Munk, William, *A Memoir of the Life and Writings of John Ayrton Paris* (London, 1857).
Munk, William, *The Roll of the Royal College of Physicians of London*, 2 vols (London, 1861; 2nd edn, 3 vols, London, 1878).
The Museum of Modern Art, *Norman Bel Geddes, War Maneuver Models Created for 'Life' Magazine* (New York, 1944).
Nagel, T., 'Ursula Begegnet Den Heiligen Drei Könige Oder Die Vision Vom Kölner Stadtwappen?', *Museen Köln* [website], http://www.museenkoeln.de/home/bild-der-woche.aspx?bdw=1998_22 (accessed 17 February 2015).
Najemy, John M., 'The Republic's Two Bodies: Body Metaphors in Italian Renaissance Political Thought', in Alison Brown (ed.), *Language and Images of Renaissance Italy* (Oxford, 1995), 237–62.
Namier, Lewis, *The Structure of Politics at the Accession of George III*, 2nd edn (Basingstoke, 1957).
Needham, Rachel, 'Narcissa Whitman Painting Defaced', *Whitman Wire* [website] (31 October 2017), https://whitmanwire.com/news/2017/10/31/narcissa-whitman-painting-defaced/ (accessed 9 June 2018).

Nelson, Robert (ed.), *Visuality Before and Beyond the Renaissance: Seeing as Others Saw* (Cambridge, 2000).
Nelson, Robert, and Richard Shiff (eds), *Critical Terms for Art History*, 2nd edn (Chicago and London, 2003).
Neubecker, Ottfried, *Heraldry: Sources, Symbols & Meaning* (London, 1999).
'New York Harbor', *Life*, 20 November 1944, 55–60.
Nicholson, Eirwen, 'Consumers and Spectators: The Public of the Political Print in Eighteenth-Century England', *History*, 81 (1996): 5–21.
'Night Landing on New Britain', *Life*, 21 August 1944, 48–56.
Nobbe, George, *The North Briton: A Study in Political Propaganda* (New York, 1966).
'North Africa: Rear', *Life*, 27 December 1943, 62–6.
Nutton, Vivian (ed.), *Medicine at the Courts of Europe, 1500–1837* (London, 1990).
Oakeley, Henry, et al., *A Garden of Medicinal Plants* (London, 2015).
O'Connell, Sheila, 'The Taste for Mezzotints', in Anthony Griffiths (ed.), *Landmarks in Print Collecting: Connoisseurs and Donors at the British Museum since 1753* (London, 1996), 134–57.
Ogbechie, Sylvester Okwunodu, *Making History: The Femi Akinsanya African Art Collection* (Milan, 2011).
Ogilvie, Brian W., *The Science of Describing: Natural History in Renaissance Europe* (Chicago, 2006).
Olian, Jo Anne, 'Sixteenth-Century Costume Books', *Dress*, 3/1 (1977): 20–48.
Onyekakeyah, Luke, *The Crawling Giant* (Bloomington, 2013).
Ortalli, Gherardo, *La pittura infamante nei secoli XIII–XVI* (Rome, 2015).
Oxford Dictionary of National Biography, ed. H. C. G. Matthew and Brian Harrison (Oxford, 2004 [ongoing]).
Panofsky, Erwin, *Three Essays on Style* (Cambridge, MA, 1995).
Parr, Martin, and Gerry Badger, *The Photobook: A History; Volume One* (London, 2004).
Paulicelli, Eugenia, 'Mapping the World: The Political Geography of Dress in Cesare Vecellio's Costume Books', *The Italianist*, 28/1 (2008): 24–53.
'Peleliu: Tom Lea Paints Island Invasion', *Life*, 11 June 1945, 61–7.
Pelling, Margaret, with Frances White, *Medical Conflicts in Early Modern London: Patronage, Physicians, and Irregular Practitioners, 1550–1640* (Oxford, 2003).
Peltz, Lucy, *Facing the Text: Extra-Illustration, Print Culture, and Society in Britain, 1769–1840* (San Marino, 2017).
Pennant, Thomas, *Additions and Corrections to the First Edition of Mr. Pennant's Account of London* (London, 1791).
Penny, Nicholas, *The Materials of Sculpture* (New Haven and London, 1993).
Perlin, Bernard, 'Liberation Will Find the Greeks Are Ready: A *Life* Artist Accompanies Commandos inside Greece', *Life*, 4 September 1944, 35–8.
Perry, Gill, and Colin Cunningham, *Academies, Museums and Canons of Art* (New Haven and London, 1999).
'Peter Hurd: He Paints U.S. Airmen', *Life*, 15 February 1943, 66–73.
Peterson, M. Jeanne, *The Medical Profession in Mid-Victorian London* (Berkeley and London, 1978).
Pettitt, Tom, 'Protesting Inversions: Charivari as Folk Pageantry and Folk-Law', *Medieval English Theatre*, 21 (1999): 21–51.
Peukert, Detlev, *The Weimar Republic: The Crisis of Classical Modernity*, trans. by Richard Deveson (Harmondsworth, 1993; German original, 1981).

Pink, Sarah, *The Future of Visual Anthropology: Engaging the Senses* (London and New York, 2006).
Pintoin, Michel, *Chronique du religieux de Saint-Denys: Contenant le règne de Charles VI, de 1380 à 1422*, ed. by M. L. Bellaguet, 5 vols (Paris, 1839).
Pocock, J. G. A., *The Ancient Constitution and the Feudal Law*, rev. edn (Cambridge, 1987).
Pointon, Marcia, *Hanging the Head: Portraiture and Social Formation in Eighteenth-Century England* (New Haven and London, 1993).
Pointon, Marcia, *History of Art: A Students' Handbook*, 5th edn (London and New York, 2014).
Pollock, Griselda, *Differencing the Canon: Feminist Desire and the Writing of Art's Histories* (London, 1999).
Porter, Roy, 'Seeing the Past', *Past & Present*, 118 (1988): 186–205.
Postle, Martin (ed.), *Johan Zoffany RA: Society Observed* (New Haven and London, 2011).
Postle, Martin (ed.), *Joshua Reynolds: The Creation of Celebrity* (London, 2005).
Puma, Fernando, *We Challenge War Art* (New York, 1943).
Rampley, Matthew, *Exploring Visual Culture: Definitions, Concepts, Contexts* (Edinburgh, 2005).
Raphael, Timothy, *The President Electric: Ronald Reagan and the Politics of Performance* (Ann Arbor, 2009).
Rasch, Heinz, and Bodo Rasch (eds), *Gefesselter Blick* (Stuttgart, 1930).
Rauser, Amelia, 'Embodied Liberty', in Bernadette Fort and Angela Rosenthal (eds), *The Other Hogarth: Aesthetics of Difference* (Princeton, 2001), 240–59.
Raven, James, *What Is the History of the Book?* (Cambridge, 2017).
Rea, Robert R., *The English Press in Politics, 1760–1774* (Lincoln, 1963).
Renn, Melissa, '"An Enduring Record": Peter Hurd's Art for *Life* Magazine', in Kirsten M. Jensen (ed.), *Magical & Real: Henriette Wyeth and Peter Hurd, A Retrospective* (Doylestown, 2018).
Renn, Melissa, 'Fine Arts under Fire: *Life* Magazine and the Display of Architectural Destruction', in JoAnne Mancini and Keith Bresnahan (eds), *Architecture and Armed Conflict: The Politics of Destruction* (Oxford, 2014), 72–85.
Renn, Melissa, '*Life* in Color: *Life* Magazine and the Color Reproduction of Works of Art', in Regina Lee Blaszczyk and Uwe Spiekermann (eds), *Bright Modernity: Color, Commerce, and Consumer Culture* (New York, 2017), 167–88.
Renn, Melissa, '*Life* in the Art World, 1936–1972', PhD diss., Boston University, 2011.
Retford, Kate, *The Art of Domestic Life: Family Portraiture in Eighteenth-Century England* (New Haven, 2006).
Retford, Kate, *The Conversation Piece: Making Modern Art in Eighteenth-Century Britain* (New Haven, 2017).
'Rich Gift of War Art', *Life*, 26 December 1960, 86.
Richmond, Colin F., 'The Visual Culture of Fifteenth-Century England', in A. F. Pollard (ed.), *The Wars of the Roses* (Basingstoke, 2001), 186–209.
Rieff Anawalt, Patricia, *Indian Clothing before Cortés: Mesoamerican Costumes from the Codices* (Norman, 1981).
R., M. [Maude Riley], 'Pictorial Reporting by Nine Who Went to War', *Art Digest*, 17/20 (1943): 6.
Roberts, Jennifer Davis, *Norman Bel Geddes: An Exhibition of Theatrical and Industrial Designs* (Austin, 1979).

Robertson, Fiona, and Peter N. Lindfield (eds), *The Display of Heraldry: The Heraldic Imagination in Arts and Culture* (Baldock, 2020).
Robertson, Fiona, and Peter N. Lindfield, 'Introduction: Speaking of Arms', in Fiona Robertson and Peter N. Lindfield (eds), *Semy-de-Lys: Speaking of Arms, 1400–2016* (Oxford and Stirling, 2016), 1–6, https://heraldics2014.files.wordpress.com/2015/12/introduction1.pdf (accessed 12 February 2019).
Robinson, Norman, *The Royal Society Catalogue of Portraits* (London, 1980).
Rose, Gillian, *Doing Family Photography: The Domestic, the Public and the Politics of Sentiment* (Farnham, 2010).
Rose, Gillian, *Visual Methodologies: An Introduction to the Interpretation of Visual Materials*, 2nd edn (London, 2007).
Rose, Gillian, *Visual Methodologies: An Introduction to Researching with Visual Materials*, 4th edn (Los Angeles, 2016).
Roy, Just Jean E., *Histoire de la chevalerie* (Tours, 1839).
Royer, Katherine Adele, 'The Body in Parts: Reading the Execution Ritual in Late Medieval England', *Historical Reflections/Réflexions historiques*, 29 (2003): 319–39.
Royle, Edward, and James Walvin, *English Radicals and Reformers 1760–1848* (Brighton, 1982).
Rubin, Miri, 'Identities', in Rosemary Horrox and W. Mark Ormrod (eds), *A Social History of England, 1200–1500* (Cambridge, 2006), 383–412.
Rublack, Ulinka, *Dressing Up: Cultural Identity in Renaissance Europe* (Oxford, 2010).
'Russian Soldiers: *Life* Artist Fredenthal Shows Soviet Army in Yugoslavia', *Life*, 5 February 1945, 83–9.
Russo, Alessandra, 'Cortés's Objects and the Idea of New Spain: Inventories as Spatial Narratives', *Journal of the History of Collections*, 23/2 (2011): 229–52.
Sainsbury, John, *John Wilkes: The Lives of a Libertine* (Aldershot, 2006).
Salicrú i Lluch, Roser, *Documents per a la història de Granada del regnat d'Alfons el Magnànim (1416–1458)* (Barcelona, 1999).
Santa Cruz, Paul H., *Making JFK Matter: Popular Memory and the Thirty-Fifth President* (Denton, 2015).
'Santa Fe at War', *Life*, 7 December 1942, 92–5.
Scallen, Catherine, *Rembrandt, Reputation, and the Practice of Connoisseurship* (Amsterdam, 2004).
Schmidt, Hans, *Architektur-Photographie: Unter besonderer Berücksichtigung der Plastik und des Kunstgewerbes* (Berlin, 1902).
Schorske, Carl, *Fin-de-Siècle Vienna: Politics and Culture* (New York, 1979).
Secousse, Denis-François (ed.), *Mémoires pour servir a l'histoire de Charles II: Roi de Navarre et comte d'Evreux, surnommé le Mauvais* (Paris, 1755).
Senckenberg, Heinrich Christian von (ed.), *Selecta iuris et historiarum tum anecdota tum iam edita, sed rariora*, 6 vols (Frankfurt am Main, 1738).
Sheets, Millard, 'The Attack on Bamboo Hill', *Life*, 5 June 1944, 17–9.
Shortland, Michael, and Richard Yeo (eds), *Telling Lives in Science: Essays on Scientific Biography* (Cambridge, 1996).
Shorvon, Simon, and Humphrey Hodgson, *Physicians and War* (London, 2016).
'Sicily Invasion Goes Well', *Life*, 26 July 1943, 25–31.
Silverman, Debora, *Art Nouveau in Fin-de-Siècle France: Politics, Psychology, and Style* (Berkeley, 1989).
Simon, Jacob, 'British Portrait Painters and Their Canvas Sizes, 1625–1850', *National Portrait Gallery* [website] (April 2013), https://www.npg.org.uk/research/programm

es/artists-their-materials-and-suppliers/three-quarters-kit-cats-and-half-lengths-british-portrait-painters-and-their-canvas-sizes-1625-1850/ (accessed 19 June 2018).
'Sinking of *Wasp*: A Painting for *Life* by Tom Lea', *Life*, 5 April 1943, 48–9.
Smith, Pamela, 'Art, Science, and Visual Culture in Early Modern Europe', *Isis*, 97/1 (2006): 83–100.
Smith, Pamela, *The Body of the Artisan: Art and Experience in the Scientific Revolution* (Chicago and London, 2004).
Solkin, David, *Art on the Line: The Royal Academy Exhibitions at Somerset House, 1780–1836* (New Haven, 2002).
Spangenberg, Cyriacus, *Ander Teil des Adelspiegels* (Schmalkalden, 1564).
'Speaking of Pictures . . . These Are Notes from Peter Hurd's Sketchbook', *Life*, 19 June 1944, 12–4.
Speck, Catherine, *Beyond the Battlefield: Women Artists of the Two World Wars* (London, 2014).
Spiegelman, Art, *The Complete Maus* (London, 2003; first published 1986 and 1991).
Stallabrass, Julian, *Contemporary Art: A Very Short Introduction* (Oxford, 2006).
Stamm, Rainer, 'Moderne, vornehme Massenartikel: Die Blauen Bücher des Verlags Robert Langewiesche', in Manfred Heiting and Roland Jaeger (eds), *Autopsie: Deutschsprachige Fotobücher 1918–1945; Volume Two* (Göttingen, 2014), 168–87.
Starkey, Kathryn, 'Visual Culture and the German Middle Ages', in Kathryn Starkey (ed.), *Visual Culture and the German Middle Ages* (New York, 2005), 1–12.
Steiner, Zara, *The Lights That Failed: European International History 1919–1933* (Oxford, 2005).
Steorn, Patrick, 'Caricature and Fashion Critique on the Move: Establishing European Print and Fashion Culture in Eighteenth-Century Sweden', in Evelyn Welch (ed.), *Fashioning the Early Modern: Dress, Textiles, and Innovation in Europe, 1500–1800* (Oxford, 2017), 255–78.
Stewart, Frank Henderson, 'What Is Honor?', *Acta Histriae*, 8/1 (2000): 13–28.
Stewart, Robert G., *Robert Edge Pine: A British Portrait Painter in America, 1784–1788* (Washington, DC, 1979).
Stow, John, *A Survey of London*, ed. by William John Thoms (London, 1842).
Strathern, Paul, *Quacks, Rogues and Charlatans* (London, 2016).
Strickland, Matthew, '"All brought to nought and thy state undone": Treason, Disinvestiture and the Disgracing of Arms under Edward II', in Peter R. Coss and Christopher Tyerman (eds), *Soldiers, Nobles and Gentlemen: Essays in Honour of Maurice Keen* (Woodbridge, 2009), 279–304.
Strong, Roy, *Painting the Past: The Victorian Painter and British History* (London, 2004).
'Studio War Art', *Life*, 12 June 1944, 76.
Sturtevant, William, and David Beers Quinn, 'This New Prey: Eskimos in Europe in 1567, 1576 and 1577', in Christian F. Feest (ed.), *Indians and Europe: An Interdisciplinary Collection of Essays* (Aachen, 1987), 61–140.
Suchenwirt, Peter, *Werke aus dem vierzehnten Jahrhunderte*, ed. by Alois Primisser (Vienna, 1827).
Sunderland, John, 'Mortimer, Pine and Some Political Aspects of English History Painting', *Burlington Magazine*, 116 (1974): 317–26.
Sutter, Rolf E. (ed.), *Identität in Genealogie und Heraldik/Identity in Genealogy and Heraldry/La notion d'identite en genealogie et en heraldique* (Stuttgart, 2012).
Tang, Xiaobing, *Visual Culture in Contemporary China: Paradigms and Shifts* (Cambridge, 2015).

Taylor, Francis Henry, 'Foreword', in *War Art, A Catalogue of Paintings Done on the War Fronts by American Artists for 'Life'* (Chicago, 1943), 3.
Thiry, Steven, 'The Emblazoned Kingdom Ablaze: Heraldic Iconoclasm and Armorial Recovery during the French Wars of Religion, 1588–95', *French History*, 27/3 (2013): 323–50.
Thiry, Steven, *Matter(s) of State: Heraldic Display and Discourse in the Early Modern Monarchy (c. 1480–1650)* (Ostfildern, 2019).
Thomas, Peter D. G., *John Wilkes: A Friend to Liberty* (Oxford, 1996).
Thompson, E. P., *Customs in Common* (New York, 1991).
Thompson, E. P., *The Making of the English Working Class* (New York, 1963).
Thompson, E. P., 'Rough Music Reconsidered', *Folklore*, 103/1 (1992): 3–26.
Thompson, Richard, *Curiosities from the College Museum* (London, 2016).
'Three Americans', *Life*, 20 September 1943, 34–5.
Traub, Valerie, 'Mapping the Global Body', in Peter Erickson and Clark Hulse (eds), *Early Modern Visual Culture: Representation, Race, and Empire in Renaissance England* (Philadelphia, 2000), 44–97.
Tschichold, Jan, *Die neue Tyopgraphie: Ein Handbuch für zeitgemäß Schaffende* (Berlin, 1928).
Tucoo-Chala, Pierre, 'Les honneurs funebres d'Archaumbaud de Foix-Béarn a Orthez en 1414', *Revue de Pau et du Béarn*, 5 (1977): 5–30.
Tumblety, Joan (ed.), *Memory and History: Understanding Memory as Source and Subject* (Abingdon, 2013).
'Two Artists Hitchhiked to Normandy', *Life*, 9 October 1944, 58–60.
Uglow, Jenny, *Hogarth: A Life and a World* (London, 1997).
Umberger, Emily, 'Art and Imperial Strategy in Tenochtitlan', in Frances F. Berdan et al. (eds), *Aztec Imperial Strategies* (Washington, DC, 1996), 85–108.
Van Leeuwen, Jacoba (ed.), *Symbolic Communication Late Medieval Towns* (Leuven, 2006).
Van Mander, Karel, *The Lives of the Illustrious German and Netherlandish Painters*, ed. and trans. by Hessel Miedema et al. (Doornspijk, 1994).
Varga, Margit, 'Britain Mobilizes Her Artists, What about America?', *Magazine of Art*, 34/6 (1941): 298–304.
Varga, Margit, '*Life*'s Art Program', in Elizabeth McCausland (ed.), *Work for Artists* (New York, 1947), 118–22.
Vattel, Emmerich de, *Le droit de gens, ou principes de la loi naturelle* (Leiden, 1758).
Vaughan, Louella, *Grave and Learned Men: The Physicians, 1518–1660* (London, 2016).
Vaughan, Louella, and Richard Thompson, *Ever Persons Capable and Able: The Physicians, 1660–2018* (London, 2017).
Vecellio, Cesare, *Clothing of the Renaissance World: Europe, Asia, Africa, the Americas; Cesare Vecellio's Habiti Antichi et Moderni*, ed. and trans. by A. R. Jones and Margaret Rosenthal (London, 2008).
Vital, Laurent, 'Relation du premier voyage de Charles-Quint en Espagne', in M. Gachard (ed.), *Collection des voyages des souverains des Pays-Bas: Volume Three* (Brussels, 1881), 1–316.
Vulson de La Colombière, Marc de, *Le vray théâtre d'honneur et de chevalerie, ou le miroir héroique de la noblesse*, 2 vols (Paris, 1648).
Wagner, Anthony, *Heralds of England: A History of the Office and College of Arms* (London, 1967).

Wainwright, Loudon, *The Great American Magazine: An Inside History of 'Life'* (New York, 1986).
Walpole, Horace, *Correspondence*, ed. by Wilmarth Sheldon Lewis, 48 vols (New Haven, 1932–83).
Walsingham, Thomas, *Chronicon Angliae: Ab anno Domini 1328 usque ad annum 1388*, ed. by Edward M. Thompson (London et al., 1847).
The War against Japan (New York, 1945).
Ward, Janet, *Weimar Surfaces: Urban Visual Culture in 1920s Germany* (Berkeley and Los Angeles, 2001).
Webster, Charles, *The National Health Service: A Political History*, 2nd edn (Oxford, 2002).
Webster, Mary, *Johan Zoffany, 1733–1810* (New Haven and London, 2011).
Weiditz, Christoph, *Authentic Everyday Dress of the Renaissance: All 154 Plates from the 'Trachtenbuch'*, ed. by Theodor Hampe (New York and London, 1994).
Weigel, Hans, *Habitus Praecipuorum Populorum tam Virorum quam Feminarum Singulari Arte Depicti* (Nuremberg, 1577).
Wells, Liz (ed.), *Photography: A Critical Introduction*, 2nd edn (London, 2000).
Wendorf, Richard, *The Elements of Life: Biography and Portrait-Painting in Stuart and Georgian England* (Oxford, 1990).
West, Shearer, *Guide to Art* (London, 1996).
West, Shearer, *Portraiture* (Oxford, 2004).
West, Shearer, 'Wilkes's Squint: Synecdochic Physiognomy and Political Identity in Eighteenth-Century Political Culture', *Eighteenth-Century Studies*, 33/1 (1999): 65–84.
Westerhof, Danielle Marianne, 'Deconstructing Identities on the Scaffold: The Execution of Hugh Despenser the Younger, 1326', *Journal of Medieval History*, 33 (2007): 87–106.
Wheeler, Monroe (ed.), *Britain at War* (New York, 1941).
White, Hayden, 'Historiography and Historiophoty', *American Historical Review*, 93 (1998): 1193–9.
Whitley, W. T., *Artists and Their Friends in England*, 2 vols (London, 1928).
Wick, Rainer K., 'Mythos Bauhaus-Fotografie', in Rainer K. Wick (ed.), *Das Neue Sehen: Von der Fotografie am Bauhaus zur subjektiven Fotografie* (Berlin, 1991).
Wickham, Chris, 'Problems in Doing Comparative History', in Patricia Skinner (ed.), *Challenging the Boundaries of Medieval History: The Legacy of Timothy Reuter* (Turnhout, 2009), 5–28.
Williams, Raymond, *Keywords: A Vocabulary of Culture and Society*, rev. edn (London, 1983).
Willumson, Glenn G., *W. Eugene Smith and the Photographic Essay* (Cambridge, 1992).
Wilson, Bronwen, *The World in Venice: Print, the City, and Early Modern Identity* (Toronto, 2005).
Wilson, Kathleen, *The Sense of the People: Politics, Culture and Imperialism in England, 1715–1815* (Cambridge, 1998).
Wilton, Andrew, *The Swagger Portrait: Grand Manner Portraiture in Britain from Van Dyck to Augustus John* (London, 1992).
Winkler, Klaus-Jürgen, *Bauhaus, Moderne in Weimar 1919–1933* (Weimar, 1995).
Wohnbauten und Siedlungen aus deutscher Gegenwart (Königstein im Taunus and Leipzig, 1928).

Wolstenholme, Gordon (ed.), *The Royal College of Physicians of London: Portraits* (London, 1964).
Wolstenholme, Gordon, and John Kerslake, *The Royal College of Physicians of London: Portraits Catalogue II* (Amsterdam, Oxford and New York, 1977).
'Women at War', *Life*, 5 June 1944, 74–9.
Woodall, Joanna (ed.), *Portraiture: Facing the Subject* (Manchester, 1997).
Woodcock, Thomas, and John Martin Robinson, *The Oxford Guide to Heraldry* (Oxford, 1990).
Woodward, Jennifer, *The Theatre of Death: The Ritual Management of Royal Funerals in Renaissance England, 1570–1625* (Woodbridge and Rochester, 1997).
Word and Image: A Journal of Verbal/Visual Enquiry (1985–).
Yates, Frances A., *The Valois Tapestries* (London, 2013).
Young, James, *The Texture of Memory: Holocaust Memorials and Meaning* (New Haven and London, 2000).
Zimmerman, Claire, *Photographic Architecture in the Twentieth Century* (Minneapolis and London, 2014).

Index

Page references for illustrations appear in *italics*.

agency 1, 20, 57, 132, 147–8
Akenside, Mark 72, 79
Albrecht II, Duke of Austria 37
American Federation of Arts 134 n.4, 144
Amman, Jost 59, *65*
Anne of Bohemia, consort of Richard II, king of England 34
anthropology 7, 13, 132 n.45
archaeology 7, 19, 113
Archambaud of Foix-Béarn 38
architecture 5, 7, 20, 25, 51, 71, 73–6, 110–32, 138, 141, 151, 155, 158
art 2, 3, 4, 6, 7–10, 11, 12, 13, 14, 15, 16, 17, 19, 25, 26, 37 n.56, 55 n.36, 59, 68 n.2, 77, 78 n.26, 80, 81, 89, 96–8, 100, 105, 106 n.47, 107 n.50, 108, 111, 120–1, 127, 128, 132 n.45, 133–57, 161, 164, 167
Artstor 163
attention 1, 2, 3, 6, 10, 12, 17, 72, 73, 75, 82, 105, 106, 109, 125, 147, 149, 151, 155–7, 162, 166
audiences 2–4, 11, 13, 20, 45, 56, 59, 60, 93, 97, 152, 153
Augusta, Princess Dowager of Wales 92, 95

Baillie, Matthew 75, 78, 80
Baillie, Sophia 75, 77, 80
baroque 5, 155, 161
Barthes, Roland 126
Bauhaus 8, 115, 121–31
Baxandall, Michael 3 n.4, 14–15, 27, 72 n.11, 161
Beaton, Cecil 11
Bel Geddes, Norman 139–41
Benedict XIII, anti-pope (Pedro de Luna) 33
Benjamin, Walter 10 n.20, 126
Bernat de Vilarig 35
Berndt, Johann Oswald 101–2

Biddle, George 135 n.12, 136, 137
Billings, John Shaw 134, 135 n.12, 141
Binford, Julien 135 n.12, 137, 144
Bohrod, Aaron 138, 141, 144
Boissard, Jean-Jacques 47
Boorde, Andrew 60, 63
Braun, Georg 48
British Empire 88, 90
British Museum (London) 77 n.22, 78, 89, 95, 98 n.35, 99, *100*, 101, 102 n.40, *103*, 104, 105, 107 n.51, 162
Burdett, Francis 108
Burke, Edmund 92
Burke, Peter 14, 110

canon 7, 8, 19, 55, 57, 58, 111, 148
Carroll, Lewis 12
Cavendish, Georgiana, Duchess of Devonshire 108
Chanel 155
Chaplin, Arnold 86–7
Chaplin, Margaret Douie 86–7
Charles I, king of England 81, Pl. 6
Charles II, king of England 78
Charles V, Holy Roman Emperor 45, 48, 52, 56, 58, 60
Charles the Bold, Duke of Burgundy 35
China Design Museum (Hangzhou) 8 n.16
chivalry 27 n.7, 31, 32, 35, 37
Clinton, Edward, Earl of Lincoln 62, 63 n.65
Coates, Robert M. 142
coat of arms, *see* heraldry
collecting/collectors/collections 2–3, 4, 5, 7, 9, 15, 16, 19 n.35, 46, 48, 49, 56, 57, 59, 63, 68–87, 95, 96, 101, 104, 105, 107, 134, 142 n.49, 144 n.63, 145, 148, 152, 153, 160, 162–3
College Art Association 164

comparative analysis   4, 19, 28, 50, 52 n.22
connoisseurs/connoisseurship   1, 7, 89, 95, 154
conservation   2
context/contextualization   2–6, 12, 13, 18, 19–21, 28, 31, 34, 37–41, 52, 57, 76–7, 102, 105, 132, 147–8, 150, 154, 155, 157–61, 164, 166
Cooper Hewitt, Smithsonian Design Museum (New York)   8 n.16
Copley, John Singleton   96
Cortés, Hernán   50, 53, 55, 56
costume   7, 19, 45–67, 96
Cotterell (tobacconnist)   103–5
Craig, Tom   135, 138

Davis, Floyd   135 n.12, 141, 144
Department of Defense (US)   145
description   2, 5–6, 16, 70, 148, 157–9, 163, 164, 166–8
design/designer   1, 2, 3, 4, 5, 8, 11–12, 13, 17, 20, 39, 48, 56, 60, 62, 67, 70, 71, 74, 77, 98, 107, 110, 111, 112, 114, 116, *118*, *119*, 120–3, *124*, 127, *128*, *129*, *130*, 131, 133, 134, 139, 155, 158, 165
Desprez, François   46, 48, *49*, 59, 60, 67
digital media   2, 3, 11, 13, 146 n.74, 151, 153, 163, 165, 166
discourse   20, 46, 60, 108, 110, 113–14, 116, 119–25, 129, 131, 132, 149
Doré, Gustave   12
dress, *see* costume
du Guesclin, Bertrand   35, 38

Eberhard III, Count of Württemberg   37
Edward II, king of England   33
Edward VII, king of the United Kingdom of Great Britain and Ireland and Emperor of India   77 n.23
Edwards, Elizabeth   110, 132 n.45, 145 n.69
ethnography   6, 19, 45, 46, 47, 48 n.10, 50, 51, 52, 54 n.34, 56–9, 66, 67, 111

European Union   43
extra-illustration   86, 87 n.50

Farage, Nigel   43, 44
Farre, Frederick John   *84*, 86–7
Fieger, Karl   123
Fiennes, James, Lord of Saye and Sele   36–7
Foucault, Michel   20, 113–14, 131
Foundling Hospital (London)   98
Fox, Charles James   108
Fredenthal, David   135 n.12, 138, 143 n.56
Freedberg, David   2 n.1, 27, 37
Froissart, Jean   33, 36
Froschauer, Johann   54

gender   25, 153, 167
genre/s   1, 3, 4, 7, 8, 10, 12, 13, 14, 15, 18, 19, 20, 46 n.2, 47 n.7, 49, 59, 68 n.1, 72, 81, 97, 102, 105–7, 117, 149–51, 158
Geoffrey de Marisco   39
George I, king of Great Britain and Ireland   91
George II, king of Great Britain and Ireland   91
George III, king of Great Britain and Ireland   89, 91, 93 n.13, 94, 97
Getty Images   163
Gómez de Figueroa   35
Grailly, Jean de   32
Gropius, Walter   112, 115 n.18, 123, 127
Grover, Allen   139

Hakluyt, Richard   48
Halford, Henry   78, 86
Hannah, Robert   81–2, Pl. 6
Harvey, William   68–9, 71–5, 78, 81–2
Heartfield, John   122 n.35
Heere, Lucas de   62–3, *64*
Helmschmid, Kolman   50
Henry III, Count of Nassau-Dillenburg   58
Henry VII, king of England   34
Hepburn, A. J.   135
heraldry   19, 25–44, 88, 104, 150

Hersey, John 138
Hogarth, William 77 n.22, 86, 100, 102, 106
Hogenberg, Franz 48
honour 19, 25–44, 60, 65
Hunter, John 77
Hunter, William 3, 16–17, 77, 80–1
Hunterian Museum (Glasgow) 16
Hurd, Peter 135 n.12, 138, 141, 142

iconography 15, 43, 46, 59–62, 67, 100, 108, 150–1
identity 4, 5, 11, 19, 20, 27, 29 n.16, 33, 46, 47, 51, 52, 57–9, 62, 63, 67–87, 116, 154, 159
institutions 4–5, 7–11, 15–18, 20, 42–3, 68–87, 89, 98, 105, 142, 148, 154, 157–8, 162–5

Jewell, Edward Alden 142
jewellery 1, 56, 57, 95, 155, 156
John II, Count of Wied 29
John II, king of France 32
John III, Duke of Bavaria 29, Pl. 1
John V, Count of Nassau 28
John of Gaunt, Duke of Lancaster 36
Judmann, Hans 29

Keere, Pieter van den 48
Kennedy, John F. 41
keyword 147, 162
knowledge 6, 41, 45, 46, 50, 52, 56–9, 63, 66–7, 69, 71, 82, 89 n.2, 113–14, 117, 120, 129, 131, 132, 150, 167
Kuh, Katharine 144

Langewiesche, Karl Robert 115–16
Laning, Edward 135 n.12, 137, 138, 141
La Rocque, Jean-François, sieur de Roberval 48
Larsen, Roy 145
Lasdun, Denys 70 n.4, 73, 74, 87
Latour, Bruno 132
Lawrence, Thomas 78
Lea, Tom 133, 134, 135, 138, 139, 141, 142, 143 n.56, 144, 145
le Despenser, Hugh 33
Leonardo Da Vinci 152

Linacre, Thomas 87
Lissitzky, El 122 n.35
Longwell, Daniel 133, 134, 136–7, 145 n.68, 146
Loos, Adolf 121
Louis, Landgrave of Hesse 29, Pl. 2
Luce, Henry R. 134 n.4, 135, 136, 139, 145, 146

McCloy, John J. 136, 137
Mackintosh, Charles Rennie 155
Macmichael, William 75, 78 n.25
Mander, Karel van 62–3
maps 1, 8, 47, 48, 56, 86, 140, 141
March, Walter 128
Martin, Fletcher 135 n.12, 137, 138, 141, 144, 146
Martyr d' Anghiera, Peter 55
Master of the Housebook 25, 26, 43
Maximilian I, Holy Roman Emperor 31
Mead, Richard 3 n.3, 16 n.30, 71, 72 n.10, 78, 83
media 1, 4, 8–9, 10, 11, 13, 14, 18, 19 n.35, 20, 28, 41 n.73, 46, 59, 67, 70, 74, 77, 102, 150, 151, 153, 154, 156, 159, 161, 164, 166
medium 2, 3, 4, 5, 8, 10, 11, 20, 41, 46, 79, 89, 101, 113–14, 117, 145 n.69, 146, 149, 151, 152, 157, 164
Mellquist, Jerome 142
Mendelsohn, Erich 112, *118*
Metropolitan Museum of Art (New York) 133, 134 n.4, 141–4
Meyer, Adolf 112, 115, 122, 123 n.36, *124*, 127, 128–9, *130*
Mies van der Rohe, Ludwig 112
Moctezuma, emperor of Mexico 52, 56
modernism 112, 121, 150, 161
Moholy-Nagy, László 115
Monet, Claude 152
Montaigne, Michel de 60
Muche, Georg 129,
Müller-Wulckow, Walter 115–17, 120–2
Munk, William 69 n.3, 71 n.9, 75 n.16, 78 n.26, 86–7

Museum of Modern Art (New York)   12, 134 n.4, 135 n.11, 139 n.37, 140, 141 n.43
museum/s   4, 5, 7, 8, 9, 12, 14, 16, 18, 42–3, 89, 133, 134 n.4, 135 n.11, 143, 148, 151, 153, 155, 157, 159, 160, 162, 163

National Gallery of Art (Washington, DC)   136, 141, 144
National Health Service (United Kingdom)   76
National Museum of African American History and Culture (Washington, DC)   4
National Portrait Gallery (London)   5, 89
Neville, Sir Thomas   38

Paris, Matthew   38–9
Paul Mellon Centre for Studies in British Art   4
Paxton, Worthen   139
periodization   5, 155, 157, 160–1, 167
Perlin, Bernard   135 n.12, 137
Philip VI, king of France   32
Philippe de Crèvecoeur   32
photographs/photography   1, 2, 3, 6, 10–12, 20, 77 n.21, 78, 82, 86, 110–47, 150–4, 161–4, 167
Pierrepont, Henry, Marquis of Dorchester   75
Pine, Robert Edge   96, 97–8, 99, 100–2, 104, 105, Pl. 7
Poole, David   82 n.43
Poor, Henry Varnum   135 n.12, 136
Porter, Roy   88, 108
portraits/portraiture   2, 3, 5, 6, 20, 40, 42, 43, 48, 50, 68–87, 89, 90, 96–108, 111, 113, 138, 149, 151
Prentice, Pierrepont   134
print   1, 3, 7, 11, 18–20, 28, 45, 46, 48, 49, 57–9, 66–8, 71, 72, 77–80, 82, 85–9, 92, 93, 96, 98–108, 111, 115, 116 n.22, 128, 130, 134, 138, 141, 143, 144, 145, 148, 151–3, 155, 159, 163, 164
provenance   2, 15, 58, 78, 129, 148, 152
Puma, Fernando   142–4

Radcliffe, John   75, 78
Reagan, Ronald   41
reception   13, 19, 90, 102, 112, 126, 132, 151–4, 159
Reindel, Edna   135 n.12, 137
reproduction   13, 20, 90, 98, 104, 109, 134 n.7, 141 n.47, 142, 144, 146, 152–3, 163, 165
Reynolds, Joshua   80, 96, 97, 104 n.42, 108
rhetoric   13, 21, 46, 59, 66, 92, 119, 153–4, 166
Ribera, Juan de   56
Richard II, king of England   34
Richard Neville, Earl of Salisbury   38
Ripa, Cesare   150
Römer, Hans (the elder)   58–9
Römer, Hans (the younger)   50 n.18, 58–9
Rose, Gillian   132
Royal Academy of Arts (London)   4, 78, 80, 81, 97, 105–6, 108
Royal College of Physicians (London)   20, 68–87
Royal Institution of Great Britain (London)   81
Royal Society (London)   78, 83 n.45
Rutz, Caspar   47

Scheemakers, Peter   71–2
Schmidt, Hans   117 n.26, 126
Schorske, Carl   17
Second World War   9, 20, 133–47
Sharp, William   103
Sheets, Millard   135 n.12, 137, 143 n.56
Sickingen, Franz von   31
Sidney, Algernon   99–100
Silverman, Debora   17–18
skill/s   1, 3, 7, 10, 15, 47, 81, 92, 96, 136, 137, 151, 154–5, 158, 166
Sloane, Hans   16 n.30, 78, 83
Society of Artists of Great Britain (London)   98
Somervell, Brehon   136
Sommerfeld, Adolf   128
Spangenberg, Cyriacus   39
Speed, John   48
Spiegelman, Art   13, 15
Starkey, Kathryn   27

Straubinger, Isaac 29
Straubinger, Saydro 29
Strock, George 141
Stuart, Charles Edward 91
Stuart, John, third Earl of Bute 91, 92, 94–6, 107
style 5, 7, 8, 14, 17–18, 46, 48, 52, 57, 59–61, 63, 67, 112, 113, 121, 131, 137, 154, 155, 158, 160–2, 164
Suchenwirt, Peter von 37

Taut, Bruno 112
Taylor, Francis Henry 141, 142 n.48
technology 3, 10, 11, 13, 17, 89, 90, 109, 111, 112, 121, 126, 131, 161
Tenniel, John 12
Thomas, Byron 135 n.12, 138, 144
Thompson, Edward K. 134, 136
Thompson, E. P. 34 n.41, 93, 95, 96 n.23
Thornton, Bonnell 105
Tschichold, Jan 122 n.35, 127
Turner-Warwick, Margaret 82 n.43

Ulrich V, Count of Württemberg 37
University of Glasgow 3, 16
US Army 133, 136, 144, 145 n.68
US Navy 134, 144, 145
US Treasury 143

Varga, Margit 134 n.4, 135
Vecellio, Cesare 46 n.2, 49, 63, 66
Vespucci, Amerigo 54

Victoria and Albert Museum (London) 4
visual culture 2 n.1, 4, 6–13, 18, 19, 27, 40, 41, 44, 45–7, 50, 58, 59, 66–87, 105, 107, 132, 148, 150–6, 158, 166–8
Vital, Laurent 48, 60

Walpole, Horace 95, 105
Walsingham, Thomas 36
Warbeck, Perkin 34
War Department Art Advisory Committee (US) 136
Watson, James 98, 99, 101–2
Weiditz, Christoph 45, 48, 50–60, 67, Pl. 3
Weigel, Hans 46, 48 n.13, 59, 60–3, 65–7
Weimar Republic 20, 110–32
Wellcome Library (London) 77 n.22
White, Hayden 110, 113
Whitman, Narcissa 42, 43
Whitman College, Washington 42, 43
Wilkes, John 6, 20, 88–109, Pl. 7, Pl. 8
Wilkes, Mary 105, 107 Pl. 8
William de Marisco 39
Williams, Raymond 147

Yale Center for British Art 3
Yale University Press 16

Zoffany, Johan 80–1, 90 n.3, 105–7, 108, Pl. 5
Zuazo, Alonso de 55